Elementary Latin: The Basic Structures   Part I

ELEMENTARY LATIN: THE BASIC STRUCTURES

Part I

edited by

GRACE A. CRAWFORD

and

Clara W. Ashley
Jane M. Infield
Frederick F. Kempner

Foreword by Waldo E. Sweet

Ann Arbor: The University of Michigan Press

Published in the United States of America by
The University of Michigan Press and simultaneously
in Toronto, Canada, by Ambassador Books Limited

Manufactured in the United States of America

FOREWORD

The authors have asked me to write a few words setting down my own reactions to this revision of material with which I was intimately connected from 1948 to 1953. In what ways, in short, does it differ from the *Experimental Materials* of 1953?

After using the *Experimental/Materials* for one year, I plunged further ahead in unorthodox lines, resulting in the publication in 1957 of *Latin: A Structural Approach*. My purpose was not so much to write a textbook for the average teacher as to try out new techniques, and my present experience with programmed learning is a continuation of this search. At one time or another I have discarded almost all of the traditional methods, but if I could find nothing better to replace them with I have returned to them. The authors of this revision, however, have dedicated themselves to the task of rewriting the earlier material so that it would be of use to the maximum number of teachers and students, a praiseworthy task. The outstanding feature of the book, however, is still the fact that like its predecessor it relies upon modern linguistic analysis rather than the traditional semantically based grammar. In order to make the book as useful as possible, however, they have kept the traditional terminology.

The basic assumption of the traditional grammarians was the existence of a universal grammar to which all languages conformed, although some were noticeably more "irregular" than others. English and Latin were both said to have gender, although there is nothing in English which corresponds to the arbitrary choice of adjective in *bonus vir, bona fēmina,* and *bonum oppidum;* English uses "good" with "man," "woman," and "town" without change and therefore does not have gender. The pronoun system of "he," "she," and "it" has nothing in common with Latin gender except the terms "masculine," "feminine," and "neuter."

The assumption of the structural linguists, on the other hand, is that language systems are totally different systems, although they may resemble one another *in partibus*. In constructing materials for foreign language learning the linguist analyzes both languages, the target language and the language to be learned. By comparing the two analyses—by laying one grid on top of the other, so to speak—he can observe where the points of difficulty lie and can also suggest an economical order of presentation of items. But linguistics per se does not tell us how to teach these structures; methodology lies rather in the fields of psychology and pedagogy. It is true that a more accurate understanding of the problems may suggest new techniques; however, we cannot speak of a "linguistic method" of learning a language but only of materials that are linguistically oriented. This book offers teachers both exercises that are new (like Pattern Practice) and those that are traditional (like English to Latin prose composition). The teacher is thus free to choose and experiment.

The traditional assumption that Latin and English shared a common grammar led to three major weaknesses in textbooks: 1) the explanations were not clear because in stressing alleged resemblances they obscured the real difficulties; 2) unaware of the importance of word order in English the authors wrote Latin in a fixed word order so that students, used to word order as a signal in English, were relying upon word order as a signal, instead of inflections; and 3) vocabulary items were given a one-to-one correspondence which they do not in fact possess.

This book presents the student with a corpus of Latin material which accurately represents the Latin language along with a variety of exercises. In my opinion it should do a lot to advance the cause of Latin.

Waldo E. Sweet

The University of Michigan

EDITORS' NOTE

This book is a complete and thoroughgoing revision of the *Latin Workshop Experimental Materials*, Book One, published in 1953. The editors, former members of the Workshop, have tried to make a more orderly, organized textbook, with many more study tools and new types of material added. The original reading material has been kept, but thoroughly revised and reduced in vocabulary load.

Like its predecessor, the text is intended for those who want to try applying some of the findings of linguistics to their work, but are not yet ready to forego a traditional terminology; for those who want to use oral pattern practice; for those who want stress on the practical; for those who want good reading material; for those who want variety in the approach to the problem of teaching elementary Latin.

Our greatest debt, of course, is to Professor Waldo E. Sweet, of The University of Michigan, who brought this whole development into being, who made the original materials possible, and who has been tireless in his patience and help in the process of this revision.

The contributions of the members of the 1952 and 1953 Workshops at The University of Michigan (under a Carnegie Grant) are still evident in the new book. They are, in addition to the editors of this text: Sister Mary Donald, Margaret Forbes, Rev. Charles Herkert, Eleanor Huzar, Eileen Johnson, Edith Kovach, Austin Lashbrook, Joan Madsen, Malcolm McLoud, Stanford Miller, Gerda Seligson, John Shepard, Lawrence Springer, Hilton Turner, Myra Uhlfelder, Laura Voelkel, Richard Walker, Evelyn Way, Elizabeth White.

Thanks are due those teachers, former members of other workshops, who have used the material in stencil form and made many helpful suggestions: Mary Babic, Ann Horton, Marion Williamson. The material has also been in constant use in the classes of Clara Ashley and Grace Crawford.

We should also like to express our gratitude to those students of Edwin O. Smith School, Storrs, and of Hartford Public High School who typed many manuscript and stencil pages, and to all the Latin students in these, Newton High, and other schools who have manfully endured stencils for the past five years, in the interest of perfecting the materials.

PREFACE FOR TEACHERS

Since the form and content of this book differ considerably from those of most current texts, it seems advisable to explain the purpose, contents, and possible ways of using the materials.

The text is intended to give the student familiarity with the most important structures, basic to an understanding of what he will read in Latin authors. In some schools these basics can be covered in one year, in some, a year and a quarter or a year and a half may be needed, in others, two years may be taken, particularly for younger students in grades 7 and 8.

The fact that Latin is a language, a tool for communicating thought, is implicit in all the material; the goal of reading to comprehend the thought content is always kept in view; the reading material is based on Latin writers from the very beginning with direct quotations and the narrative selections adapted in varying degrees from ancient sources. Much more attention is given to materials for practicing structures and forms than to discussion of them; the approach is inductive; the units are broad and comprehensive in content. There is opportunity to use ear and tongue as well as eye and pen.

One of the most distinctive features of the book is the arrangement of the material in what may be called a "horizontal" rather than a vertical organization. In the presentation of nouns, this means that nouns of five declensions are presented simultaneously, but only in the nominative and accusative case at first; next, all are taken in the ablative, then in the plurals of these cases. The genitive and dative are reserved until after work has been done on verbs. The horizontal organization places the emphasis on "what case" rather than "what declension." Since 85 per cent of noun use is in the nominative, accusative, and ablative cases, this corresponds to frequency of use. Similarly with verbs: the third singular form is used as a "crutch" until the basic noun work is done, then, the present tense of all conjugations is taken. Frequency of use determines the taking up of the perfect tense long before the imperfect and others. In the organization of material, then, the stress is on frequency and therefore usefulness. The most used forms are taken up first and practiced the most. This procedure, we are sure, after years of use, offers no problems to students and makes for a better balanced picture of the language from the start.

There is an abundance, not to say a superabundance, of practice material. Each lesson on structure has about a hundred sentences, exclusive of connected reading or quotations. At the outset it is vital that you as a teacher realize that *not* all classes need to do all the practice work in every lesson. How much you do will depend upon what you intend to cover in the year, the speed and ease with which your students grasp the material, and what you omit to use for review purposes. Probably no group should ever do all of any one lesson; surely no one should do all of all of them. Why then the abundance? It is there to allow you to make choices, to select the types of drill which best suit you and your class, to do more work on points that a group finds difficult (a factor which will differ to some extent from year to year, from class to class, and from teacher to teacher). The keynote is FLEXIBILITY.

As we have implied, it is also advisable, even with review lessons provided, to leave some items for review purposes before tests, at the year's end, or at the start of the next year. Some might care to leave the sections labeled "optional" for this; others, the English sentences; others, the detailed work on word study—or something else.

Some teachers may prefer more of the written work, some more of the oral; in fact, the text can be used entirely without oral pattern practice, great though the advantage of that procedure seems to most users; conversely, it can be used with chiefly oral work and reading, and little written if that is preferred. For a fast class, a minimum of practice may be needed (never practice to the point of boredom!); however, when the thoughtful student who may not have quite understood a point pleads, "Can you let me try it once more?" it is very useful to have additional practice material available.

For younger students, especially in grades 7 and 8, the oral practices should be shortened and fewer exercises given because of their shorter attention span. If half a practice does not suffice to gain the desired mastery, the second half may be given in a subsequent assignment. For older and more sophisticated students than the average, more use of quotations, including optional readings, and less of the exercises may be the best procedure.

In short, just remember in your planning that *no one* is expected to do all of every lesson—the book is just not designed that way.

Now we will take up each item in the lessons and explain its relation to the whole plan, the values to be derived, and suggested ways of using each one.

Introductory Lessons

The introductory lessons do not need to be covered in their entirety before work on the regular lessons begins. Some of the basic concepts about language which they contain should be understood at the very outset; other items are placed there more for convenience of reference than for necessary use at the start. This is especially true of the pronunciation rules on pages 7 and 8. It is usually best for a student to learn pronunciation by imitation of a live model, the teacher, reinforced perhaps by one heard on tape. The preliminary practices are good for training the ear to fine distinctions. They may, however, be equally well used after a couple of months of study, when the early meticulous attention to sounds and accuracy of pronunciation and spelling begin to wear off. The section on the history of Latin can be done at any convenient time. Also the information on the reading content of the book may be done informally by the teacher as each type of story occurs, or it may be read when the first connected reading is reached, or at the outset, or in a review of the reading content.

The inclusion of the Aztec problems may puzzle you. Experience has shown us that it affords excellent practice to develop a grasp of the idea of a highly "synthetic" language— where a single "word" or unit has a complex formation and meaning which would require several words to express in a language such as English. There is an advantage in objectivity gained from working on this concept out of the context of Latin or any familiar situation.

None of the exercises or problems in the introductory lessons are meant to offer material for learning in the same way as the content of regular lessons; they are there to suggest ideas, concepts, principles, or background. The only things which should carry over to the regular lessons are the general concepts—and the Roman numerals (which may be learned as they occur in the regular lessons).

ANSWERS TO PROBLEMS IN INTRODUCTION

Problem I

1. The sound represented by a hook
2. ni-
3. ti-
4. -coka-
5. -mayana-
6. -s

Problem II

1. komit-
2. -meh
3. -sosol
4. -cīn
5. petat-
6. ikal-
7. -wewe
8. -kōyame

Problem III

1. -k, -k-
2. ti-
3. -k-, k-
4. kin-, -kin-
5. ni-
6. -eh
7. -ita-
8. -s

Notice that the first and second persons are added to the beginning of the word, while the third person is added to the end.

Problem IV

1. By adding the sounds -s, -z, or -iz.
2. When the subject is singular, the verb has the sounds -s, -z, or -iz.
3. By adding the sounds -t, -d, or -id.
4. None
5. Position before the verb.
6. Position after the verb.

Problem V

1. -t
2. Anywhere
3. -m
4. Long vowel and -s
5. -s or no ending after vowel
6. can(i)
7. terre-
8. parv-
9. By having an ending which shows same form

Regular Lessons

There are forty-four regular lessons. At the beginning of each lesson there are *quotations* from writers of Latin—ancient, medieval, even modern. (An effort has been made to avoid any later quotations which violate the structures of classical Latin and so might confuse students.) These quotes are given as they occur in the text of the author named, except for a few omissions marked " . . . ," or the few marked "adapted" where the changes are minimal to make them intelligible out of context, etc. The word order is that of the original source— not "regularized" to conform to an artificial concept of Latin word order, as is sometimes done in quoting.

Many quotations are taken from such collections as:

Jakob Werner, "Lateinische Sprichwörter und Sinnsprüche des Mittelalters," Heidelberg, 1912, and

Wilhelm Binder, "Novus Thesaurus Adagiorum Latinorum," Stuttgart, 1861.

Since the quotations are intended to serve as models of the structure or forms in the lesson, and since they recur frequently in the exercises, it is advisable that students learn them, although some of the more abstract or sophisticated may be omitted for younger or slower pupils.

The *Statement of Purpose* is meant to focus the students' attention on the major structural item in the lesson as a whole.

In each of the first six lessons there are one or two *pictures* to introduce vocabulary and present a simple situation. The pictures are usually described in a simple paragraph which the students can read at the stage before they can handle even a simple anecdote. The major importance of the picture is that it serves as a basis for oral question and answer, practicing the structure being taught in the lesson.

In the rest of the book, from Lesson Ten on, the pictures serve to present some of the vocabulary in graphic form and the "contextual orientation" of the narrative of the lesson. Presenting some of the vocabulary in this way has the value of breaking away from verbal equivalency only: "E-Q-U-U-S" = "H-O-R-S-E," by equating "equus" to . The pictures throughout may help students avoid misunderstandings of the setting or general background of a narrative. Any and all of them may be used as a basis for oral question and answer in preview or review of the reading lesson.

Filmstrips of the pictures will be available. Use of them in the classroom serves to focus attention of all the class on the item at hand better than when each student is using his own book. Also questions may be asked without the student seeing the answers in the text.

In general, the development of vocabulary or structure from the pictures is best done in the classroom under the guidance of the teacher, not assigned for preparation. Then such questions may be reviewed and studied for rapid oral response as an assignment. Often it is valuable to interweave the presentation of structure in the Pattern Reading with the picture material, or even take up the Pattern Reading first, especially in Lessons One through Six.

Oral question and answer in the Latin language (always being sure the student understands what is being said, but *not* "translating") is an excellent means of establishing firmly the basic elements of a Latin sentence and the function of such items as case forms of nouns. The process of substitution of a correct case in answer to a set interrogative word is a relatively simple, but valid drill. If the question words seem a bit artificial, it is of no great moment; pupils soon learn to realize that they are intended to point up matters of structure—that *quem* calls for an object, *quo modo* for an ablative expressing a feeling, etc.

The purpose of the *Pattern Reading* is to provide an introduction to the new structure, which can be handled inductively. The *sample sentences* (A) provide illustrations of the main structural features, used in sentences with meanings given, so that the students, guided by the teacher, may perceive for themselves just what is involved. The concepts that a student develops for himself and perceives through his own efforts of analysis and thought are the ones that he remembers best. Inductive presentation usually more than repays the extra time it takes. While it takes less time for the teacher to make an explanation, which may be lucid and often brilliant, and set a rule to be followed, the student tends to become passive; the more active his participation in the analysis as well as the practicing, the better the results. It is for this reason that no analysis of structure is given in the text of the lesson. Summaries of the most important points of structure are made in Appendix B, on the page to which reference is made in the lesson. This material, however, is best used in reviewing a lesson after it has been worked out inductively. (However, there is nothing in this format to prevent a teacher from making any explanation he desires at any point where he may prefer to do so.) The structure questions are intended as a guide either to the first inductive working out of the lesson or as a later checkup to see that important or difficult points are understood. Many more questions than those given should be asked and the students' own questions encouraged, especially at this early stage. Many of us believe thoroughly and tell students, "The more stupid the question seems, the more it needs to be asked and answered at once!"

As a further aid at this point, form charts are given when it seems useful to isolate forms that must be learned in a given lesson from the necessarily rather large number of forms summarized in Appendix C. In general the categories of forms follow the traditional pattern, except for the order of noun cases; here the order of nominative, accusative, ablative, dative, genitive follows the order in which they are taught, the order of frequency of occurrence (except for genitive being more frequent than dative), and puts similar forms together in paradigms the greatest number of times. The determining factor, here as in the order of presentation of most items, is frequency of usage; ease of memorization as a paradigm is secondary but useful.

The practice sentences (B), the core of the Pattern Reading, are intended for rapid practice in recognition of forms or structures, their meaning and use. This may be arrived at by discussion, question and answer, or explaining the meaning, or all three. This section is best used chiefly for classroom practice, rather than for a student working on his own. The reason for the large number of sentences (20 to 30) is to allow each pupil in a class at least one opportunity to try a sentence for himself—it is not intended that each student laboriously work out all thirty in detailed preparation. Neither is it necessary to do all the practice in a small or quick class—where it may be well to skip some sentences that are very simple and do a few at the end which may be more difficult. Also, some of these practices (notably in Lessons Three, Six, Eight, Nine, Eleven, Twelve, etc.) lend themselves to taping for rapid oral drill, if this type of exercise works well for you and your particular class. In this form they can be used for practice outside of class, after an understanding of the meaning and structure is assured.

In summary, in Pattern Reading especially, it is important to keep the talking about the language to a minimum and to stress practicing and using the forms and structures, with just enough generalizing and organizing into orderly patterns or paradigms as is necessary to give a basis for a carry-over into use in future situations.

The *Exercises* may be used for oral or written practice: picture drills and metaphrases lend themselves best to oral work, while the form developers and English-to-Latin sentences are best written; question-and-answer and multiple choice may be done equally well either way. Some exercises may be done in class, some assigned for homework, or part of an exercise may be done in class and part as preparation. If the particular work is well understood, it is not necessary to do all of each exercise (but do not always avoid the later and harder sentences). If still more practice is needed, a type of exercise you find helpful to your students can be expanded. Another way to expand the drill possibilities is to go back to an earlier lesson and, using the pictures or sentences, add the new item: for example, add adjectives to nouns in the sentences, change sentences to passive form, change singulars to plurals, etc., in a context where the familiarity with the material may be very helpful especially to the slower students.

Metaphrases, as is explained to students in the first metaphrase exercise of Lesson One, are not completion exercises (they are always labeled and a dotted line used for the omission, not a blank as in completions). They are partial sentences to be studied for the relationships of the words given, without all the material provided which could easily make the meaning clear from the vocabulary, without sufficient attention to the structure. They may be completed after the other essential work is done.

The English-to-Latin sentences practicing a given structure are placed in the lesson which follows, not in the lesson where the structure is taught. In this way some review of the previous lesson is provided, and the hardest type of exercise is deferred until the structure and vocabulary are quite familiar.

Pattern Practice is intended for rapid oral response. Many users find that it works best as the final exercise on structure, after practice has been done in other ways; it is the step taken for mastery. It is highly successful when done with the aid of a tape recorder, with the student listening and practicing in a language laboratory and reciting to the tape in class. If the tape is not used, the speed of response tends to break down; however, it can be done without the recorder. The sentences are carefully built so that the vocabulary burden is minimal and the focus is on the structure. If the practice is shortened for junior high groups, be sure to omit total "frames" of sentences, not to interrupt the sequences. The sentences should also be taped out of the set order, with longer pauses, so that there is not mere rote response to the order itself. These rapid, correct responses give students an assurance and pleasure in achievement that contribute greatly to their progress. Tapes of the practices will be available.

The *Reading Sections (LĒCTIO)*, other than the little paragraphs describing pictures, begin at Lesson Ten. Thereafter each lesson has a reading and a total of eight lessons are entirely reading, with only word study, vocabulary, and occasionally a very small item of forms such as an irregular verb in one or two tenses. The anecdotes, stories, or essays which make up most of the readings are based on ancient sources, much modified at the start, gradually working up to material very close to the original, with the last one edited only to the extent of omissions and some vocabulary modifications. About twelve of the readings consist of collections of quotations or short unedited selections such as fables, short poems, and part of one medieval dialogue.

Especially in the first experiences with connected reading, it is probably advisable to read at least part of a story with the class as a group, helping them with such new problems as transition words, carry-over of subject, etc. It is also advisable to help with the interpretation of the quotations for a time, for isolated sentences out of a context have some disadvantages in spite of the merits of brevity and genuineness. If this is done, reviewing what has been read, completing the story or set of quotations, answering the questions in *Respondē Latīnē* on the stories, and vocabulary work make useful assignments for individual out-of-class work.

The work on the reading may be done in whatever way the teacher wishes. We would, however, suggest that it is very profitable to discuss the sense of what is said, to determine accuracy of reading by question and answer in English and in Latin, rather than simply to "translate." The poor English or garbled phrases of a poor "transliteration" do not serve nearly so well the aim of reading to understand a thought as do the other methods suggested. It is most important, whatever method is used, to be sure that the reading has *meaning* for the student and that the Latin is comprehended in the order and way in which it was written. To aid the latter aim, filmstrips with the stories in sense-unit lines will be made available.

Still more reading practice is provided by *Supplementary Reading* in Appendix A. These stories fit in after Lesson Fifteen at intervals indicated in the lessons and may be used any time after the lesson indicated (that is, the structures and vocabulary are geared to do so).

There are also *Optional Reading* sections in each regular lesson which illustrate the structure of the lesson. They may keep some quick minds occupied while others drill structure, or be done by the class with the teacher, or done in review. The vocabulary is not limited to the lesson vocabulary words.

If a teacher wishes to cover Parts I and II in a year (through subjunctives), the supplementary and optional reading and even some of the reading lesson material may have to be by-passed, or perhaps used later in review.

The *Word Study* items are related directly to the vocabulary of the lesson, but they are not random or casual. In the course of the total group of word study sections almost all the important prefixes have been taken up, many of the common suffixes, the most usual patterns of change in adapting Latin words to English spelling and use, and the common semantic shifts. Some items, of course, are introduced merely as a matter of interest, or to suggest avenues of interest to students. The words suggested as derivatives are by no means exhaustive; here again the intention is to suggest rather than complete the possibilities. After the first few lessons, the more obvious derivatives are often left to the student to mention. Probably these items are best gone over in class by students and teacher together. If some parts are assigned, the students should have access to an English dictionary in which derivation is given. One of the best smaller dictionaries for this purpose is the *Thorndike-Barnhart Desk Dictionary*.

Vocabulary, listed at the end of the lesson, includes those words the student should be sure to know upon completion of the lesson. After Lesson Nine these are not all of the words used in the lesson. As soon as it is comprehensible to the student, and therefore practical, the necessary information about the Latin word is given here. Nouns are listed by nominative and ablative forms until Lesson Twenty-one on genitives, and the change is made then to genitive, in deference to dictionary usage which they must cope with later on. Verbs are listed at first by third singular forms, then, as soon as possible, by two and then four principal parts. Partly because of these changes, and partly because of the absence of English meanings (also as an aid to derivation work), it is highly desirable that students keep a notebook of vocabulary. In it can be kept the possible meanings of a word, which may be added to as new meanings in new contexts occur. A real effort has been made to use words in widely varying senses, so that students will not develop the erroneous concept of one-word-one-meaning, in spite of what is said in the Introductory Lessons. This is also the reason for the omission of meanings in the vocabulary listings.

In Lessons One to Nine it is possible for the student to find a meaning for all words by observing the quotations, sample sentences, and obvious items in the pictures. From Lesson Ten on, pictures, quotations, and sample sentences provide much of the vocabulary. Many other words in the readings are obvious from derivatives. Words used only occasionally or expressions likely to cause trouble are taken care of in the *notā bene* section. A few remaining words, chiefly adverbs on the "vocabulary-to-be-learned" list will have to be given by the teacher or looked up in the vocabulary provided at the end of each volume.

In line with the thinking set forth in the introductory lessons, we feel it is inadvisable to "drill vocabulary" in the sense of giving "a" meaning for a word. The time is far better spent in reading and seeing the words over and over in a context.

There are some *variations of the form* of the lessons. Those lessons which consist almost wholly of reading have already been mentioned. Some lessons (adjectives, participles, indirect statements) are divided into two parts because of the length and complexity of the contents; yet they do form a whole and are better kept as a unit so that, for instance, students realize at once that there are two types of adjectives, etc.

The nine review lessons are placed at strategic points, but the exercises may be reserved for testing times, end of year review, or otherwise used as the teacher sees fit. It is suggested, however, that the quotations, few vocabulary words, and practices on paradigms included in them not be neglected, or even be used in connection with the immediately preceding lessons.

Appendix A, as already noted, contains supplementary reading.

Appendix B contains summaries of the forms and constructions used in the book. The summaries are designed to fit in with the order and organization of the text, but are most appropriately used in reviewing after the practicing and using in context has been done.

The descriptions are structural but are made easier for the teacher who does not have linguistic training by the avoidance of linguistic terminology and by using or making possible the use of traditional terminology.

Appendix C contains the complete form charts for the material covered in the book.

The end vocabulary contains all words used in any part of the book; that at the end of Part I contains the words used in that part, including those used in Part I but assigned for learning in Part II.

CONTENTS

INTRODUCTORY LESSONS

ONE 1-5	How we learn to understand a language How English works Grammar Structure Differences in sound	
TWO 6-19	Sounds of Latin Differences in vocabulary Difference in the way languages fit together Differences based on context Similarities	Pronunciation Practice I, II Problems I-V
THREE 20-25	History of the Latin Language Cognates, Loan Words, Derivatives	Pronunciation Practice III
FOUR 26-27	Reading and Literature	

LESSONS

ONE 28-33	Picture paragraphs QUIS EST? FĒMINA VESTEM LAVAT	Subject and object (nominative, accusative singular) *Pattern Practice One*
TWO 34-39	Picture paragraphs QUID EST? AGRICOLA LABŌRAT	Neuter nouns; predicate nominative *Pattern Practice Two*
THREE 40-45	Picture paragraph MĪLES RŌMĀNUS	Ablative singular - adverbial uses *Pattern Practice Three*
FOUR 46-51	Picture paragraphs HARĒNA IN VIĀ	Ablative; more adverbial uses; place prepositions *Pattern Practice Four*
FIVE 52-56	Picture paragraphs LUPUS ET AGNUS IN AQUĀ	Adverbial accusative; prepositions *Pattern Practice Five*

INTRODUCTORY LESSON ONE

You are starting a new and challenging experience—the study of the Latin language. For some of you this is your first experience with a foreign language; others may have had some contact with a different tongue in school, at home, in your grandparents' or friends' homes, or from living in another country. Whatever your experience or lack of it, there are facts and ideas which will help you in your study of language if you come to understand them at the beginning.

First of all, Latin is a *language*. While it is not one in which large numbers of people now conduct daily conversation (though people certainly can and do communicate fluently in Latin), we must always remember that for many hundreds of years it was the speech of thousands of people, subjects of that great empire of Rome which ruled most of the Western world. People worked and fought, talked politics and philosophy, made love, and wrote poetry in this language. The record of what they thought and said has come down to us: it is a priceless part of the heritage of our civilization. We have inherited not only most of our *words* for important ideas but also many of the *ideas* themselves about life, liberty, democracy, religion, and science from the writers and speakers of Latin. The Latin language has truly been called the "main vehicle of Western culture." At a time of great challenges and deep thinking about our way of life, it is of the utmost importance that we should have as clear an understanding as possible of the sources of our ideas and ideals. One of the most important keys to that understanding is the language which transmitted them, namely, Latin.

Since Latin is a language, it must be taught and studied as one—not merely as a collection of symbols on a printed page but as speech and a way of communicating thought. What does this mean for your study of it? It means that you will work in it orally as well as by reading and writing, that you will be constantly observing how ideas are expressed and thoughts communicated.

A. How we learn to understand a language

What makes the difference between languages? *What do we have to study in order to learn another language?* To answer this question we should do some thinking about the process involved in learning our own. Since we were very young when we began learning it, we don't remember exactly how we came to understand English. By the time we were five or six years old, we had a working knowledge of our native language, even though we could not yet read or write—and, of course, we did not know a very large number of the words of the language. All of us are still learning words and we can still remember a little of the process of learning to read and write; therefore, we are apt to think of learning to read, spell, and understand new words as being the chief element involved in learning another language. But are words alone the answer? How do we arrive at the meaning of a statement? Let's examine how just one simple English sentence works.

Alice watched the little rabbit in the garden.

Of what does a sentence consist? Of *sounds* (or letters representing sounds) formed into words, which in turn are organized into a sentence which gives a message. The sentence creates a picture in our minds at once. It may not be the same picture for all of us: the rabbit may be of various colors; it may be sleeping, eating, or loping along; Alice may be young or old, pretty or plain; the garden well kept or weed filled, with flower beds or a vegetable patch. Yet these pictures in the minds of various people have several basic features in common: a girl or woman is observing a small rabbit in an outdoor spot among growing things. How do we get this picture in our minds?

Some of the *individual words* create pictures—rabbit, garden, little, watched—that is, we have come to associate the sounds of these words with certain "contents" familiar to all speakers of English. In the case of "rabbit," we probably saw a live one or a picture in a book when we were about two years old and we heard someone pronounce the word. Perhaps at first we thought it meant any small animal and called a dog "rabbit" the next time we saw one. Gradually, by being corrected, we learned to associate the word with the right animal. By the same sort of process the other words acquired "meaning" for us.

But does this account for the statement the sentence makes? Do the individual words tell us who watched whom? Clearly it was Alice who observed the rabbit, not the rabbit who watched Alice. Who was little? The rabbit, not Alice or the garden. How do we *know* this? Not from anything yet mentioned about the individual words, but it must be something very definite because we do not have any doubt about the meaning. As we think about it, we must realize that the *order of the words* provides this information. To test this, switch "Alice" with "rabbit": "The rabbit watched little Alice" gives quite a different picture. Test it still further: "Alice rabbit the little watched the garden in" becomes nonsense. It is the order of the words that tells us who did the watching, who was watched, and where they were.

We also know that only one rabbit was involved by the fact that the word used is "rabbit," not "rabbit*s*" (the absence of the -*s* on rabbit). We know that the action took place at some time in the past by the -*ed* on "watch*ed*." Changes in the *form of words* affect the total meaning.

The two remaining words in the sentence, though short, do their part in establishing the meaning: "the" and "in." "In" tells us that the garden was the location of the action and "the" establishes that we are talking about a particular rabbit or garden previously mentioned or known. Words like this help group the other words of a sentence and establish relationships between them, rather than create pictures of their own. Such *function words* are the mortar that binds the bricks (content words) together into a meaningful whole.

Then if we think how our sentence would sound as spoken aloud, the tone of voice, the placing of stress, or the pauses would contribute something more to the meaning—an attitude such as doubt, amazement, pleasure, or displeasure. Try saying the sentence aloud stressing different words each time, pausing at different points and using different tones. You will find that a great variety of attitudes can be expressed even about a simple situation such as this.

Finally, you may be one of those who have been picturing all along a special Alice, rabbit, and garden. This may be because you have a little sister named Alice who keeps rabbits, or it may be because you have read Lewis Carroll's book *Alice in Wonderland* and a sentence such as this immediately recalls his vivid and unforgettable characters. It is in this way that broad general experience and wide reading affect our understanding of all that we encounter.

To return now to our original questions, "Of what does the sentence consist?" "How does it work to convey meaning?", we can now summarize our answers. The summary might well serve as a description of how English sentences in general work and of what we learn when we learn to understand a language.

B. How English works

1. The sentence we have been talking about (or any sentence in any language) consists of *sounds* spoken aloud or represented on a page by groups of letters. Of all the possible sounds that human speech organs can produce, only certain selected ones are used to convey meaning in English. We learn to recognize the sounds that are customarily used in English, to produce them in a way understandable to others, and how they combine. (For example, we never use in English the *ü* or the gutteral *ch* sounds common in German; we soon recognize words containing them as non-English words. Also the combination *rd* occurs in the middle or end of a word—ga*rd*en, gua*rd*—but never at the start.)

2. These individual sounds combine into larger units that have meaning. In English these units are *words* or *word parts* that combine to form many different words (e.g., *boy*; the *-ish* in *boyish*, the *-ness* in *boyishness*; the *-s* in *boys*; the *tom* in *tomboy*). We learn the words and word parts and what they mean and how meaningful combinations that change their form are made.

3. The individual words are fitted together into a larger unit or sentence which gives a statement or message to us. We learn what the patterns of the sentence are, how words are related to one another in the pattern, and so the complete meaning of the sentence by:

    a. *order of words* ("Alice watched the rabbit." differs from "The rabbit watched Alice." Also a "vegetable garden" differs from a "garden vegetable.")

    b. *certain letters* (*sounds*) regularly *added* to words or *changed* in words (watch, watch*ed*; t*a*ke, t*oo*k; rabbit, rabbit*s*)

    c. *function words*. These are few in number ("and," "in," "the," "is," "will").

    d. *intonation*. pitch, tone, and stress (hard to represent in writing except by variations of type and punctuation. Intonation shows the difference between a *garden city* and *Garden City*).

4. By far the largest number of words are *content words*, words that convey pictures or meaning. They are listed in dictionaries, catalogued, and defined. We keep on learning these all the time we use a language, long after we have mastered its other aspects.

5. Words occur in connection with a wide variety of situations in a great many *contexts*. In this way they acquire a tone or flavor which influences our concept of the meaning in a new use. Context gives a deeper meaning or value to words; we learn this only by wide reading and experience. (For example, to a city child "garden" may lack the variety and richness of possibility that it has for a country person; an Alice you dislike may prejudice you, unjustly, toward a character in a story. Those who have read *Alice in Wonderland* have a much more vivid picture in mind when they hear a sentence like the one we analyzed.)

These same elements go to make up any sentence, paragraph, or book in English—and, in varying proportions, they are the factors that make up a language and that must be studied in learning a new one. Perhaps you have noticed that a term often used in connection with language study has been omitted from our discussion so far: grammar. What is "grammar" in English or any language? Perhaps you have been told that there is a lot of grammar to learn in Latin. Like many terms this one is used to cover more than one thing.

C. *Grammar*

"Grammar" as you use it now in your English class deals chiefly with a fairly high level of discrimination, learning the most effective ways to speak and write. There are in English, as in any language, various differences of usage which indicate level of education, social group, home town, and even age. Some of these are not generally acceptable as good usage. ("I don't want no help." indicates lack of education; "Who done it" is acceptable only in some country communities or in humorous reference to mystery stories.) This kind of study is possible only for a person who knows a language quite well; a number of years' experience with it is necessary before you are in a position to pick among various usages. So while this kind of grammar is useful to you in dealing with your native language, it is not the point at which you begin in the learning process.

Another very common meaning of "grammar" is the technical description given to the way a language works. Many people feel that this is the important thing in learning another language: that if they can "quote the rules" they know the "grammar" of the language. Description is important (it is a study in itself) and some technical terms are certainly helpful in working with a second language; they can save a great many words of explanation and speed up our learning. But knowing *about* a language does not necessarily mean knowing it; and surely this is not the way we learned language naturally when we were learning our own. In fact there are many languages spoken in the world today which have never been described at all; yet they are used and spoken, and many fluent speakers of English know nothing about the technical description of the workings of their own language.

What is the "grammar" that does apply to the beginner—the child learning his native speech or the beginning learner of a second language? It is the basic patterns of sound, word, and sentence, the *structure* and operation of the language which those who are native or fluent in it handle automatically. This you must be able to do before you can describe a language or make fine discriminations of usage. In English it means being able to use without hesitation the correct word order, endings, function words, and intonation, which a six-year-old can do when he is ready for school.

D. *Structure*

To prove to yourself that this is true, that you have mastered the structure of English, try answering the following questions about the first two lines of the poem "Jabberwocky" from *Alice Through the Looking Glass*.

> 'Twas brillig, and the slithy toves
> Did gyre and gimble in the wabe.

1. What gyred and gimbled?

2. Where did the gyring and gimbling take place?

3. What did the toves do?

Your knowledge of the sentence patterns of English will provide some of the answers for you (although you might not all have the same answers). What are the significant features of structure that appear in these two lines? First, there is the presence of the well-known function-words *was, and, the, did, in.* Second, the order of these words in relation to the nonsense words is not haphazard, but that of a standard English sentence. For example, *did* suggests that *gyre* and *gimble* could be verbs (or certain kinds of nouns); *the* indicates that *slithy toves* is probably an adjective noun combination; the *-s* on *toves* looks very much like a plural *-s*. If the lines had been read aloud such features as pitch, stress, and pauses would have provided additional clues.

These lines, therefore, which seem like complete nonsense at first are found to have considerable sense, what we might call "structural sense." As Alice herself says, "Somehow it seems to fill my head with ideas--only I don't know excatly what they are!" The "ideas" which Alice had were structural ideas, but of course, with nonsense content words Alice received a nonsense message. If you would like to see one person's substitutions of content words for the nonsense words, read the chapter entitled "Humpty Dumpty" in *Alice Through the Looking Glass*.

It is this kind of mastery of the structure of the language that must be a person's first concern in learning a new tongue. Descriptions of the language will be used to help, but will not substitute for, the acquisition of the ability to use the language; refinements of usage will come for the advanced student.

The descriptions used here will be chiefly those that will help in acquiring mastery over fundamental structure, not those which can only be made after you know the meaning of the material. For instance, it is hot helpful to a person who does not know English to be told that a noun may be defined as "the name of a person, place, or thing," or even to add "or quality or idea"—however true this statement may be. What a beginner learning English needs to know is how to recognize that a certain word (of unknown meaning) in the sentence is a noun. If it distinguishes singular from plural form (usually by '-s') and can fit into a frame like one of these, it is a noun:

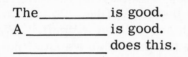

The_____ is good.
A _____ is good.
_____ does this.

If a word fits into a frame like one of these it is a verb:

The man _____ s the house.   The men _____ the house.
The man _____ s there.   The men _____ there.
A man _____ s wise.   The men _____ wise.

An adjective fits into both of these frames. (Some words used as adjectival modifiers fit only into the first example.)

The _____ man came.   The man is _____ .

These distinctions of form and environment of words are more useful than definitions of meaning or listing. What, for instance, is *garden*? The *garden* is beautiful (noun). He *gardens* every Saturday (verb). I have a new *garden* chair (adjectival).

QUESTIONS ON LESSON ONE

1. What are the most important factors that make up a language?

2. What determines the pattern of English sentences?

3. How can you recognize a noun in an English sentence? a verb? an adjective?

4. What are possible meanings of "grammar"?

5. Why is the study of Latin important today?

INTRODUCTORY LESSON TWO

In the first part of this introduction, we outlined what makes up a language, what we did in learning our own, what we study when we want to learn another. We saw that we must study the sounds, the formation or shaping of words, the patterns of sentences, as well as the meanings of words in many contexts. What we must next realize is that *languages are different* not in one but in all of these respects; they use different sets of sounds and ways of forming words, different sentence patterns and word order, as well as different words for things. There are degrees of difference. Where a language chances to be similar to our own the learning may seem to be easier, if we are not lulled into expecting too much similarity; more useful, however, is to see just how unlike your own a new language can be, and to accept this fact. Once it is accepted and you neither fight nor ignore the differences, the whole task becomes far simpler.

A. *Differences in sound*

No two languages ever use exactly the same sets of sounds. There may be many similar sounds, but there is never exact identity. For example, in English we distinguish sounds of *l* and *r* whereas in some other languages (among them Korean) people do not make any distinction. In English, "root" and "loot" are two different words with entirely different meanings. This seems entirely obvious to us, but a Korean learning English has a hard time to hear and make this distinction, for to him they are alike. To take another example, our letter *p* stands for several different sounds, with and without a "puff." Which sound we use makes no difference in meaning to us. We make the puff when we say "pot," but not when we say "spot." (If you don't believe this try saying the words with your hand before your mouth so that you can feel the difference which you probably cannot hear, since it makes no meaningful distinction.) In some other languages, however, the puff of air or lack of it is important. In Chinese *Pa* with the puff means "eight," without it, it means "white." In French the puff is never used; you will not speak French well unless you learn to omit the puff on such words as "Paris."

Writing systems represent the various sounds by symbols or letters. Ideally each sound should be represented by only one letter and each letter should stand for one set of sounds. Some languages (e.g., Spanish, Czech, Finnish) have a writing system that fits the sounds very accurately, but in English the alphabet fits very poorly, as we know only too well from our many spelling problems. Who would ever guess that *pair, pear*, and *pare* were pronounced alike? Or that the *-ough* was different in *cough, through, tough*, and *though*? Latin, however, is a language for which the alphabet is almost, but not quite, a perfect fit. Latin spelling therefore is very easy since we know just what sound each letter represents.

B. *The sounds of Latin*

We are able to reconstruct quite accurately the pronunciation of Latin used by the ancient Romans. This should be learned correctly from the very beginning.[1] While we don't have the

---

[1] The pronunciation outlined here is as close as we can get to that used in ancient times. Pronunciation gradually changed during the Middle Ages and more modern times. The later style of pronunciation is used today in Italy and by the Roman Catholic Church in its ritual and sometimes in its schools. In some countries, Latin is pronounced as if it were the native language. Lawyers today in our country use the Anglicized (English-like) pronunciation for their Latin—a pronunciation no Roman would have understood. So, while different pronunciations are correct in different situations, in this book we are going to use the system most like that of the ancient Romans whose works you will read.

problem, even in the oral use of Latin, of making ourselves understood by a native speaker, we should follow as well as we can what we know to have been true of ancient Latin sounds. We must be especially careful to make those distinctions which are meaningful in Latin. Accuracy of pronunciation will make for speed and accuracy in your understanding of the language in the classroom, and for a greater appreciation of the quality of Roman writing in your later work.

The best way to learn to pronounce is to listen to and imitate your teacher in class and on recordings. With practice, you can soon learn to read aloud with ease and to write Latin from dictation. It may be of help to you to keep in mind the following facts about Latin pronunciation.

1. There are no "silent letters" in the Latin writing system. *Stultē* and *quīnque* each have two syllables; the final *e* is sounded.

2. The same letter almost always represents the same sound.[2]

   c has a hard sound (like k) in *octō* and *decem*.

   g has a hard sound not only in *grammatica* but also in *vigintī*.

   s has the hissing sound, as in "horse" (not a buzz as in "bees") in both *sēdecim* and *prīmus*.

3. Latin consonants have in general much the same sound as the equivalent English consonants. There are two important exceptions:

   The letter *v* has the sound of the English *w*

   The letter written as *j* in this book has a sound similar to English *y* as in "young." It is sometimes written as *i*, although it is a consonant.

4. In Latin there is a distinction between long and short consonants; long consonants are indicated by a double letter, short ones by a single letter. This contrast is important because it often shows a difference in meaning; *calidus* means "warm," *callidus*, "clever."

5. There is a similar and very important difference between long and short vowels. Each of the five long vowels is represented with a length mark or macron (ā, ē, ī, ō, ū); the short vowels appear without marking (a, e, i, o, u). Since we do not make distinctions in this way in English, this is the feature of Latin pronunciation which will need the most practice. The contrasts are often very important in showing differences in meaning. The following chart will give you *approximate* English equivalents of the ten vowel sounds—they are *not* exact. You will need to listen to these sounds. If you know French, Spanish, or Italian your task is easy—simply pronounce these vowels much as you do in those languages. It is not possible to give adequate directions for pronunciation on the printed page. The best procedure is to imitate your teacher closely.

---

[2]Exceptions are *qu* (kw) as in *quīnque*, b = p as in *urbs*.

VOWEL CHART

long				short
ā	about as in f*a*ther ——————→ FĀTA ←—————— about as in *a*gain	a
ē	about as in th*e*y —————————→ CĒDET ←————— about as in p*e*t	e
ī	about as in mach*i*ne ————————→ FĪNIT ←————— about as in s*i*t	i
ō	about as in c*o*ne —————————→ CŌNOR ←———— about as in n*o*r	o*
ū	about as in r*u*de —————————→ LŪDUS ←———— about as in f*u*ll	u
	(cf. *noon*)	

*the short o is least like the English sound; listen to it carefully.

6. There are three vowel combinations or diphthongs which have sounds different from those of the separate vowels.

ae	about as in *ai*sle_____	AEQUUS
au	about as in th*ou* _____	AUGET
oe	about as in b*oy* _____	POENA

These sounds can be practiced with a tape. The following practices may also be practiced with tape until you have learned to recognize and distinguish the sounds.

PRONUNCIATION PRACTICE I

Purpose: to distinguish length

canum	regī	liber	hŏc	dūcī	stultē	īra
cānum	regī	līber	hŏc	dŭcī	stulte	īra
cānum	rĕgī	liber	hoc	ducī	stultē	īrā

solum	vultus	fīlia	modo	vēnit	dūceris	rēxeris
sōlum	vultūs	fīliā	modō	venit	dūcēris	rēxeris
solum	vultus	fīlia	modo	vēnit	dūceris	rēxerīs

dedī	īdem	notus	longā	fugit	hic
dēdī	īdem	notus	longā	fūgit	hic
dedī	idem	nōtus	longa	fugit	hīc

anus	summus	colis	callidus	erās	cūrō
annus	summus	collis	calidus	errās	currō
annus	sumus	collis	callidus	errās	cūrō

PRONUNCIATION PRACTICE II

Purpose: to distinguish diphthongs and some short vowels

fīliae	pauca	poenās	foedus	laudō	aula	caelō
fīliī	paucae	pōnās	foedus	lūdō	aula	cēlo
fīliae	paucae	poenās	fīdus	lūdō	āla	caelō

nāta	et	at	omnis	avis	ulter	eae	domine
nauta	et	ut	omnis	ovis	alter	eī	domina
nāta	at	at	amnis	avis	alter	eae	domina

C. *Differences in vocabulary*

Languages also differ, not only in having different words for things, but in the fact that a word in one language is rarely, if ever, the exact equivalent of a word in another. Words usually have an area of meaning and the entire area is not usually covered by just one word in another language. Take as an illustration the word "time" in English and its frequent Latin equivalent *tempus*.

Both *tempus* and "time" mean what is indicated in the overlap area in the diagram. The other meanings of *tempus* require other English words to express the idea; the other meanings of "time" require other Latin words as equivalents. If you ask "What is the word for time in Latin?" the response would be "What kind of time?" If you mean a "period of time," the word is *tempus*; if you mean "What time is it?" the word is *hōra*; if you mean "He stayed a long time," the word is *diū*. All these ideas are outside the area of *tempus*.

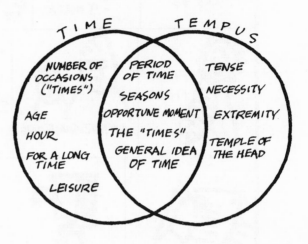

Some words are used in a wide variety of senses. What, for example, does "take" mean in English? The picture on page 10 illustrates some of the very different actions we lump under "take." It is hardly surprising that no single word in Latin, French, or German covers this same wide range.

Sometimes one language does not have a single word to take care of many actions of a similar sort while another does have such a single general word. In Chinese there is no one word for "carry." Before a speaker of Chinese could answer your question, "What is the Chinese word for carry?" he would have to know what was to be carried and how it was to be carried. There are about thirty possible situations and words, some of which are illustrated on page 10. It would strike a speaker of Chinese as exceedingly comical if you were to use *nye*, "to carry between thumb and forefinger," in speaking of an article like a trunk. From his point of view *we* describe very different actions by the word "carry."

Most languages have many multiple meaning words. For instance, what is the meaning of the German word *Zug*? If you look it up in a good dictionary, you will find about a hundred different entries, some of which are illustrated on page 11. How does a speaker of German know what is meant? By the context in which it is used, just as you have no trouble knowing what "take" means.

Finally there is a picture illustrating some of the meanings of the Latin word *gerit*. What does *gerit* mean? It all depends upon the situation in which it is used. Words acquire new shades of meanings through the situations in which they occur and the combinations in which they are used with other words.

Not all words in all languages have as wide a range of meanings as these, but you may never assume that a meaning which you have met is the only one possible for any given word. You must always be on the alert for new extensions and variations of meaning.

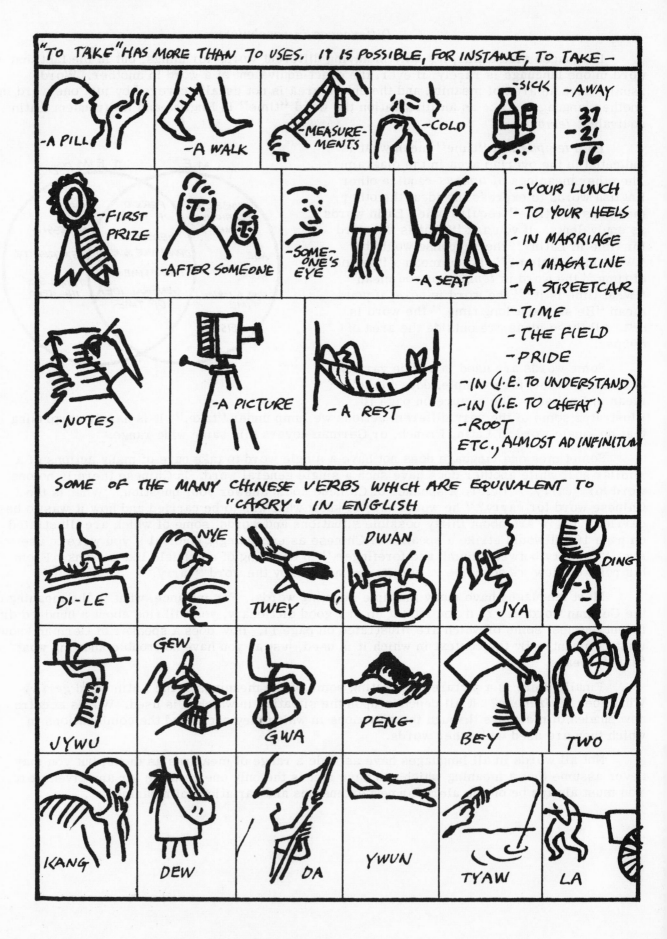

"TO TAKE" HAS MORE THAN 70 USES. IT IS POSSIBLE, FOR INSTANCE, TO TAKE—

-A PILL   -A WALK   -MEASUREMENTS   -COLD   -SICK -AWAY

$$\frac{\begin{array}{r}37\\-21\end{array}}{16}$$

-FIRST PRIZE   -AFTER SOMEONE   -SOMEONE'S EYE   -A SEAT

- YOUR LUNCH
- TO YOUR HEELS
- IN MARRIAGE
- A MAGAZINE
- A STREETCAR
- TIME
- THE FIELD
- PRIDE
- IN (I.E. TO UNDERSTAND)
- IN (I.E. TO CHEAT)
- ROOT
ETC., ALMOST AD INFINITUM

-NOTES   -A PICTURE   - A REST

SOME OF THE MANY CHINESE VERBS WHICH ARE EQUIVALENT TO "CARRY" IN ENGLISH

DI-LE   NYE   TWEY   DWAN   JYA   DING

JYWU   GEW   GWA   PENG   BEY   TWO

KANG   DEW   DA   YWUN   TYAW   LA

HERE ARE SOME OF THE 100+ USES OF THE GERMAN WORD "ZUG"...

ZUG = "HERD"

ZUG = "FLOCK"

ZUG = "TRAIN"

ZUG = "JOINT"

ZUG = "WHIFF"

ZUG = "PROCESSION"

ZUG = "MOVE"

ZUG = "STROKE"

ZUG = "SHOAL"

ZUG = "RANGE"

ZUG = "ROW"

ZUG = "PEDAL"

ZUG = "BLAST"

ZUG = "BELL-PULL"

ZUG = "GULP"

SOME OF THE MANY MEANINGS OF THE LATIN VERB "GERERE"

TUNICAM GERERE
TO WEAR A TUNIC

PERSONAM GERERE
TO PLAY A ROLE

TIBI MOREM GERERE
TO OBEY OR TO HUMOR YOU

CLIPEUM GERERE
TO CARRY A SHIELD

SE HONESTE GERERE
TO BEHAVE HONORABLY

BELLUM GERERE
TO WAGE WAR

SQUALENTEM BARBAM GERERE
TO HAVE A MESSY BEARD

CORONAM GERERE
TO WEAR A CROWN

AMICITIAS GERERE
TO BE FRIENDLY

SAXA GERERE
TO CARRY STONES

RES GERERE
TO RULE

ODIUM GERERE
TO HATE

FRUGES GERERE
TO PRODUCE CROPS

ONERA GERERE
TO BEAR BURDENS

FORTEM ANIMUM GERERE
TO BE BRAVE

D. *Differences in the way languages fit together*

Just as languages differ in the sound and meaning of words, so do they differ also in the way words are fitted together into larger units to convey a message. We have seen that in English much of the meaning is carried by the *order of the words,* and, to a lesser extent, by changes in the formation of words, function words, etc. Many languages make much more extensive use of changes in the form of words and much less use of word order than we do. Latin is one of them. Examine the Latin pair:

manēmus	"we are remaining"
manēs	"you are remaining"

Each is made up of three segments or parts:

man-	the idea of "remain"	*-mus*	"we" do the action
-ē-	indicating the kind of verb	*-s*	"you" (one person) do the action

Notice that while in English "we" and "you" are separate words which indicate the subject or doer of the action, the Latin *-s* and *-mus* are endings which are always joined to a base or stem of a verb to indicate the corresponding subject.

Form change is not restricted to the end of a word. Note the following Latin pair:

manēbimus	"we will remain"
mānēbāmus	"we remained"

These are the two new segments: *-bi-*   "in the future"
                                     -bā-   "in the past"

Here, we have change within a word.

There can also be change at the beginning of a word.

currit	"he runs"
*cu*currit	"he ran"

To show you how these various changes work, here are some problems from a dialect of Aztec, spoken in Mexico. See if you can find out what segment of the word has a certain meaning.

PROBLEM I

Aztec word	English meaning
ničoka	"I cry."
ničoka?	"I cried."
nimayana	"I am hungry."
nimayana?	"I was hungry."
nimayanaya	"I was hungry (and still may be)."
timayana	"You (sg.) are hungry."
nimayanas	"I will be hungry."
tičoka	"You (sg.) will cry."
ničokaya	"I was crying (and still may be)."
ničokas	"I will cry."

1. In this language, what is it that signals simple past time?
2. What signals the subject "I"?
3. What signals the subject "you"?
4. What is the stem of the word that means "to cry"?
5. What is the stem of the word that means "to be hungry"?
6. What signals future time?

(Explanation of symbols: "č" stands for something like the "ch" in *chair;* the hook stands for a sound something like the sound that some people have in place of the "t" in *mountain* when they pronounce it "moun'en." The other sounds are something like the sounds that these letters have in English. Their exact quality you would have to learn from someone who speaks Aztec.)

If you had trouble picking out the Aztec word parts, here is a suggestion. Compare the forms of the Aztec words and the English meanings. What is the difference in form between the first two Aztec words? It is the sound that we have represented by the little hook. And what is the difference in meaning? It is apparently the difference between present and past time. Then what is the answer to the first question?

As a check on this answer, look for another pair which has this same contrast in form. You will find that the third and fourth items show the same contrast.

Here's another problem from a similar dialect.

PROBLEM II

Aztec word	English meaning
ikalwewe	"his big house"
ikalsosol	"his old house"
ikalcīn	"his little house"
komitwewe	"big cooking pot"
komitsosol	"old cooking pot"
komitcīn	"little cooking pot"
petatwewe	"big mat"
petatsosol	"old mat"
petatcīn	"little mat"
ikalmeh	"his houses"
petatmeh	"mats"
komitmeh	"cooking pots"
kōyamecīn	"little pig"
kōyamewewe	"big pig"
kōyamemeh	"pigs"

(The mark over some of the vowels means that the vowel is held longer than the ones without it. This difference is very important in some languages. The sign "c" represents a sound something like *ts* .)

Find the word segments that have the following meanings:

1. "cooking pot"	3. "old"	5. "mat"	7. "big"
2. plural	4. "little"	6. "house"	8. "pig"

Here is a third set, taken from a different dialect of Aztec.

PROBLEM III[3]

Aztec word	English meaning
-ita	stem of verb "to see"
nikita	"I see it."
kita	"He sees it."
kinita	"He sees them."
kitas	"He will see it."
kitak	"He saw it."
tikinita	"You (sg.) see them."
nikitak	"I saw it."
nikinitak	"I saw them."
kitakeh	"They saw it."
kinitakeh	"They saw them."
tikitas	"You (sg.) will see it."
kitaya	"He was seeing it."
tikitaya	"You (sg.) were seeing it."
kitaskia	"He would see it."
nikitaskia	"I would see it."

(There is no set of letters to show the subject "he." Sometimes the *absence* of any symbol indicates a particular form.)

Identify the letters that have the following meanings:

1. past time	5. "I" as subject
2. "you" as subject	6. "they" as subject
3. "it" as object	7. stem of verb "see"
4. "them" as object	8. future time

Returning to English, notice the form changes in these sentences:

[3] See page xi for answers. From E. A. Nida, *Morphology* (Ann Arbor, 1949).

PROBLEM IV

The dog loves the girl.
The girl loves the dog.
The dogs love the girl.
The girl loves the dogs.
The girls want the dog.
The girl wanted the dog.
The girls wanted the dog.
The dog loves the cat.

The cat loves the dog.
The cats loved the dog.
The horse likes the girl.
The horse liked the girl.
The horses liked the girl.
The dog teases the horse.
The dogs tease the horses.

In answering the following questions, be sure to consider the *sounds* rather than the written letters.

1. How are the plurals of nouns formed in English?
2. What change appears in the present form of the verb when the number of the subject changes?
3. How is past time shown?
4. What changes occur in the past form of the verb when the number of the subject changes?
5. What is the signal for subject?
6. What is the signal for object?

You will now write the same sentence in a transcription which will indicate the sounds. It is necessary to do this since the English alphabet is not adequate to indicate the pronunciation of all words.

In the first place, English has nine vowel sounds and twenty-four consonant sounds, which we try to spell with an alphabet of only twenty-six letters. In the second place, the spelling we use represents in many cases the pronunciation of some five hundred years ago. All languages are constantly changing, but our modern spelling does not usually show these changes.

ðə gərl ləvz ðə dɔg	The girl loves the dog.
ðə dɔg ləvz ðə gərl	The dog loves the girl.
ðə gərl ləvz ðə dɔgz	The girl loves the dogs.
ðə dɔgz ləv ðə gərl	The dogs love the girl.
ðə gərlz want ðə dɔg	The girls want the dog.
ðə gərl wantid ðə dɔg	The girl wanted the dog.
ðə gərls wantid ðə dɔg	The girls wanted the dog.
ðə dɔg ləvz ðə kat	The dog loves the cat.
ðə kat ləvz ðə dɔg	The cat loves the dog.
ðə kats ləvd ðə dɔg	The cats loved the dog.
ðə hors layks ðə gərl	The horse likes the girl.
ðə hors laykt ðə gərl	The horse liked the girl.
ðə horsiz laykt ðə gərl	The horses liked the girl.
ðə dɔg tijziz ðə hors	The dog teases the horse.
ðə dɔgz tijz ðə hors	The dogs tease the horse.

Looking now at the special transcription, try to answer the six questions, using the symbols and treating it like a foreign language. Do you see that there are three ways of forming plurals? Three ways of forming the past tense?

With this background you are now ready to tackle a problem from Latin. Examine the statements as you did before.

PROBLEM V

Latin sentence	English meaning
Cunīculus canem videt.	The rabbit sees a dog.
Cunīculum canis pellit.	The dog chases the rabbit away.
Canem rāna videt.	A frog sees the dog.
Pellit rānam canis.	The dog chases the frog away.
Canis rānum pellit parvam.	The dog chases the little frog away.
Parvum canem videt equus.	A horse sees the little dog.
Cunīculus rānās terret.	The rabbit scares the frogs.
Equōs canis videt.	The dog sees the horses.
Equum canis videt.	The dog sees a horse.
Cunīculus rānam videt.	The rabbit sees a frog.
Parva videt rāna cunīculum.	The little frog sees the rabbit.
Equus canēs videt.	The horse sees dogs.
Videt canēs parvus equus.	The little horse sees the dogs.

Now try the following questions:

1. What ending indicates a verb in Latin?

2. Where does the verb come in a sentence?

3. What ending shows a singular object?

4. What ending shows a plural object?

5. There are two different endings to show a singular subject. What are they?

6. What is the segment that means "dog"?

7. What is the segment that means "scare"?

8. What is the segment that means "horse"?

9. What is the segment that means "small"?

10. How does Latin show what noun an adjective goes with?

These illustrations from Latin and English should show you that the two languages use changes of form and changes in word order in quite different ways. To see if you have recognized these differences, answer the following questions:

1. What signals a subject in Latin? in English?
2. What signals an object in Latin? in English?
3. How do you know what noun an adjective goes with in Latin? in English?
4. Which language relies more on word order as a signal of the construction of a sentence?

We have now seen that languages differ in their way of fitting a sentence together: they do not signal subjects, persons, verbs, and so forth in identical ways. English relies heavily on word order, as well as on function words, Latin less on these and more on changes of the form of words. You will succeed in your study of Latin more easily if you understand and accept this fact as basic to your work.

E. Differences based on context

These differences related to context are reflections of differences between our culture and that of the people whose language we are studying. In the case of students of Latin, the more we read about Rome and Romans, especially in their own language, the more we are able to understand their culture and point of view, the more meaningful the context of our reading becomes to us. Sometimes, until we are familiar with the Roman way of life, even after we have arrived at a meaning for a sentence, we feel as if we do not really understand it.

Take for example:

1. *pater familias*: "father of a family"

    The American image of a family is of father, mother, and children living co-operatively in their home. The Roman image would have been of a large household, including unmarried relatives, possibly a son and his wife, and a sizable group of slaves. The head of this household held the right of life and death over his *familia*, and, while he never exercised it in the times of which we know, the possession of such complete power led to a respect and awe which does not enter much into modern attitudes.

2. "Fourth of July": to us is a national holiday, the words evoke images of patriotic celebrations, flags, parades, family picnics, fireworks, etc.; to people of most other countries, it is just a day in the month of July. It would have been necessary to explain in detail to a Roman the differences from his holidays, most of which had basically a religious origin and were celebrated differently.

This matter of increasing our understanding of context will continue long after we understand the basic construction of the language and know meanings of a good many words. It is perhaps the most challenging and interesting side of language study, especially to those who have gone beyond the elementary stages.

F. Similarities

We have spent a good many pages talking about the differences between languages. What, if anything, do they have in common? If they are so different, does learning another language do any good for us in our understanding of language as such or in our command of our own mother tongue?

All languages of a related group or language family—Latin and English are both members of one big related family (see Section III)—have many basic similarities. The family group to which both belong has the same "parts of speech" (nouns, verbs, etc.), distinguishes singular and plural number, has tenses of verbs, etc. The same basic elements go to make up a thought unit or sentence. Within this broad framework come the differences we have been stressing.

There are also the things that are somewhat similar, but not *exactly* alike. These can be a problem to the student. For instance, take the matter of gender. In French all nouns are masculine or feminine, including pens, ink, houses, as well as persons. In Latin there are three genders but they relate primarily to the form class of the noun, so that most inanimate objects are masculine or feminine; only words with certain special characteristics are neuter. In English, on the other hand, we follow a system of natural gender. But you will hear more of this later; just remember that when something sounds as if it were similar to English, don't necessarily expect it to be exactly the same.

The very fact of seeing how other languages operate and convey meaning helps us to understand better how language in general works and so to have a better appreciation of how

English works. It gives us a perspective that no person who knows only one language can have, for the contrasts between languages make us see the patterns of structure all the more clearly.

There is, finally, one very important carry-over from Latin to English. There is an unusually close relationship between Latin and English vocabulary, even though English is not one of the Romance languages which are direct descendants of Latin. We have taken a *very* large number of Latin words and word elements—roots, prefixes, and suffixes—into English, sometimes in combinations that existed in Latin, sometimes in new ones. The great majority of words for scientific matters, new inventions, and for our advanced, more abstract ideas are Latin in origin (or Greek, which comes to us in Latin form). The Latin vocabulary you learn will enrich your understanding of English; some Latin words will seem familiar because of related English words. Let us take only one very incomplete example:

Latin *scrībere*, "write;" other stems *scrīps - scrīpt-*, "wrote," "written."

English derivatives: scribble, scribe, script, scripture
transcribe, transcription
inscribe, inscription
describe, description, descriptive
descriptively, prescribe, prescription, etc.
(at least 50 words can be found.)

There are, then, these kinds of similarities between Latin and English; there are many differences of structure. We have a rich inheritance in vocabulary which many people feel has been in itself a very great reward for their study of Latin (in addition to the reasons mentioned on page 1). We have been stressing the differences in this introduction because, at the start of your study of a language, it is these, not the similarities, that can cause you problems if you do not realize they are going to be there. Coming newly to the study of a foreign language, you may well have believed that the same letter always stands for the same sound, that one word in the new language will always exactly equal another in your own, that the languages are going to be fitted together in the same way (you know now that these are completely false and misleading conceptions). In that case, if only likenesses were emphasized, it would merely serve to mislead you further. Then, when you begin to discover the hard realities of differences, you are very likely to become disillusioned and discouraged. You might even want to criticize the language as "queer" and "illogical." You would be tempted to complain, "Why did they have to say it *that* way?" But if you have been prepared to accept differences, you will find them interesting and you will progress smoothly and rapidly.

As you approach this challenging task of learning the Latin language, you should realize that it will require time and effort, daily study, careful mastery of details. But, of course, you also realize that any worthwhile undertaking requires effort. It is also rewarding. The thrill of accomplishment, the interest in the mastery of a new mode of expression, the many doors opened to new ideas, new perspective in your thinking, new understanding of what a wonderful thing language itself is—all this will be well worth the effort that you give to it. Good luck! *Fēlīcitās!*

QUESTIONS ON LESSON TWO

1. Do all languages which have the same writing system use the same sets of sounds for the letters represented?

2. What is the best way to learn the sounds of Latin—or any foreign language?

3. What system of Latin pronunciation is taught in this book?

4. Does one word in English have just one exact equivalent in Latin?

5. Does Latin or English make more extensive use of changes in the form of words to convey meaning?

6. What did you learn by doing the Aztec and English exercises?

7. What effect does context have in the meaning of a word?

8. Wherein lies the closest relationship between Latin and English?

9. What is the greatest difference between them?

10. Enumerate the ways in which any two languages are different from one another.

INTRODUCTORY LESSON THREE

A. *History of the Latin Language*

Naturally students of Latin are interested in the Latin language and should know something about when, where, and by whom it has been used. It has had a remarkably long history, unusually wide use, and far-reaching influence in the Western world.

The history of any language is the history of people. About 1000 years before the birth of Christ, groups of people belonging to a Caucasian race migrated from central Europe into Italy. (They were one of many related groups that moved at different times into most of Europe, Persia, and India.) They were simple shepherd folk who settled in the hills, or herders who settled in the plains of central Italy, gradually coming to till the soil and build their homes. The groups that settled there had names such as Oscans, Umbrians, Sabines, and Latins. Their languages were described by these same names, and the areas where they settled were named from them. Thus, the Latins, *Latīnī*, lived in the area of *Latium* and spoke the *lingua Latīna*.

These people grew gradually in prosperity and power, especially the Latins who became noted for their hardihood in war and devotion to the state. One city, Rome, became the leader, first of the other Latins, then after many years and many wars, the head of central Italy, and finally of the entire peninsula. By this time, between 300 and 200 B.C., their language was becoming the language of Italy and most of the people gradually began to think of themselves as "Romans" (except the Greeks in the South who kept their own language and laws and who had a civilization so far in advance of that of Rome that the Greeks became the teachers of the Romans).

These Romans of Italy not only defended themselves successfully against other invaders from the north (Celtic and Germanic peoples) but also won supremacy over the sea traders of the Western Mediterranean, the Carthaginians. They then dominated the area, developed commerce, and began to rule large provinces which bordered that sea. Finally by the first century B.C. they conquered the older civilizations and lands of the Eastern Mediterranean, even Egypt. Their power extended over the civilized world of that time, except for the Far East (Persia, India, China, etc.). This area, roughly equal in size to the U. S. A., remained united under Roman sway for some 500 years. The people of these lands had to be able to understand Latin, the official language of the Empire, in order to understand the laws by which they were governed or to carry on official business (Greek was used extensively in the East, but with this exception, the *official* language was Latin). People all over the Roman Empire were educated in this language and the great writers of the times, no matter whether they were born in Spain, Asia Minor, or North Africa, wrote in Latin (some in Greek). Latin was truly the language of the Western world.

During the time of the Roman Empire the teachings of the Christian Church spread rapidly through the ancient world. Its spread was made easier because of the world-wide peace and order maintained by Rome, the ease of travel and communication, and the use of a universal language. Latin was the language of the church services, teaching, and the Vulgate Bible, officially published in the Western Church in the fifth century after Christ. Gradually the political power of Rome weakened; by 600 A.D. the Empire of the West, and even Italy, had surrendered to the waves of migration of Germanic tribes from the north and to forces of disintegration within. In the chaotic conditions which resulted, the Church was the chief influence in the preservation of law, order, and a degree of civilization. Latin continued to be

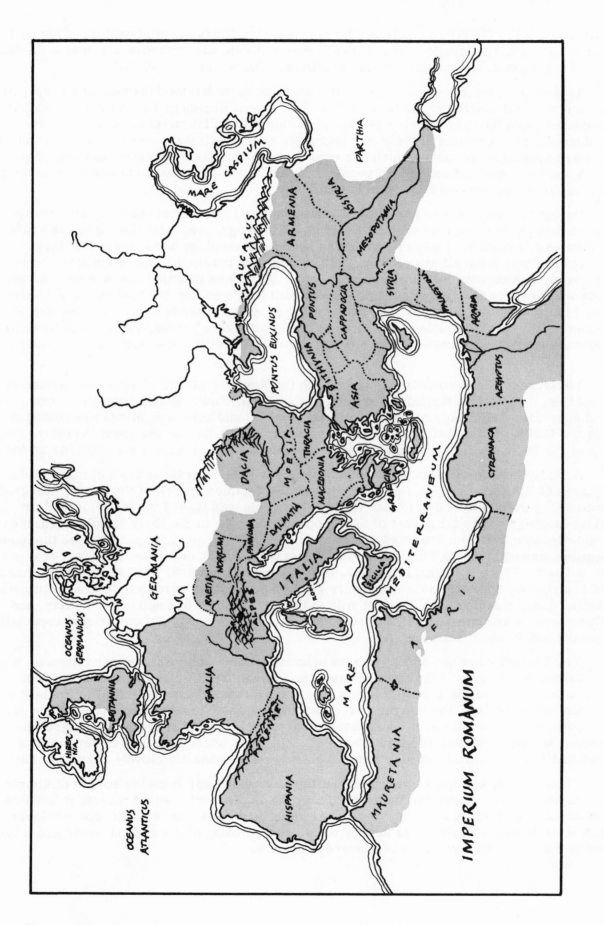

the language of the Church, not only for its services, but for the administration of law and in all its relations in the Middle Ages. In the Roman Catholic Church today it remains the language of the Mass and of documents issued officially for world-wide distribution.

As new governments emerged, they too used Latin, understood throughout Europe, for their international relations. As late as 1600 A.D. Queen Elizabeth was conversing with the ambassador from Spain in Latin. The rise of strong nationalist powers, however, which insisted upon the introduction of their own languages in international conferences, led to the use of modern languages, no one of which has ever gained complete acceptance as the medium of international communication. (Many people feel that one of the great barriers to communication today is the absence of a common language.)

During the later Middle Ages with a reawakening of interest in learning, universities began to develop in Europe as centers for study of theology, law, medicine, and, gradually, other areas of learning. Their beginnings as schools of theology and the fact that they attracted students from all over Europe both helped to maintain the use of Latin as the language of instruction until well into modern times. While this practice has now been largely abandoned except in Catholic seminaries, one result has been that the basic body of technical terms in law, religion, medicine, and many of the sciences is made up of Latin words. Many creative writers of the Middle Ages, some of the Renaissance period, and a few in modern times have continued to write in Latin. Many universities still issue degrees and citations in Latin.

Today, then, Latin continues to be used in the Roman Catholic Church, and spoken in its seminaries; it is used in formal documents, and in legal, medical, and scientific terms. As new discoveries and inventions appear, names for them and their operations are coined from Latin and Greek words. Latin is studied in modern schools so that the great literature and ideas of the ancient world may be read and understood, for they have a message for us today.

Actually the life of Latin does not stop there; it lives in several ways in many of the languages of Western Europe. As we have seen, the common speech of the people was gradually changing even in the later Roman times. The Bible was issued in the "Vulgate" or popular language. With the advent of new peoples in Europe in the early Middle Ages, the changes became even more marked and gradually out of the common speech arose the modern languages, among them the Romance group of languages which developed as direct descendants of Latin. These Romance languages, Italian, French, Spanish, Portugese, and Rumanian, have many features of structure and a very great proportion of words which are modifications of Latin. Latin has also played a vital role in the development of English vocabulary, and, as we have seen in sections I and II, has contributed a high percentage of our words, especially in the various fields of learning.

The English language, which is in its origins (Anglo-Saxon) a Germanic language, was first influenced by Latin at the time Britain was converted to Christianity. Later, when William the Conqueror in 1066 A.D. brought Norman French (based on Latin) to England with his court and overlords, the merger of the two brought about the development of a new phase of English, a step toward our present day language. The revival of learning, the growth of advanced studies, and modern science have all done their share in adding to our stock of Greek and Latin derivative words. In vocabulary we are unusually closely related to Latin.

Thus we see, in a quick overview, that the Latin language, once the speech of simple, migrant shepherds, became the language of a world empire and a world church; it lives on in modern times both in its own right and as parent of languages spoken in Europe and large parts of the Western world. It is the key to an understanding of the ancient world and a better comprehension of our own which is descended from it.

B. Cognates, loan words, derivatives

The words which have come into English from Latin are, for the most part, classified as *derivatives*. An example of many English derivatives from a basic Latin word *scrībere*, to write, (plus various Latin and non-Latin prefixes and suffixes) was given on page 16. Such examples can be multiplied hundreds of times over.

Words borrowed from another language without change are called *loan* words. Such, for example, are *senator, actor, maximum, sine die, finis*.

In addition to these, there are a few words which have a basic similarity, not because they were taken from Latin into English, but because of the fact that both languages stem from a common ancestor language, called by scholars *Indo-European* (because the majority of the languages of India and Europe are descended from it). The languages are cognate or related languages. Words which reflect this are those for family relationships, simple ideas and actions, low numbers, and a few pronouns. For example, the English word "mother" is a cognate for the Latin word *māter*, since both are descended from the Indo-European word for mother (along with Greek *mētēr*, Sanskrit *matr*, Celtic *mothair*, German *mutter*). The word "maternal" is a derivative from Latin *māter*; when British children refer to their mothers as "mater" they are using a loan word.

Numerals are an interesting illustration of cognates and derivatives. Numbers from 1 to 10 in all Indo-European languages are similar enough to show that they are *cognates*. These same numbers in the Romance languages are based directly on Latin; that is, they are direct *derivatives* and therefore much closer in form to the Latin words.

COGNATE NUMERALS

	LATIN	GREEK	SANSKRIT	SLAVIC	CELTIC	GERMAN	ENGLISH
I	ūnus	ἕν	eka	-	aon	eins	one
II	duō	δύο	dva	duva	da	zwei	two
III	trēs	τρεῖs	tri	trys	tri	drei	three
IV	quattuor	τέτταρες	catur	chetyre	pedwar	vier	four
V	quīnque	πέντε	pancan	penki	pump	fünf	five
VI	sex	ἕξ	shah	shest	se	sechs	six
VII	septem	ἑπτά	saptan	septuni	seacht	sieben	seven
VIII	octō	ὀκτώ	ashtan	osztuni	ochd	acht	eight
IX	novem	ἐννέα	navan	-	naoi	neun	nine
X	decem	δέκα	dagan	deszimt	deich	zehn	ten

DERIVATIVE NUMERALS

	LATIN	ITALIAN	FRENCH	SPANISH	PORTUGESE	RUMANIAN
I	ūnus	uno	un	uno	um	un
II	duō	due	deux	dos	dois	doi
III	trēs	tre	trois	tres	trez	trei
IV	quattuor	quattro	quatre	cuatro	quatro	patru
V	quīnque	cinque	cinq	cinco	cinco	cinci
VI	sex	sei	six	seis	seis	sesse
VII	septem	sette	sept	sieto	sete	septe
VIII	octō	otto	huit	ocho	oito	opt
IX	novem	nove	neuf	nueve	nove	noua
X	decem	dieci	dix	diez	dez	zeco

PRONUNCIATION PRACTICE III

Purpose: to practice Latin pronunciation, using numerals, both those used for counting (cardinals) and for showing the order (ordinals).

A.

Cardinals	Ordinals	Cardinals	Ordinals
I ūnus	prīmus	VI sex	sextus
II duo	secundus	VII septem	septimus
III trēs	tertius	VIII octō	octāvus
IV quattuor	quārtus	IX novem	nōnus
V quīnque	quīntus	X decem	decimus

Note also C *centum* (100) and M *mille* (1,000).

B. Practice further, after you have memorized the numerals, by doing orally some problems in addition (I et I = II) and subtraction (I dē II = I).

Addition questions:

Quot sunt ūnus et ūnus?   Ūnus et ūnus sunt_____ .
Quot sunt duo et trēs?   Duo et trēs sunt _____ .

Subtraction questions:

Quot sunt ūnus dē duōbus?   Ūnus dē duōbus sunt _____ .
Quot sunt quattuor dē decem?   Quattuor dē decem sunt _____ .

You have probably been noticing also the English derivatives from these Latin numerals. Among the most interesting are the month names of September, October, November, and December. According to the Roman numerals from which they are derived, the numbers of these months do not correspond to their present place in the calendar. The reason is this: in the earliest Roman calendar there were only ten months, with the year beginning in March. Later two months were added, but at the beginning, not the end, of the year, yet the Romans kept the original names, and we have inherited them. (The other month names and other features of the Roman calendar are an interesting part of our heritage from Rome. Look it up in a good classical dictionary or the pamphlet entitled *The Roman Calendar* by Prof. Van L. Johnson.)

PROBLEM

Try your hand at derivation by explaining the relationship in meaning to the Latin source word of these English words based on the Latin numerals:

> unit, union, unify, unity, unite; dual, duel, duet, deuce; primary, primitive, primer, prime; second, secondary; trio, triangle, triplet, trey; quadrangle, quart, quarter, quartet; quintet, quintuplet; sextet, septet; octet, octave; decimal; cent, century, percent, centennial; millenium.

(Work with derivation will form the chief part of the section entitled "Word Study" in each lesson in this book.)

QUESTIONS ON LESSON THREE

1. Who were the first speakers of Latin? Where did they come from? Where did they settle?

2. In what area was Latin spoken about 200 B.C.? By the first century A.D.?

3. How long was the Roman Empire in existence?

4. Why was Latin important in it?

5. What effect did the use of Latin have on the growth of the Christian Church? What effect did the Church have on Latin?

6. When did Latin cease to be used as the language of governments? Why?

7. In what fields of learning is Latin especially important?

8. In what ways is Latin used today?

9. Explain its importance in English vocabulary.

10. Distinguish between cognate, loan word, and derivative.

INTRODUCTORY LESSON FOUR

Reading and literature

Several different types of Latin reading material are contained in this book. All of it is designed to acquaint you with the way the ancient Romans, and also people of succeeding ages, used this language and with a few of the things they wrote. Naturally the materials we use must be graded according to your growing knowledge of Latin structure and vocabulary.

At the beginning of each lesson are one or more brief quotations, just as they were said by a Latin writer.[1] They are intended primarily to illustrate the point of structure being studied in the lesson, secondarily for their interest in ideas or aptness in relation to a picture or story. Beginning in Lesson 12 groups of such quotations are used as the main reading section. Also, in most of the other lessons, there is a section called "Optional Reading" made up of quotations of the same sort—to be used as your teacher wishes. All direct quotations are taken from writers of Latin, some of them early, some of them well-known names in Latin literature, some of them later writers, even from the Middle Ages and Renaissance. The important thing is that they are verbatim quotations as a "native" user of the language expressed himself. (Some of the names of well-known writers your teacher will tell you about or ask you to look up as you meet them.)

It is obvious that at the beginning stages of learning a language you can understand only relatively simple sentences using a few structures and your vocabulary is very limited. Therefore in the first nine lessons the connected reading is limited to a description of what is going on in pictures in the text. After that, it is possible to read short paragraphs and stories that have some point or meaning. From Lesson 10 on, the connected reading is for the most part based on stories, facts, and anecdotes found in the writings of Latin authors. At first these are adapted a good deal; gradually the changes necessary are fewer and fewer, until finally there are selections which are changed only very slightly or not at all from the original. The "stories" or, more properly, various kinds of narratives belong to one of several types.

One type of story, developed among almost all peoples at an early time, is the *folk tale*. Frequently such tales were told orally and written down later. Many of them are simply "good stories" that have been popular in many different ages and many widely separated places, with different details, according to where they were told. They are usually little anecdotes illustrating character, simple but interesting situations, or humor which is appealing to audiences of any kind in any place.

Typical of the tale which has appeared in many lands in various forms is the story of the baby and the dog in Lesson 10. This story probably originated in India; it has made its way into the folklore of many nations of Europe, with variations in the kind of animal and weapon involved. There is even a backwoods American version with a wolf and a shotgun! Various versions of the story of the donkey were current in Germany during Renaissance times. The one related by the famous Renaissance humanist Erasmus in a letter to a friend is used as the basis for the version in Lesson 13. There are several old jokes or humorous anecdotes retold

---

[1] If even a word has been changed (so that the sentence can stand alone out of its paragraph context) this is indicated by the note "adapted." While we have used quotations from later writers, we have tried to avoid giving any which contain constructions an ancient Roman would not have used so as not to confuse you.

—for example, "No News" in Lesson 22—and tales with a "moral" as the "Treasure in the Vineyard" in Lesson 16.

A specialized branch of the folktale is called the *fable*. The best known type of fable is that in which animals talk and act like people. The beast fable, known in Oriental literature, is perhaps most familiar in the work of the Greek writer Aesop. The beast stories we read have been taken from the Latin of Phaedrus. Many of these fables were based on those of Aesop. Some fables in Part I have been adapted and are in prose; in Part II, the "Wolf and Lamb" and others are in verse form exactly as Phaedrus wrote them. On the surface, fables are simple stories which can be understood and enjoyed by readers of all ages. The stories also have a more subtle point, revealing human character faults or teaching a moral lesson. They have remained popular through the ages; indeed such phrases as "sour grapes" indicate that they have become a byword. You will no doubt be able to see very readily around you the type of characters revealed in the fables. In modern times we still like the fable and are still creating creatures like Pogo, Mickey Mouse, and Uncle Remus' animals to point out our own human failings and good qualities.

These two types of stories were chiefly intended to entertain. Rather different in origin and purpose are tales classified as *myths*. While later Roman writers told them chiefly for their value as stories, they originally had a serious association with the ancient gods. These stories were often told to explain strange things in nature that were not understood in early days or to show the supernatural power of a god. The Greeks, who originated most of them, were highly imaginative people and embroidered the tales with all sorts of imaginative details. The Roman poet Ovid, who loved good stories like these and told them well, has left us a collection of myths woven together into a long poem about "transformations." (Each story in the *Metamorphoses* had to contain some transformation of person, god, or object.) A number of the myths you will read, such as *Midas* and *Phaethon*, are based on Ovid's poem.

Closely related to myths are *legends*, stories of heroic men of old times. They may be to some extent involved with the gods and supernatural happenings, but the emphasis in the story is on the human persons. Sometimes these are stories of real people, somewhat exaggerated or made more glamorous or heroic than was likely to have been the case; yet they are the forerunners of factual history. Some are highly romantic tales, like that of *Pyramus and Thisbe*; some are of old Roman heroes like the Horatii triplets who were historical persons, perhaps just a little idealized. In the story of Regulus it is still a little hard to disentangle legend from fact; by the time we get to the story of "Caesar and the Pirates" we are on the solid, factual ground of history.

Romans were proud of their history and the good men of their "olden days"; they felt that the writer of history should set examples of strength and virtue before people of his own day (as Livy did) as well as tell accurately the facts or events that had occurred. Besides history, there were, of course, many other types of prose written in Roman days—speeches on political issues, letters, essays. There were many kinds of poems, too, ranging from highly personal love lyrics to a long epic glorifying the greatness of Rome's origins and destiny (Vergil's *Aeneid*). There were plays (chiefly comedies), satires on the life of the times, speeches defending men accused of murder, and essays on how to treat slaves, how to win friends, make love, or run a farm. In short, all the interests and activities of an age teeming with life, activity, and very human people are represented in Roman literature.

There will be samples of some of these in the early stages of your reading, and mastery of the fundamentals set forth here will open to you the opportunity to read widely in many of the kinds of writing that interest you. It is time now to begin your Latin lessons.

LESSON ONE

Vestis virum facit. —Erasmus "Clothes make the man."[1]

Manus manum lavat. —Petronius "One hand washes the other": i.e., co-operation is necessary.

Purpose: To learn simple sentences; subject and object (nominative and accusative)

I QUIS EST?[2]

canis   puer   equus
canem   puerum[3] equum

Canis est. Puer est. Equus puerum videt. Puer canem videt. Equum puer nōn videt. Equum nōn videt canis. Puerum videt.

1. Quis est? Canis est.
2. Quis est? Puer est.
3. Quis est? Equus est.

4. Quid agit equus? Puerum videt equus.
5. Quid agit puer? Canem videt.
6. Quid agit canis? Puerum videt canis.

7. Quem puer videt? Canem puer videt.
8. Quis puerum videt? Canis puerum videt.

9. Quem videt canis? Puerum videt canis.
10. Quis canem videt? Puer canem videt.
11. Quem videt equus? Puerum videt equus.

12. Videtne equus puerum? Videt.
13. Videtne equus canem? Nōn videt.

14. Videtne equum puer? Nōn videt.
15. Videtne canem puer? Videt.

[1]These quotations are taken directly from the works of well-known writers of Latin. They are intended not only to be read but to be learned by heart as "real life" models of the feature of Latin structure studied in the lesson. They will also be used in exercises throughout the book.

[2]The pictures, with the labels, will help in the understanding of new words. The little paragraph with it will describe what appears in the picture. These will be "reading lessons" until you have learned enough Latin to read an interesting story. The questions in this case (*"Quis est?"*"Who is it?" or *"Quid est?"*"What is it?" or *"Quid agit?"*"What is he doing?") will provide for rapid oral handling of Latin.

[3]A Roman boy wore a tunic as pictured here; men,too, used just tunics for active work on farms or in shops. Roman men who were citizens wore the formal robe or toga in public on special occasions. For pictures and descriptions of ancient dress see a good book on Roman customs such as M. Johnson's *Roman Life* (1957 edition).

II PATTERN READING

The pattern reading introduces important features of Latin structure. After some samples (A), there are easy sentences to read (B), based on simple vocabulary; they seem very much alike but contrast in some important element. Reading them will afford practice on the feature being studied. The questions (C) will also help in understanding the structure.

A. Sample sentences

1. Equus canem spectat.   The horse looks at the dog.
   Canem equus spectat.   The horse looks at the *dog*.
   Canem spectat equus.   The *horse* looks at the dog.
   Spectat canem equus.   The horse *looks* at the dog.

2. Spectatne puer equum?   Is the boy looking at the horse?

3. Equus fēminam pellit.   The horse chases the woman away.

4. Puella virum nōn audit.   The girl does not hear the man.

B. Practice sentences

1. Vir puerum spectat.
2. Puerum vir spectat.
3. Puellam vir videt.
4. Videt puellam puer.
5. Fēmina puerum pellit.
6. Canem fēmina nōn pellit.
7. Fēmina canem audit.
8. Fēminam canis audit.
9. Auditne fēmina puellam?
10. Equum puella spectat.
11. Puella equum spectat.
12. Nōn pellit puellam canis.
13. Pellitne puella puerum?
14. Canis virum audit.

C. Questions on structure

1. How do the words in each of these pairs differ from one another?

canis	puella	vir
canem	puellam	virum

2. What common endings do you find for the nouns used as objects here (accusative case)?

3. What common signal do you find on the end of the verbs in this lesson?

4. What is the difference in meaning between *videt* and *videtne*?

5. How is emphasis expressed in Latin? in oral English? (On the printed page, English words that are emphasized are in italics.)

See Appendix B, pages 188-90.

III   EXERCISES (written or oral)

A. FĒMINA VESTEM LAVAT

fēmina
fēminam

canis
canem

vestis   vir
vestem   virum

Be able to answer all the questions in Latin (1-3 about the picture, 4-5 about the model sentences).

1. Fēmina vestem lavat.
   Quis lavat?   Fēmina lavat.
   Quid lavat?   Vestem lavat.
   Quid agit fēmina?   Vestem lavat fēmina.

2. Canem pellit vir.
   Quis pellit?   Vir pellit.
   Quem pellit vir?   Canem pellit vir.
   Pellitne vir canem?   Pellit.

3. Fēminam vir nōn videt.
   Videtne fēminam vir?   Nōn videt fēminam vir.
   Quem nōn videt?   Fēminam nōn videt.
   Quis nōn videt?   Vir nōn videt.

4. Vestis virum facit.
   Quid virum facit?   Vestis facit.
   Quem facit vestis?   Virum facit vestis.
   Facitne vir vestem?   Nōn facit.

5. Manus manum lavat.

Quid lavat manus?	Manum lavat.
Quid manum lavat?	Manus lavat.
Lavatne manus manum?	Manus manum lavat.

B. Ask the Latin question that will get the italicized word or words as an answer.

1. *Equus* puerum spectat.
2. *Canem* puer spectat.
3. *Equum* nōn spectat canis.
4. *Manus* manum lavat.
5. *Audit* puella virum.
6. *Vir* puerum audit.
7. *Lavat* fēmina *canem*.
8. *Puella* manum lavat.
9. *Puerum* canis pellit.
10. *Vestem* lavat vir.
11. *Videt* puellam puer.
12. *Vestem facit* puella.

C. Metaphrase the following partial sentences.

To metaphrase means to explain the structure of each Latin word as it occurs in the sentence before the total sentence is known. Thus "*Vestem fēmina.* . . ." is metaphrased in this way: *vestem* (object form), "something is done to the clothes"; *fēmina* (subject form), "a woman does something to the clothes." (If the verb—e.g. *lavat*—were known in a short sentence such as this, its meaning would make the relationship of the nouns obvious: the only possibility is that "the woman washes the clothes." If only the nouns are seen, then you must examine endings to determine their place in the sentence.) This is the vital first step in understanding any Latin sentence, long or short, and should become automatic in all your reading. Once the structure of the sentence is understood, the meaning can be developed easily and accurately. In a metaphrase exercise it is interesting to complete the sentence, but this is not the real point; the important thing is to understand the structure and relationship of the words given.

1. Equus virum. . . . . .
2. Virum puer . . . . . .
3. Vir canem . . . .
4. Canis manum . . . . .
5. Equum manus . . . . .
6. . . . . . .equus puerum.
7. Manum. . . . . . . puer.
8. Fēminam vestis . . . . .
9. . . . . . vestem puella .
10. Canis puellam . . . . . .

D. Make one simple, match-stick drawing which will illustrate all of these situations at one time.

1. Puer equum videt.
2. Canem equus videt.
3. Puerum nōn videt canis.
4. Canis equum nōn videt.

E. Give the Latin equivalent.

1. The dog sees the man.
2. The boy chases a horse away.
3. Is the woman washing clothes?
4. The man does not hear the boy.
5. He is watching the dog.

IV   PATTERN PRACTICE ONE

This type of exercise gives practice in the different sentence patterns that occur in Latin. In some, a short English sentence is given first, on the left, with the equivalent Latin sentence on the right. In others, a Latin sentence may be given to be changed in some way. These should be studied, with or without the help of tapes or records, so that the response can be repeated rapidly, regardless of the order in which sentences are given.

1.	He is watching the dog.	Canem spectat.
2.	The man is watching the dog.	Vir canem spectat.
3.	The man is watching the boy.	Vir puerum spectat.
4.	He sees the boy.	Puerum videt.
5.	The dog sees the *boy*.	Puerum canis videt.
6.	The dog sees the *girl*.	Puellam canis videt.
7.	The woman *does see* the girl.	Videt fēmina puellam.
8.	The woman chases the girl away.	Fēmina puellam pellit.
9.	The woman chases the *horse* away.	Equum fēmina pellit.
10.	The *boy* is chasing the horse away.	Equum pellit puer.
11.	The boy is chasing the dog away.	Puer canem pellit.
12.	The *girl* does not chase the dog away.	Canem nōn pellit puella.
13.	The girl hears the dog.	Puella canem audit.
14.	The girl hears the *man*.	Virum puella audit.
15.	The man hears the girl.	Vir puellam audit.
16.	The *boy* does not hear the man.	Virum nōn audit puer.
17.	The boy hears the *dog*.	Canem puer audit.
18.	The boy *is washing* the dog.	Lavat puer canem.
19.	The girl is not washing the dog.	Puella canem nōn lavat.
20.	The girl washes the clothes.	Puella vestem lavat.
21.	The woman washes the clothes.	Fēmina vestem lavat.
22.	The woman *makes* the clothes.	Facit fēmina vestem.
23.	The man does not make clothes.	Vestem vir nōn facit.
24.	Clothes make the man.	Vestis virum facit.

V OPTIONAL READING

These optional readings are also made up of quotations from Latin authors, ancient, medieval, and modern. They purposely contain words you have not met. It is more important at this stage to identify the structure—parts of speech, cases, relationships of words—than to give English meanings.

> Diēs diem docet. - in Burton (*Anatomy of Melancholy*)
> Experientia docet. - Tacitus (adapted)
> Mōnstrat viam. - Ennius (in Cicero), used as a motto

VI WORD STUDY

Most of the Latin words used in this lesson resemble English words, for a great part of our English vocabulary is based on Latin. Because this relationship is so important, a section of each lesson will be devoted to a study of words and their relation to one another in the two languages.

1. For instance, it is easy to connect Latin *canis* with English "canine." These words have a part in common (the stem *can-*, meaning "dog"). The "-ine" ending corresponds to a Latin *-īnus* ending (both are adjective-forming suffixes). Latin *canīnus*, "dog-like"; English "canine."

2. *Pellit* has many derivatives which appear in English in combination with such prefixes as *re-*, *com-*, *ex-*, and others: "repel," "compel," "expel." The second "l," which is lost as a final letter, appears in "repelling," "compelling," "expelled."

3. What other words in this lesson combine with "-ine" to form English words?

4. What nouns combine with another adjective-forming ending, "-ile," to make English words?

5. What Latin word is in "lavatory" and "lave"?

6. What English words are suggested by *manus*? by *vestis*?

7. From what Latin words do these English words come: audible, inspect, evident?

VII VOCABULARY (used in this lesson)

Nouns		*Verbs*		*Function Words*
fēmina, fēminam	canis, canem	lavat	facit	nōn
puella, puellam	vestis, vestem	spectat		-ne (?)
			audit	
equus, equum	manus, manum	videt		quis, quem (?)
puer, puerum			est	quid, quid (?)
vir, virum		agit		
		pellit		

LESSON TWO

Philosophum nōn facit barba. —Plutarch
    (Latin translation)

"A beard does not make a philosopher."

Auctor opus laudat. —Ovid

"An author praises (approves of) his own work."

Purpose: to learn neuter nouns and predicate nominatives

I   QUID EST?

aedificium
aedificium

flūmen
flūmen

magnum animal   parvum animal
magnum animal   parvum animal

Equus est animal. Magnum animal est. Magnum animal flūmen videt. Flūmen equum dēlectat. Aedificium parvum est. Aedificium puerum dēlectat et aedificium puer laudat. Vir puerum audit; fēminam nōn audit vir. Femina puerum virumque spectat. Parvum animal canis est. Equum nōn spectat parvus canis. Magnum animal canis nōn videt.

1. Quis est?	Equus est; est magnum animal.
2. Quid est?	Flūmen est.
3. Quid magnum animal videt?	Flūmen videt.
4. Quid equum dēlectat?	Flūmen equum dēlectat.
5. Quid puerum dēlectat?	Aedificium puerum dēlectat.
6. Quid puer laudat?	Aedificium puer laudat.
7. Spectatne aedificium fēmina?	Nōn spectat aedificium.
8. Quem audit vir?	Puerum audit.
9. Quis equum nōn spectat?	Canis equum nōn spectat; parvum animal equum nōn spectat.
10. Videtne magnum animal canis?	Nōn videt magnum animal canis.

34

II   PATTERN READING

A.   Sample sentences

1. Nōmen est.   It's a name.
    Fēmina nōmen audit.   A woman hears the name.

2. Est magnum corpus.   There is a large body.
    Sed vir corpus nōn videt.   But the man does not see the body.

3. Vir philosophus est.   The man is a philosopher.

4. Oppidum est parvum.   The town is small.

5. Fēmina oppidum et flūmen laudat.   The woman is praising the town and the river.

6. Fēminam puellamque oppidum   The town pleases the woman and the girl.
    dēlectat.

B.   Practice sentences

1. Nōmen virum dēlectat.   8. Equus flūmen videt.

2. Nōmen vir laudat.   9. Equum flūmen dēlectat.

3. Animal puer pellit.   10. Nōn laudat oppidum puella.

4. Animal puerum pellit.   11. Nōn dēlectat oppidum puellam.

5. Spectatne puella aedificium?   12. Virum animal spectat.

6. Aedificium nōn spectat.   13. Vir animal spectat.

7. Corpus lavat puer.   14. Laudatne vir opus?

15. Nōn opus sed auctōrem laudat vir.

C.   Questions on structure

1. How do neuters differ from other nouns?

2. How can you tell whether *animal* is nominative or accusative in a sentence?

3. In the sentence *Vir oppidum videt* could *oppidum* be the subject? Give your reason.

4. In the sentence *Vir philosophus est* why are both nouns nominative?

For two nominatives with *est* see Appendix B, page 190 and the exercises on page 36. For gender see Appendix B, page 189.

III EXERCISES

A. Study the questions and answers based on the picture and model sentences.

AGRICOLA LABŌRAT

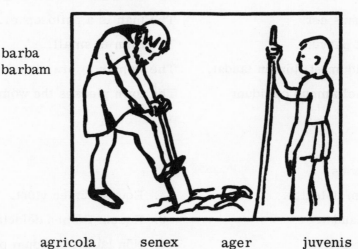

barba
barbam

agricola	senex	ager	juvenis
agricolam	senem	agrum	juvenem

1. Quis est vir?   Agricola est vir.
2. Estne vir senex?   Vir senex est.
3. Quid gerit agricola?   Barbam gerit agricola.
4. Estne puer?   Nōn est puer. Juvenis est.
5. Quid agit juvenis?   Juvenis agricolam spectat.

6. Quid agit senex?   Senex labōrat et agrum fodit.
7. Labōratne juvenis?   Nōn labōrat sed stat.
8. Spectatne agricola juvenem?   Nōn spectat juvenem.
9. Estne agricola juvenis?   Nōn juvenis, sed senex est.
10. Facitne barba agricolam?   Nōn facit.

11. Facitne barba philosophum?   Nōn facit.
12. Quis labōrat?   Agricōla laborat.
13. Quis nōn labōrat?   Juvenis nōn labōrat.
14. Quid senex fodit?   Agrum senex fodit.

B. Metaphase the following:

1. Aedificium senem . . . .   6. Vir opus . . . .
2. Auctor corpus . . . .   7. . . . . -ne juvenis nōmen?
3. Animal philosophum . . . .   8. . . . . -ne animal puella?
4. Puella fēminam . . . .   9. Agrum . . . . agricola?
5. Oppidum virum . . . .   10. Auctor senem . . . .

C. Supply in the blank the appropriate case of the noun in parentheses. Be able to give a reason for your choice.

1. Puella _____ nōn spectat. (equus, equum)
2. Canem _____ nōn laudat. (philosophus, philosophum)
3. Agricola _____ est. (juvenis, juvenem)
4. _____ nōn videt juvenis. (manus, manum)
5. _____ vir est. (senex, senem)
6. Senex _____ lavat. (barba, barbam)
7. _____ nōn labōrat. (fēmina, fēminam)
8. Stat _____ (agricola, agricolam)
9. Fēmina _____ facit. (vestis, vestem)
10. Estne philosophus _____ ? (vir, virum)

D. Give the answers to the questions based on each of these sentences.

1. Vir agricola est; magnam barbam gerit.
    Quis est agricola?
    Quid gerit agricola?
    Quis est vir?

2. Est juvenis; agrum spectat.
    Quis est?
    Quid agit juvenis?
    Spectatne juvenis agrum?

3. Parvum aedificium spectat puer.
    Spectatne parvum aedificium puerum?
    Quid puer spectat?
    Quis spectat?

4. Juvenis videt corpus.
    Quid videt?
    Quis videt?
    Videtne corpus juvenem?

5. Virum oppidum dēlectat.
    Quid dēlectat?
    Quem dēlectat?
    Dēlectatne oppidum vir?

6. Auctor opus laudat.
    Quis laudat?
    Quid laudat?
    Laudatne auctor opus?

7. Auctōrem dēlectat opus.
    Quem dēlectat?
    Quid dēlectat?
    Dēlectatne auctor opus?

8. Philosophus agrum et oppidum laudat.
    Quis laudat?
    Quid laudat?
    Laudatne oppidum agrum?

E. Give the Latin equivalent.

1. The girl makes clothes.
2. Does the horse hear the man?
3. The woman chases the dog away.
4. She is not looking at (her) hand.
5. The boy sees a girl.

IV   PATTERN PRACTICE TWO

1. The old man is not a philosopher.   Senex philosophus nōn est.

2. The old man praises the philosopher.   Senex philosophum laudat.

3. The old man praises his name.   Senex nōmen laudat.

4. The name pleases the *old man*.   Senem nōmen dēlectat.

5. His beard pleases the *old man*.   Senem barba dēlectat.

6. The old man wears a beard.   Senex barbam gerit.

7. Does a beard make him an old man?   Facitne barba senem?

8. A *beard* does not make a philosopher.   Philosophum nōn facit barba.

9. The philosopher is not a farmer.   Philosophus nōn est agricola.

10. Is an animal a farmer?   No.   Estne animal agricola? Nōn est.

11. The animal chases the farmer away.   Animal agricolam pellit.

12. The farmer chases the *animal* away.   Animal agricola pellit.

13. The farmer doesn't chase the *boy* away. Puerum agricola nōn pellit.

14. The boy is not working hard.   Puer nōn labōrat.

15. Is the boy standing still?   Statne puer?

16. Does the boy see the body?   Videtne puer corpus?

17. The boy *does* see the body.   Videt puer corpus.

18. The boy is digging up the body.   Puer corpus fodit.

19. The boy is digging the field.   Puer agrum fodit.

20. The field is pleasing to the *boy*.   Puerum ager dēlectat.

21. The field pleases the young man.   Ager juvenem dēlectat.

22. The building pleases the young man.   Aedificium juvenem dēlectat.

23. The work does *not* please the young man. Nōn dēlectat opus juvenem.

24. The youth does not praise the work.   Juvenis opus nōn laudat.

25. The author approves of the work.   Auctor opus laudat.

26. The author is a man.   Auctor vir est.

V   OPTIONAL READING

Homō locum ōrnat, nōn hominem locus. — Medieval
Lūx et vēritās — Motto (Yale University)
Nūmen, lūmen[1] — Motto (University of Wisconsin)

---

[1] Two nominatives can signal the A = B construction without a verb.

VI   WORD STUDY

1. Some Latin words come into English without any change in spelling: for example, *opus* and *animal*. What does "opus" mean in English?

2. Other Latin words appear in English with slight changes in spelling: *aedificium* becomes "edifice," *auctor* "author." How have these words changed in meaning?

3. What English words come from *laudat*? from *labōrat*? from *philosophus*?

4. *Corpus* has many English derivatives. Explain the relationship in meaning between *corpus* and "corpse," "corps," "corporal" (noun and adjective), "corporation."

5. The adjective-forming suffix "-ile" (Latin *-īlis*) was used in Lesson I. To what nouns in this lesson can it be added to form adjectives?

6. The Roman Senate was made up of older men, elders, called "senators" (from *senex*); they acted as advisers to Roman magistrates and performed some legislative functions.

7. There are other examples of word relationship within the Latin language itself. For instance, *puella* ("girl") is the feminine counterpart of *puellus* ("little boy"), a diminutive form of *puer* ("boy"). By adding the ending *-cola* ("cultivator") to a form of *ager* ("field") the noun *agri - cola* ("cultivator of the field") is formed.

8. What relationship in meaning is there between "fossil" and *fodit?* between "barber" and *barba?*

VII   VOCABULARY

Nouns[2]

agricola, agricolam m.
barba, barbam f.

ager, agrum m.
philosophus, philosophum m.

aedificium, aedificium n.
oppidum, oppidum n.

auctor, auctōrem m.
juvenis, juvenem m.
senex, senem m.

animal, animal n.
corpus, corpus n.
flūmen, flūmen n.
nōmen, nōmen n.
opus, opus n.

Adjectives

magnus, magna, magnum
parvus, parva, parvum

Verbs

dēlectat
labōrat
laudat
stat

gerit

fodit

Function Words

et
-que
sed

---

[2]Gender designations are given the nouns in this lesson. The fact that neuter nouns have a different form pattern shows that it is necessary to know genders. The m./f. distinction will show its importance when you are required to use adjectives. Meanwhile the adjective variations caused by differences in gender will appear in your reading (*canis magnus, animal magnum, manus magna*). Learn the genders as you learn the nouns. The nouns of Lesson I have the following genders: those ending in *-a* are feminine, those in *-r* and *equus* are masculine, *canis* is either m. or f., *vestis* and *manus* are f.

LESSON THREE

Vorēnus [1] *gladiō . . . . rem gerit.* —Caesar   "Vorenus carries on the combat (matter, affair) with his sword."

Hieme et aestāte —Cicero   "Winter and summer" (at all times)

Purpose: to learn something of the ablative case

I MĪLES RŌMĀNUS

gladius
gladium
gladiō

hostis	mīles Rōmānus
hostem	mīlitem Rōmānum
hoste	mīlite Rōmānō

Juvenis mīles Rōmānus est. Mīles Rōmānus gladium habet. Tenet gladium manū. Hostis etiam gladium habet. Hostis gladium manū tenet. Hostis est vir. Hostis etiam mīles est sed Rōmānus nōn est. Mīles Rōmānus cum hoste pūgnat. Gladiō hostem vulnerat mīles Rōmānus. Mīlitem Rōmānum hostis gladiō nōn vulnerat. Rōmānus laetus sed hostis trīstis est. Rōmānus laetus est quod hostem vulnerat. Hostis trīstis est quod nōn vulnerat Rōmānum. Rōmānus cum hoste bene pūgnat; manū [2] vincit. Cum Rōmānō hostis male pūgnat; nōn vincit. Mīles Rōmānus rem bene gerit.

---

[1] Vorenus, a brave centurion in Caesar's army, rescued a fellow officer who was in difficulty by his heroic action in entering the fight. For details about the Roman army see a good book on Roman life.

[2] In a new sense, not "by his hand," but "by the strength of his hand" or "by his forcefulness."

1. Quis est juvenis? Mīles Rōmānus est juvenis.
2. Quid mīles tenet? Gladium mīles tenet.
3. Quis est hostis? Vir est hostis.
4. Quōcum pūgnat mīles? Cum hoste mīles pūgnat.
5. Quō īnstrūmentō hostem mīles vulnerat? Gladiō hostem vulnerat.
6. Quōcum pūgnat hostis? Cum Rōmānō pūgnat hostis.
7. Vulneratne hostis militem Rōmānum? Nōn vulnerat.
8. Vulneratne mīles Rōmānus hostem? Vulnerat.
9. Vincitne hostis? Nōn vincit.
10. Quid agit mīles Rōmānus? Rem gerit mīles Rōmānus.

II   PATTERN READING

A.   Sample sentences

1. Vir saxum manū habet. The man has a stone in his hand.
2. Quō īnstrūmentō agricola agrum fodit? With what is the farmer digging the field?
   Pālā agricola agrum fodit. The farmer digs the field with a spade.
3. Juvenis laetus est quod bene labōrat. The youth is happy because he is working well.
4. Quōcum labōrat? Cum agricolā. With whom is he working? With the farmer.
5. Quandō mīles pūgnat? Aestāte. When does the soldier fight? In summer.
6. Hōc diē mīles hostem trīstem vulnerat. The soldier wounds his unhappy enemy on this day.

B.   Practice sentences

1. Hostis cum mīlite rem gerit.
   Quis rem gerit? Hostis rem gerit.
   Quōcum rem gerit? Cum mīlite rem gerit.
   Quid agit hostis? Cum mīlite rem gerit hostis.

2. Mīles hostem gladiō vulnerat.
   Quis hostem vulnerat? Mīles hostem vulnerat.
   Quem vulnerat? Hostem vulnerat.
   Quō īnstrūmentō vulnerat? Gladiō vulnerat.
   Quid agit mīles? Hostem gladiō vulnerat mīles.

3. Vir canem pellit eō diē.
   Quem pellit? Canem pellit.
   Quandō canem pellit? Eō diē canem pellit.
   Quid vir agit? Canem vir pellit.
   Pellitne canis virum? Nōn pellit.

4. Cum juvene hieme senex labōrat.
   Quōcum labōrat? Cum juvene labōrat.
   Quid agit senex? Cum juvene labōrat senex.
   Quis labōrat? Senex labōrat.
   Quandō labōrat senex? Hieme labōrat senex.

5. Mīles manū gladium tenet.
   Quis tenet gladium?   Mīles tenet gladium.
   Quid tenet?   Gladium tenet.
   Tenetne gladium manū?   Tenet gladium manū.

6. Aestāte agrum pālā fodit agricola.
   Quis fodit?   Agricola fodit.
   Quid fodit?   Agrum fodit.
   Quandō fodit agricola?   Aestāte fodit agricola.
   Quō īnstrūmentō fodit?   Pālā fodit.

7. Juvenis cum hoste saxō pūgnat.
   Quō īnstrūmentō pūgnat?   Saxō pūgnat.
   Quōcum pūgnat?   Cum hoste pūgnat.
   Pūgnatne juvenis?   Pūgnat.
   Quis pūgnat?   Juvenis pūgnat.

8. Aestāte et hieme puella cum fēminā vestem manū facit.
   Quid facit?   Vestem facit.
   Quis facit?   Puella facit.
   Quōcum vestem facit?   Cum fēminā vestem facit.
   Quandō facit vestem?   Aestāte et hieme facit vestem.
   Quō īnstrūmentō facit vestem?   Manū facit vestem.

C.   Questions on structure

1. What signals for the Latin ablative case do you find?
2. How is the ablative case related to the verb?
3. What idea is expressed by *gladiō vulnerat*? by *eō diē*? by *cum hoste*?
4. What seems to be the general idea in the use of the ablative case?

See Appendix B, page 191.

III   EXERCISES

A.   Answer in Latin these questions about the picture on page 36.

1. Quis barbam habet?
2. Vulneratne hostem mīles Rōmānus?
3. Estne senex mīles?
4. Quis gladiō vulnerat?
5. Quis nōn bene pūgnat?
6. Quōcum pūgnat hostis?
7. Quem vulnerat mīles?
8. Quid manū tenet hostis?
9. Quō īnstrūmentō Rōmānus rem bene gerit?
10. Quō īnstrūmentō hostis pūgnat?

B.   Ask the Latin questions that will get the italicized word or words as an answer.

1. *Cum agricolā* fodit juvenis.
2. *Saxō* puer equum male vulnerat.
3. *Cum sene* fēmina stat.
4. *Philosophum* rēs dēlectat.
5. *Fēmina* vestem bene lavat.
6. *Pellit/canem* mīles.
7. *Barbam* nōn gerit fēmina.
8. *Hieme* nōn labōrat agricola.
9. *Gladiō* rem gerit.
10. *Mīles* vir est.

C. Supply in each blank a suitable form of the word in parentheses. (Which of the possible parts of the sentence is missing?)

1. _____ gladiō vincit. (mīles)
2. Manū _____ puer tenet. (equus)
3. Mīles cum _____ pūgnat. (agricola)
4. Barbam agricola _____ lavat. (manus)
5. Vir mīlitem vulnerat _____ . (aestās)
6. Cum _____ puer stat. (juvenis)
7. _____ fodit pālā agricola. (ager)
8. _____ spectat senex. (fēmina)
9. Habetne nōmen _____ . (auctor)
10. Equus est _____ . (animal)
11. Nōn habet equum _____ . (hostis)
12. Juvenis virum _____ dēlectat. (opus)

D. Give the Latin equivalent.

1. The young man hears the name.
2. The old man wears a beard.
3. The farmer is a philosopher.
4. The work pleases the old man.
5. The woman is an author.
6. An animal is chasing the horse away.
7. The farmer does not see the body.
8. Is the woman standing?
9. Does she approve of the house (building)?
10. A girl is looking at the river and the town.

IV   PATTERN PRACTICE THREE

1. The girl pleases the woman.

Puella fēminam dēlectat.

2. The girl pleases the woman on this day.

Puella fēminam eō diē dēlectat.

3. The girl pleases the woman with her name.

Puella fēminam nōmine dēlectat.

4. The girl pleases the woman with her clothes.

Puella fēminam veste dēlectat.

5. The girl is wearing the clothing.

Puella vestem gerit.

6. The girl is wearing the clothing in the winter.

Hieme puella vestem gerit.

7. The girl is wearing the clothing in the summer.

Aestāte puella vestem gerit.

8. The girl does *not* carry on the matter.

Nōn gerit puella rem.

9. *The soldier* carries the matter on well.

Rem bene gerit mīles.

10. *The soldier* carries on the combat with a sword.

Rem gladiō gerit mīles.

11. *The soldier* fights with a sword.

Gladiō pūgnat mīles.

12. *The soldier* is fighting with an enemy.

Cum hoste pūgnat mīles.

13. An *enemy* fights with the soldier.

Cum mīlite pūgnat hostis.

14. An enemy is wounding the soldier.

Hostis mīlitem vulnerat.

15. His enemy is wounding the soldier with a sword.

Hostis mīlitem gladiō vulnerat.

16. The soldier is wounding the *enemy* with a sword.

Hostem mīles gladiō vulnerat.

17. The soldier conquers his *enemy*.

Hostem mīles vincit.

18. A soldier conquers the *enemy* with his sword.   Hostem mīles gladiō vincit.

19. The soldier conquers the *enemy* on this day.   Hostem mīles eō diē vincit.

20. The soldier conquers the *enemy* by his forcefulness.   Hostem mīles manū vincit.

21. Has the soldier a sword?   Habetne mīles gladium?

22. The soldier *does* have the sword in his hand.   Habet mīles gladium manū.

23. The soldier has a rock in his hand.   Mīles saxum manū habet.

24. A man has a rock in his hand.   Vir saxum manū habet.

25. The man hurts the soldier with a rock.   Vir saxō mīlitem vulnerat.

V   OPTIONAL READING

Hostem manū . . . . . sternit.   —Vergil (adapted)
Necessitās nōn habet lēgem.   —St. Bernard (?)
Victōria Concordiā crēscit.   —Motto
Puer . . . lūsū . . . impedit opus.   —Ovid (adapted)

VI   WORD STUDY

1. What English adjective is formed from the Latin word *hostis*?

2. What ending change is necessary to make an English word from *Rōmānus*?

3. Point out the relationship in meaning of these words to *mīles*: militia, militant, military, militarize.

4. What is a "tenet" of a church?

5. How does the flower called "gladiolus" (or "gladiola") get its name?

6. The adverbs *bene, male,* and *nōn* are often used in English as prefixes. Show how the prefix affects the meaning of these words: benefactor, malnutrition, nonsense. Find two additional words containing each of these prefixes.

7. The ablative form of *rēs* is used in English: "re" or "in re" means "in the matter of," "concerning."

VII   VOCABULARY

Nouns[1]	*Adjectives*	*Function Words*
pāla, pālam, pālā f.	laetus, laeta, laetum	etiam
	Rōmānus, Rōmāna, Rōmānum	bene
gladius, gladium, gladiō m.	trīstis, trīste	male
saxum, saxum, saxō n.	*Verbs*	quod
aestās, aestātem, aestāte f.	pūgnat	cum + abl.
hiems, hiemem, hieme f.	vulnerat	
hostis, hostem, hoste m.		quō īnstrūmentō (?)
mīles, mīlitem, mīlite m.	habet	quōcum (?)
	tenet	quandō (?)
diēs, diem, diē m. (f.)		
rēs, rem, rē f.	vincit	

[1] The ablative forms of nouns in Lessons 1 and 2 are as follows:
   like *pāla*: fēminā, puellā, agricolā, barbā
   like *gladius*: equō, philosophō; also: puerō, virō, agrō
   like *saxum*: aedificiō, oppidō
   like *hostis*: cane, veste, juvene; also: auctōre, sene
   note especially: corpus, corpore   animal, animālī
                      flūmen, flūmine
                      nōmen, nōmine   manus, manū
                      opus, opere

LESSON FOUR

Gladiātor in harēnā capit cōnsilium.
   —Seneca

"The gladiator forms his plan in the arena" (on the spot).

Purpose: to learn more about the ablative case (with prepositions)

I HARĒNA

spectātor
spectātōrem
spectātōre

gladiātor   harēna   servus
gladiātōrem   harēnam   servum
gladiātōre   harēnā   servō

PATTERN READING

A.   Sample sentences

1. Quō modō gladiātor pūgnat?
   Cum studiō pūgnat.

   How does the gladiator fight?
   He fights eagerly (with enthusiasm).

2. Ubi gladiātor pūgnat?
   In harēnā gladiātor pūgnat.

   Where does the gladiator fight?
   The gladiator is fighting in the arena.

3. Ab harēnā vir cum dolōre ambulat.

   The man walks away from the arena reluctantly (with regret).

4. Spectātor procul tumultum audit.   The spectator hears an uproar at a distance.

5. Unde servus pede prōcēdit?   From where is the slave going on foot?
   Ex harēnā servus pede prōcēdit.   The slave is going out of the arena on foot.

B.   Be able to answer these questions based on the arena picture.

   1. Quis est mīles?   Gladiātor est mīles.
   2. Ubi est gladiātor?   In harēnā est gladiātor.
   3. Quid gladiātor agit?   Gladiātor pūgnat.
   4. Quō īnstrūmentō gladiātor pūgnat?   Gladiō gladiātor pūgnat.
   5. Quandō gladiātor pūgnat?   Eō diē gladiātor pūgnat.

   6. Quōcum gladiātor pūgnat?   Cum gladiātōre pūgnat.
   7. Quō modō gladiātor pūgnat?   Cum studiō gladiātor pūgnat.
   8. Ubi capit consilium?   In harēnā capit cōnsilium.
   9. Quō modō capit cōnsilium?   Cum studiō capit cōnsilium.
   10. Quid tenet gladiātor?   Gladium tenet gladiātor.

   11. Quō īnstrūmentō gladium tenet?   Manū gladium tenet.
   12. Quid agit servus?   Ambulat servus.
   13. Unde prōcēdit servus?   Ex hārēnā prōcēdit servus.
   14. Quō īnstrūmentō prōcēdit servus?   Pede prōcēdit servus.
   15. Quō modō prōcēdit servus?   Cum dolōre prōcēdit servus.

   16. Quis est vir?   Spectātor est vir.
   17. Quid spectātor agit?   Spectātor ambulat.
   18. Unde vir prōcēdit?   Ab harēnā vir prōcēdit.
   19. Quid audit vir?   Tumultum audit vir.
   20. Quō modō vir prōcēdit?   Cum dolōre vir prōcēdit.

C.   Questions on structure

   1. What prepositions show place relationships?

   2. What is the difference in idea between *cum dolōre* and *cum mīlite*?

   3. What is the difference between *in harēnā* and *aestāte*?

   4. What is the difference between *ab harēnā* and *ex harēnā*?

See Appendix B, page 192.

II   IN VIĀ

arbor
arborem
arbore

urbs
urbem
urbe

Mārcus   via   amīcus
Mārcum   viam   amīcum
Mārcō   viā   amīcō

In pictūrā est via. Eō diē in viā est equus. In equō est puer, nōmine[1] Mārcus. Puer, nōmine Jūlius, etiam in viā est. Jūlius viātor est. Mārcus etiam est viātor; sed in equō sedet. Urbem Rōmam videt. Rōma urbs est; nōn est oppidum. Ad[2] urbem in equō prōcēdit Mārcus.

Jūlius etiam ad urbem prōcēdit, sed pede, nōn in equō. Cum amīcō ambulat; laetus est puer. Rēs puerum facit laetum; cum studiō, nōn cum dolōre prōcēdit ab agrō. In agrō stat arbor; nōn procul ā viā stat. Est magna arbor; arborem videt puer.

Magnam urbem, nōmine Rōmam, laudat viātor. Viātōrem et amīcum dēlectat urbs. Aestās est. Aestāte in urbe viātor ambulat.

1. Ubi est via?
2. Ubi est equus?
3. Quid agit equus?
4. Quōcum prōcēdit equus?
5. Quis sedet?

6. Ubi sedet puer?
7. Quis est Jūlius?
8. Ubi est Jūlius?
9. Quō īnstrūmentō prōcēdit Jūlius?
10. Quandō ambulat Jūlius?

11. Quōcum ambulat Jūlius?
12. Quō modō ambulat Jūlius?
13. Unde prōcēdit puer?
14. Quid nōn procul ā viā stat?
15. Quid videt puer?

16. Quid laudat viātor?
17. Estne tumultus in viā?
18. Quid est Rōma?
19. Quandō ambulat viātor?
20. Ubi est viātor?

III   EXERCISES

A.   Answer the questions on each sentence.

1. Aestāte mīles gladiō ab aedificiō hostem pellit.
    Quem pellit?   Unde pellit?
    Quandō pellit?   Quō īnstrūmentō pellit?
    Quis pellit?

[1] *nōmine*, "in name," "named"
[2] *ad*, to (see next lesson for use)

2. Hieme in oppidō puer puellam cum studiō videt.
   Quandō videt?   Quō modō videt?
   Ubi videt?   Quis videt?
   Quem videt?

3. Spectātor cum amīcō pede prōcēdit ab harēnā.
   Unde prōcēdit spectātor?   Quō īnstrūmentō prōcēdit?
   Quōcum prōcēdit spectātor?   Quis prōcēdit?

4. Cum dolōre saxum ex agrō pālā fodit servus.
   Quis fodit?   Quō īnstrūmentō fodit?
   Quid fodit?   Quō modō fodit?
   Unde fodit?

B.   Fit 20 meaningful ablative phrases into the frame:

   Vir _____ prōcēdit.

C.   Give the Latin equivalent.

   1. His enemy conquers the soldier with his sword.
   2. The farmer is digging the field with a spade.
   3. The river delights a boy in summer.
   4. The author sees the town in winter.
   5. The old man chases the animal away with a stone.
   6. Does the philosopher have a beard too?
   7. A woman is standing with the author.
   8. The girl does not hear the name well.
   9. The young fellow is not working with the old man.
   10. The man handles the situation badly on this day.

D.   Ask the Latin question that will get the italicized word as an answer.

   1. *In pictūrā* vir tumultum facit.
   2. *Arbor* puerum dēlectat.
   3. *Hieme* senex nōn labōrat.
   4. *Cum amīcō* lavat fēmina vestem.
   5. *Cum studiō* puer cōnsilium capit.
   6. *Gladiō* capit mīles hostem.
   7. *Pede* animal juvenem vulnerat.
   8. *Ē viā* canis virum pellit.
   9. *Eō diē* spectātor ab harēnā ambulat.
   10. *Auctōrem* amīcus cum studiō laudat.
   11. *In agrō* saxum nōn procul ab arbore videt.
   12. *Ab urbe* prōcēdit servus.

IV   PATTERN PRACTICE FOUR

1.	One gladiator conquers another.	Gladiātōrem gladiātor vincit.
2.	The gladiator wins in the arena.	In harēnā gladiātor vincit.
3.	The gladiator wins on this day.	Eō diē gladiātor vincit.
4.	A gladiator wins by his sword.	Gladiō gladiātor vincit.
5.	The *woman* walks out of the building.	Ex aedificiō ambulat fēmina.
6.	The *woman* walks away from the city.	Ab urbe ambulat fēmina.
7.	The *woman* is walking with a girl.	Cum puellā ambulat fēmina.
8.	The *woman* is going on foot.	Pede ambulat fēmina.
9.	The *woman* is walking in the road.	In viā ambulat fēmina.
10.	A boy is sitting on the horse.	In equō puer sedet.
11.	The boy is sitting far from the tree.	Procul ab arbore puer sedet.
12.	The boy is not sitting with his friend.	Cum amīcō puer nōn sedet.
13.	A boy is coming along with a dog.	Cum cane puer prōcēdit.
14.	A boy is coming out of the field.	Ex agrō puer prōcēdit.
15.	The gladiator forms his *plan*.	Gladiātor capit cōnsilium.
16.	The gladiator forms his *plan* on this day.	Gladiātor eō diē capit cōnsilium.
17.	The gladiator forms his *plan* in the arena.	Gladiātor in harēnā capit cōnsilium.
18.	The *gladiator* takes his sword.	Gladium capit gladiātor.
19.	He takes his sword eagerly.	Gladium cum studiō capit.
20.	He takes his sword from the slave.	Gladium ā servō capit.
21.	The soldier is wounding his enemy.	Mīles hostem vulnerat.
22.	The soldier wounds his enemy with his sword.	Mīles hostem gladiō vulnerat.
23.	The soldier wounds his enemy angrily.	Mīles hostem cum dolōre vulnerat.
24.	The soldier captures his enemy in summer.	Mīles hostem aestāte capit.
25.	The soldier captures his enemy in the town.	Mīles hostem in oppidō capit.
26.	The soldier captures his enemy eagerly.	Mīles hostem cum studiō capit.

V   OPTIONAL READING

Common phrases[1]

deus ex machinā   ex cathedrā   extempore   Fugit hōra. —Persius

[1] When these phrases are used in English they are usually given an Anglicized (English sounding) pronunciation.

VI   WORD STUDY

1. What words in this lesson come into English with very little or no change in spelling?

2. What meaning does the *-tor* Latin suffix have? On what other Latin word is each of these nouns based: *gladiātor, viātor, spectātor*?

3. Another adjective-forming suffix is "-al" (Latin *-ālis*). From what Latin words do these derivatives come: nominal, pedal, arboreal?

4. Many prefixes in both English and Latin come from Latin prepositions. What Latin prepositions do you see in these compound roots: expel, effect, absent, collaborate, inspect?

5. The English word "trivial" has an interesting origin. According to its Latin source (*tri + via*) it originally meant "pertaining to three roads," for when you stand at a crossroads you have the choice of three roads to go. Since what occurred at the crossroads—casual meetings, gossip, etc., was of little importance, it came to be called "trivial"—as we might refer to "back fence gossip."

6. The English word "arena" is derived from *harēna* which has a variant spelling *arena*. The Roman *harēna* was named from the sand used to cover the area where the fighting was done.

7. Explain the sources of: servant, dolorous, counsel, study, urban, ambulatory, sedentary, proceed, amicable, and captive.

VIII   VOCABULARY

Nouns

harēna, harēnam, harēnā   f.
pictūra, pictūram, pictūrā   f.
via, viam, viā   f.

amīcus, amīcum, amīcō   m.
servus, servum, servō   m.

cōnsilium, cōnsilium, cōnsiliō   n.
studium, studium, studiō   n.

arbor, arborem, arbore   f.
dolor, dolōrem, dolōre   m.
gladiātor, gladiātōrem, gladiātōre   m.
pēs, pedem, pede   m.
spectātor, spectātōrem, spectātōre   m.
urbs, urbem, urbe   f.
viātor, viātōrem, viātōre   m.

tumultus, tumultum, tumultū   m.

Mārcus, Mārcum, Mārcō   m.
Jūlius, Jūlium, Jūliō   m.
Rōma, Rōmam, Rōmā   f.

Verbs

ambulat

sedet

prōcēdit

capit

Function Words

quō modō   (?)
ubi   (?)
unde   (?)

procul

ā, ab + abl.
ē, ex + abl.
   in + abl.

LESSON FIVE

Nōn lupus ad studium, sed mentem vertit ad agnum. —Medieval

"The wolf turns his attention, not to study (things of the mind) but to the lamb (food, practical things)."

Purpose: to learn adverbial accusatives (with and without prepositions)

I LUPUS ET AGNUS

arbor   silva
arborem silvam
arbore   silvā

mōns
montem
monte

lupus
lupum
lupō

fōns
fontem
fonte

saxum   agnus   aqua
saxum   agnum   aquam
saxō   agnō   aquā

PATTERN READING

A.   Sample sentences

1. Arbor ad flūmen stat.   The tree stands near the river.

2. Quō lupus prōcēdit? Ad flūmen.   Where is the wolf going? To the river.

3. Lupus per silvam currit.   The wolf runs through the forest.

4. Quandō lupus venit? Hōrā tertiā.[1]   When is the wolf coming? At the third hour.

---

[1] The Roman day was divided about evenly into 12 hours, beginning at dawn and ending at dusk. Depending on the time of the year, the third hour would be mid-morning, about 9:00 A.M.

5. Quam diū currit lupus? Ūnam hōram.

How long does the wolf run? For one hour.

6. Agnus trāns flūmen currit.

The lamb is hurrying across the river.

7. Agnus in flūmine nōn natat.

The lamb is not swimming in the river.

8. Agnus in saxum prōcēdit.

The lamb is going onto the rock.

9. Agnus super aquam prōcēdit.

The lamb goes over the water.

10. Aqua sub agnō fluit.

The water flows under the lamb.

11. Fons dē monte fluit.

The spring is flowing down from the mountain.

12. Lupus caput ad agnum vertit.

The wolf turns his head to the lamb.

B. Be able to answer these questions based on the picture and quotation.

1. Ubi est lupus? — In silvā est lupus.
2. Quid agit lupus? — Currit lupus.
3. Ubi currit lupus? — Per silvam currit lupus.
4. Quō currit lupus? — Ad flūmen currit lupus.

5. Quandō venit lupus? — Hōrā tertiā venit lupus.
6. Quam diū currit lupus? — Ūnam hōram currit lupus.
7. Unde currit lupus? — Ē silvā currit lupus.
8. Quō prōcēdit agnus? — Trāns flūmen prōcēdit agnus.

9. Ubi est agnus? — Super flūmen est agnus.
10. Ubi est flūmen? — Sub agnō est flūmen.
11. Quam diū agnus currit? — Ūnam hōram agnus currit.
12. Quō lupus mentem vertit? — Ad agnum mentem vertit.
13. Quō lupus mentem nōn vertit? — Ad studium mentem nōn vertit.
14. Ubi est flūmen? — Ad silvam est flūmen.
15. Venitne lupus in flūmen? — Nōn venit lupus in flūmen.

16. Unde fōns fluit? — Dē monte fōns fluit.

17. Ubi est silva? — In monte est silva.
18. Quō īnstrūmentō currit lupus? — Pede currit lupus.
19. Quō modō lupus currit? — Cum studiō lupus currit.
20. Quō modō agnus currit? — Cum dolōre agnus currit.

C. Questions on structure

1. What prepositions pattern with a) the accusative, b) the ablative, c) both cases?

2. What idea is expressed by an adverbial accusative without a preposition?

3. With what type of verb are many of the adverbial accusatives used? (Do they pattern with transitive verbs which have direct objects? With intransitive verbs?)

4. Show the difference in idea between *in* with accusative, *in* with ablative, *ā, ab* with the ablative, *ad* with the accusative.

See Appendix B, pages 191-92.

II   IN AQUĀ

A.   Answer in Latin the questions based on the picture.

1. Ubi stat puer prīmus?
2. Quō currit puer secundus?
3. Ubi stat puer tertius?
4. Quid agit puer quārtus?
5. Ubi natat puer quārtus?
6. Quid puer prīmus spectat?
7. Quam diū spectat puer?
8. Quōcum puer natat?
9. Curritne puer ē flūmine?
10. Natatne puer sub aquā?

B.   Refer to page 34 and answer these questions:

1. What do these statements mean?
   a. *Ante* puerum ambulat vir.
   b. *Post* puerum est canis.
   c. Puer *inter* virum et canem ambulat.

2.   What case is used with the prepositions *ante*, *post*, and *inter*?

C.   Answer these questions based on the picture on page 34.

1. Ubi stat fēmina?
2. Quō prōcēdit vir?
3. Ubi est vir?
4. Ubi est canis?
5. Ubi est puer?
6. Ambulatne puer post virum?
7. Ambulatne puer post canem?
8. Ubi stat magnum animal?
9. Ubi tenet equus caput?
10. Prōcēditne equus ad aedificium?
11. Quōcum ambulat puer?
12. Venitne fēmina ex aedificiō?

III   EXERCISES

A.   Supply in the blanks the required form of the word indicated.

oppidum

1. Puer ad_____currit.
2. Puer in_____prōcēdit.
3. Puer per_____prōcēdit.
4. Puer in_____stat.
5. Puer ex_____currit.
6. Puer ab_____currit.

senex

7. Vir ante_____venit.
8. Canis post_____venit.
9. Juvenis cum_____venit.
10. Saxum sub_____est.
11. Arbor super_____est.
12. Amīcus ad_____stat.

B.   Give the Latin equivalent.

1. The man goes out of the river reluctantly.
2. A young man is walking away from the city with Julius.
3. In the picture the building is not far from the field.
4. Does Marcus watch the gladiator with enthusiasm?

5. The girl does not go out of the town in winter.
6. A slave is going away from the arena on foot.
7. The soldier defeats an enemy with his forcefulness.
8. The author does his work eagerly also.
9. The traveler causes (makes) a disturbance on the road on this day.
10. Because the philosopher has a plan, he carries on the matter successfully.

C. Make a diagram, using a square or any other pictorial device, to illustrate as many as possible of the place prepositions.

IV PATTERN PRACTICE FIVE

1. The young man runs to the river. Juvenis ad flūmen currit.

2. The young man runs into the river. Juvenis in flūmen currit.

3. The young man is swimming in the river. Juvenis in flūmine natat.

4. The young man swims out of the river. Juvenis ē flūmine natat.

5. The young man hurries away from the river. Juvenis ā flūmine currit.

6. The young man runs with his friend. Juvenis cum amīcō currit.

7. His friend comes along eagerly. Amīcus cum studiō venit.

8. His friend comes down from the rock. Amīcus dē saxō venit.

9. His friend comes at this hour. Amīcus eā hōrā venit.

10. The friend swims through the water. Amīcus per aquam natat.

11. The friend swims for one hour. Amīcus ūnam hōram natat.

12. The friend is swimming under water. Amīcus sub aquā natat.

13. He is not swimming across the water. Trāns aquam nōn natat.

14. Is a girl sitting near the water? Sedetne puella ad aquam?

15. She *is* sitting not far from the water. Sedet nōn procul ab aquā.

16. The girl *is* sitting under a tree. Sedet sub arbore puella.

17. In front of the girl stands a *dog*. Ante puellam stat canis.

18. Behind the dog stands a *man*. Post canem stat vir.

19. The *dog* stands between the man and the girl. Inter virum et puellam stat canis.

20. A traveler goes along *near* the man. Prōcēdit viātor ad virum.

21. The traveler is going *to the city*. Prōcēdit viātor ad urbem.

22. He is proceeding *into the city* on foot. Pede prōcēdit in urbem.

23. He proceeds *through the city* with a boy. Cum puerō prōcēdit per urbem.

24. He walks around *in the city* for one day. Ūnum diem ambulat in urbe.

25. On this day he is walking *out of the city*. Eō diē ambulat ex urbe.

26. He walks *away from the city* with regret. Cum dolōre ambulat ab urbe.

V   OPTIONAL READING

Common phrases

ante bellum	per annum
ante merīdiem (A.M.)	per centum
post bellum	per diem
post merīdiem (P.M.)	in memoriam
post mortem	sub rosā
ad īnfīnītum	sub poenā

VI   WORD STUDY

1. The Latin prepositions in this lesson are the source of prefixes in both Latin and English. Identify the prefixes in: invert, intervene, perspective, adventure, antecedent, postpone, superstructure, subway, transfer.

2. Give two other English words using each of these prefixes.

3. Form English words from the following, using suffixes given in previous lessons: lupus, mēns, caput.

4. How is the word "current" related in meaning to *currit*?

5. What is the relationship of *flūmen* and *fluit*?

6. Note in the Optional Reading above the common abbreviations we use for "morning" and "afternoon," and the Latin words for which they stand.

7. What is essential in an "aquarium"? What is a "capital" crime?

8. The name of "Pennsylvania" arose from joking references to Mr. Penn's *Woods*.

VII   VOCABULARY

Nouns	*Verbs*	*Function Words*	
aqua, aquam, aquā f.	natat	ad + acc.	quam diū (?)
hōra, hōram, hōrā f.		in + acc.	quō (?)
silva, silvam, silvā f.	currit	ante + acc.	
	fluit	inter + acc.	
agnus, agnum, agnō m.	vertit	per + acc.	
lupus, lupum, lupō m.		post + acc.	
	venit	sub + acc.	
fōns, fontem, fonte m.		super + acc.	
mēns, mentem, mente f.		trāns + acc.	
mōns, montem, monte m.			
		dē + abl.	
caput, caput, capite n.		sub + abl.	

FIRST REVIEW

Multum in parvō —Common phrase   "Much in little"

Virtūte et labōre[1] —Motto   "With courage and hard work"

I   VOCABULARY AND MODEL SENTENCE REVIEW

A.   Match the words in Group II to words in Group I which contrast in meaning.

Group I		*Group II*	
____ 1. ad	____ 11. juvenis	a. ā, ab	l. puer
____ 2. aestās	____ 12. laetus	b. ambulat	m. sedet
____ 3. ager	____ 13. magnus	c. corpus	n. senex
____ 4. ante	____ 14. mēns	d. dolor	o. silva
____ 5. audit	____ 15. oppidum	e. ē, ex	p. super
____ 6. bene	____ 16. puella	f. hiems	q. trīstis
____ 7. caput	____ 17. quō (adv.)	g. male	r. unde
____ 8. currit	____ 18. stat	h. parvus	s. urbs
____ 9. fēmina	____ 19. studium	i. pēs	t. videt
____ 10. in (acc.)	____ 20. sub	k. post	u. vir

B.   Supply the missing letters in these model sentences.

1. Vest __ vir __ fac __ .
2. Man __ man __ lav __ .
3. Mult __ in parv __ .
4. Auct __ op __ laud __ .
5. Vorēn __ gladi __ r __ ger __ .
6. Hiem __ et aest __ .
7. Philosoph __ nōn fac __ barb __ .
8. Gladiāt __ in harēn __ cap __ cōnsili __ .
9. Virt __ et lab __ .
10. Nōn lup __ ad studi __ sed ment __ vert __ ad agn __ .

II   STRUCTURE REVIEW

1. How is the subject of a sentence signaled in Latin? in English?
2. How is the direct object signaled in Latin? in English?
3. How do you know whether a neuter noun is in the nominative or the accusative case?
4. What ideas may be expressed by the ablative case? When is no preposition used?
5. What ideas may be expressed by the accusative case? When is no preposition used?
6. How may one emphasize certain words in Latin? in English?

---

[1] When there is a series of ablatives, as in a motto like this, or a modifying adjective the *cum*, which would be used when one word stands alone, is often omitted.

III   FORM REVIEW

A.   The combinations of nouns listed below may be used to make up Latin sentences. Examine the sample; then make up several sentences for each of the groups of nouns listed, using any cases of the nouns and whatever verbs and prepositions you wish.

Sample: from *puer, puella, canis*, and *silva* these sentences can be made:

Puer cum puellā in silvam prōcēdit.	Ē silvā puer canem pellit.
Puella cum puerō nōn labōrat.	Canem nōn dēlectat silva.
Vidētne puella silvam?	Cum cane puer nōn ambulat.
Puellam puerumque spectat canis.	

See how many you can make up from these groups of nouns.

1. agricola, equus, ager, diēs
2. fēmina, juvenis, opus, oppidum
3. manus, aestās, aedificium, vir
4. vestis, senex, hiems, urbs
5. hostis, vir, mīles, gladius

B.   Noun classification

1. You have probably noticed that nouns are grouped in a fairly consistent pattern. The basis of grouping or classification is the vowel which appears as the ablative case ending. These form classes or groups are called *declensions*. There are five Latin declensions:

   I ā   II ō   III e   IV ū   V ē
              (a special branch of
              this group has ī)

   Identify all the nouns you have had so far by the declension to which each belongs.[1]

2.   FORM CHART

                   Three cases singular of nouns

	I	II	II n.	III	III n.	IV	V
Nominative	puell*A*	equ*US*	sax*UM*	mīles	corpus	man*US*	di*ĒS*
Accusative	puell*AM*	equ*UM*	sax*UM*	mīlit*EM*	corpus	man*UM*	di*ĒM*
Ablative	puell*Ā*	equ*Ō*	sax*Ō*	mīlit*E*	corpor*E*	man*Ū*	di*Ē*

(*puer* and *vir* belong in II but have no ending in the nominative singular; *animal* is a III (n.) i-type.)

C.   Give the question that will get the italicized word or words as an answer.
1. *Saxō* parvus puer agnum pellit.
2. *Ad urbem* etiam ambulat vir.
3. *Post arborem* caput tenet lupus.
4. *Dē monte* hieme nōn fluit aqua.
5. *In agrum* currit etiam equus.
6. *In aquā* est corpus eō diē.

---

[1] It is useful to keep a notebook of words which you are expected to know. One good suggestion is to group words by parts of speech. In listing nouns you should give the nominative, ablative, and gender of each. (This is the way they will now appear in the lesson vocabulary lists, in the order of the declensions.) The ablative is not only the key to the declension, it also shows the stem for the other case forms, except the nominative (and the accusative of neuters). If you keep a notebook, your teacher may want you also to list some of the meanings you have found for the words and some related English derivatives.

7. *Cum fēminā* stat puella ūnam hōram.
8. *Sub arbore* spectātor sedet laetus.
9. *Hieme* viātor ad oppidum prōcēdit.
10. *Ante hostem* mīles Rōmānus stat.
11. *Ūnum diem* auctor philosophum audit.
12. *Servus trīstis* ex aedificiō urbeque venit.
13. *Ad studium* vir mentem vertit.

14. *Cum dolōre* rem gerit male amīcus.
15. *Agnum* lupus spectat cum studiō.
16. *Per silvam* puella cum amīcō ambulat.
17. *Ab harēnā* venit gladiātor Rōmānus.
18. *Inter arborem et aedificium* currit servus.
19. *Trāns magnum flūmen* senex prōcēdit.
20. *Ē viā* currit parvum animal.

D. Give the Latin equivalent.

1. For one hour the gladiator fights well.
2. Does the farmer come to the city on this day?
3. The wolf chases the dog over the spring into the road.
4. The slave is standing in front of the building with a friend.
5. The woman is walking painfully between the man and the boy.
6. A lamb runs across the field into the water.
7. A young man is swimming far away from the rock in the river.
8. Winter and summer the old man goes through the forest on foot.
9. Under a tree a girl is sitting sadly with a soldier.
10. A traveler is walking eagerly down the mountain.
11. Is the girl making the clothes well by hand?
12. The animal stands still and keeps his head and body (hidden) behind the tree.

IV WORD STUDY REVIEW

1. List fifteen adverbs and prepositions used as prefixes in both English and Latin. Give one example of each used in an English word.

2. The suffix *-tor* is used in both Latin and English. Give three Latin words with this ending. Give three English words, not identical to them, which use "-tor." List three other suffixes you have studied.

3. List ten English words which have undergone only slight changes from the Latin word on which each is based.

V OPTIONAL READING

Caedem tēlō . . . committit. —Quintilian (adapted)
Diem nox premit, diēs noctem. — Seneca
Diēs dolōrem minuit. —in Burton
Lupus nōn mordet lupum. —in Binder
Nātūra abhorret vacuum. — Proverb quoted by Descartes
Concordiā, integritāte, industriā — Motto
Fidē et amōre —Motto
Virtute et fidē —Motto

VI VOCABULARY

Nouns

labor, labōre m.
virtūs, virtūte f.

Adjective

multus, multa, multum

LESSON SIX

Vincit imitātiōnem vēritās. — Cicero

"Truth defeats pretense."

Numquam perīculum sine perīculō vincitur.
  —Publilius Syrus (adapted)[1]

"Danger is never overcome without (undergoing) danger."

Purpose: to learn about the passive voice and the personal ablative that patterns with it

I   MŪRUS MŪNĪTUR

pater
patrem
patre

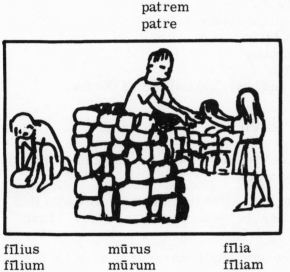

fīlius   mūrus   fīlia
fīlium   mūrum   fīliam
fīliō   mūrō   fīlia

frāter   soror
frātrem   sorōrem
frātre   sorōre

Vir mūrum mūnit. Vir pater est. Pater Lūcius appellātur. Puer est fīlius. Fīlius Pūblius appellātur. Fīlia puella est. Pater fīliam appellat Lūciam. Fīlia Lūcia appellātur. Fīlia ad Lūcium saxum portat. Saxum ā fīliā portātur. Saxum manū portātur. Saxum manū accipit pater. Cum gaudiō accipitur saxum ā patre. Ā patre cum labōre mūrus longus mūnītur. Mūrus saxō bene mūnītur. Mūrus bonus est, et longus et lātus.

Fīlius, nōmine Pūblius, magnum saxum videt. Ā Pūbliō saxum movētur manū. Pūblius Lūciam sorōrem nōn spectat. Ā frātre soror nōn spectātur. Pater cum fīliō fīliāque labōrat; cum studiō rem gerit, sed sine perīculō et injūriā. Pater fīlium fīliamque laudat. (In pictūrā nōn est māter; et servus abest.[2] Eō diē servus ā patre in oppidum mittitur. In fāmiliā[3] Rōmānā est etiam servus.)

1. Quis est vir?
2. Quis pater appellātur?
3. Quis fīlia appellātur?

Pater est vir.
Lūcius pater appellātur.
Lūcia fīlia appellātur.

---

[1] In the poetry from which this is quoted the older, contracted forms *perīc'lum* and *perīc'lō* are used.
[2] *abest = ab* (away) + *est.*
[3] The Roman *fāmilia* included all the household living under one roof, not only those related by blood or marriage (often several generations) but also the slaves. In fact the word meant originally a group of slaves. The head of the family was called the *paterfāmiliās.* See Johnson, *Roman Life,* or other reference books.

4. Quis saxum portat?   Fīlia saxum portat.
5. Ā quō portatūr saxum?   Ā fīlia portātur saxum.
6. Quō īnstrūmentō portātur saxum?   Manū portātur saxum.

7. Quis mūrum mūnit?   Pater mūrum mūnit.
8. Ā quō mūrus mūnītur?   Ā patre mūrus mūnītur.
9. Quid movet fīlius?   Saxum movet fīlius.
10. Ā quō saxum movētur?   Ā fīliō saxum movētur.
11. Quō īnstrūmentō saxum movētur?   Manū saxum movētur.

12. Quō modō rēs geritur?   Cum gaudiō rēs geritur.
13. Quōcum labōrat pater?   Cum fīliō fīliāque labōrat pater.
14. Quis est frāter?   Publius est frāter.
15. Quis est soror?   Lūcia est soror.

16. Spectatne fīlia fīlium?   Nōn spectat fīlium.
17. Spectatne soror frātrem?   Nōn spectat frātrem.
18. Ubi est servus?   In oppidō est servus.

II   PATTERN READING

A.   Sample sentences

1. Gladiātor tumultum audit.   The gladiator hears the uproar.
   Ā gladiātōre tumultus audītur.[1]   The uproar is heard by the gladiator.

2. Fīlius fīliam vocat.   The son calls the daughter.
   Fīlia ā fīliō vocātur.   The daughter is being called by the son.

3. Fīliam pater nōn terret.   The father does not scare his daughter.
   Fīlia ā patre nōn terrētur.   The daughter is not frightened by her father.
   Fīlia gladiō terrētur.   The daughter is frightened by a sword.

4. Soror saxum cum gaudiō portat.   His sister gladly carries the rock.
   Ā patre accipitur saxum.   The rock is taken (received) by her father.

5. Vēritās imitātiōnem vincit.   Truth surpasses pretense.
   Vēritāte imitātiō vincitur.   Pretense is surpassed by truth.

6. Vir servum ad urbem mittit.   A man sends his slave to the city.
   Ā virō servus ad urbem mittitur.   A slave is sent to the city by the man.

7. Soror Lūcia appellātur.   The sister is called Lucia.
   Pater Lūcius appellātur.   Her father is called Lucius.

B.   Practice sentences

1. Pater mūrum mūnit.
     Quid mūnit?   Mūrum mūnit.
     Quid mūnītur?   Mūrus mūnītur.
     Quis mūnit?   Pater mūnit.
     Ā quō mūrus mūnītur?   Ā patre mūrus mūnītur.

---

[1] Of the verbs you have studied so far, only *audit* and *mūnit* have long –*ī*– before the –*tur* passive ending. All other –*it* verbs you have studied have a short –*i*–.

2. Lupus juvenem pellit.
  Quem pellit?   Juvenem pellit.
  Quis pellitur?   Juvenis pellitur.
  Quis pellit?   Lupus pellit.
  Ā quō juvenis pellitur?   Ā lupō juvenis pellitur.

3. Gladius mātrem terret.
  Quem terret?   Mātrem terret.
  Quis terrētur?   Māter terrētur.
  Quid terret?   Gladius terret.
  Quō īnstrūmentō māter terrētur? Gladiō māter terrētur.

4. Vēritās imitātiōnem vincit.
  Quid vincit?   Vēritās vincit.
  Quid vincitur?   Imitātiō vincitur.
  Quō īnstrūmentō imitātiō   Vēritāte imitātiō vincitur.
   vincitur?

5. Perīculum cōnsiliō vincitur.
  Quō īnstrūmentō vincitur?   Cōnsiliō vincitur.
  Quid vincit?   Cōnsilium vincit.
  Quid vincitur?   Perīculum vincitur.
  Quid cōnsilium vincit?   Perīculum cōnsilium vincit.

6. Tumultus ā gladiātōre audītur.
  Ā quō audītur?   Ā gladiātōre audītur.
  Quis audit?   Gladiātor audit.
  Quid audītur?   Tumultus audītur.
  Quid gladiātor audit?   Tumultum gladiātor audit.

7. Soror servum ad frātrem mittit.
  Quem soror mittit?   Servum mittit.
  Quis mittitur?   Servus mittitur.
  Ad quem mittitur?   Ad frātrem mittitur.
  Ā quō servus mittitur?   Ā sorōre servus mittitur.

8. Agricola agrum aestāte fodit.
  Quid fodit?   Agrum fodit.
  Quid foditur?   Ager foditur.
  Quis fodit?   Agricola fodit.
  Ā quō ager foditur?   Ab agricolā ager foditur.
  Quandō ager foditur?   Aestāte ager foditur.

C. Questions on structure

1. What signal is found at the end of these passive verbs?
2. What happens to the object of the active verb when the sentence is shifted to the passive voice?
3. What happens to the subject?
4. What difference is there between a personal and a nonpersonal ablative with the passive verb?
5. Into how many groups or conjugations can verbs be classified by the vowels?
6. What kind of verb usually has passive forms? What type does not?

See Appendix B, pages 190, 192 and 197-98.

III EXERCISES

A. Metaphrase the following:

1. Gladium mīles . . . . . . t.
   Gladius mīlitem . . . . t.
   Gladius ā mīlite . . . . tur.
   Gladiō mīles . . . . tur.

4. Nōmen auctor . . . . t.
   Nōmen ab auctōre . . . . . . tur.
   Nōmen auctōrem . . . . t.
   Nōmine auctor . . . . tur.

2. Ā gladiātōre cōnsilium . . . . tur.
   Gladiātōrem cōnsilium . . . . t.
   Gladiātor cōnsilium . . . . . . t.
   Gladiātor cōnsiliō . . . . . . tur.

5. Frāter flūmen . . . . t.
   Frātrem flūmen . . . . t.
   Ā frātre flūmen . . . . . . tur.
   Frāter flūmine . . . . . . tur.

3. Ā patre māter . . . . . . tur.
   Pater mātrem . . . . . . t.
   Patrem māter . . . . . . t.
   Pater ā mātre . . . . . . tur.

6. Philosophus virtūte . . . . . . tur.
   Philosophus virtūtem . . . . t.
   Philosophum virtūs . . . . . . t.
   Ā philosophō virtūs . . . . . . tur.

B. Answer the questions below.

PUER ET PUELLA

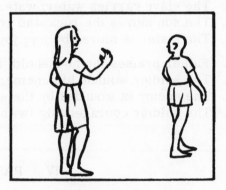

1. a. Quis puellam vocat?
   b. Quis ā puerō vocātur?
   c. Quem puer vocat?
   d. Ā quō puella vocātur?
   e. Ubi stat puer?

2. a. Quid agit puer?
   b. Quid agit puella?
   c. Vocāturne puer ā puellā?
   d. Ā quō puer vocātur?
   e. Quō īnstrūmentō vocat puella puerum?

C.   Transform the active sentence to passive.

1. Auctor opus laudat.   _____ laudātur.
2. Manus manum lavat.   _____ lavātur.
3. Mīles gladiō rem gerit.   _____ geritur.
4. Vēritās imitātiōnem vincit. _____ vincitur.
5. Viātor canem pellit.   _____ pellitur.
6. Virtūs perīculum vincit.   _____ vincitur.
7. Aedificium senex spectat.   _____ spectātur.
8. Gladiātor in harēnā cōnsilium capit. _____ capitur.

D.   Transform the passive sentence to active.

1. Ā frātre mūrus mūnītur.   _____ mūnit.
2. Ā servō aedificium vidētur. _____ videt.
3. Ā virō gladius accipitur.   _____ accipit.
4. Ā patre fāmilia laudātur.   _____ laudat.
5. Mīles virtūte dēlectātur.   _____ dēlectat.
6. Puer labōre nōn dēlectātur. _____ dēlectat.
7. Tumultus ā sorōre audītur.   _____ audit.
8. Fīlius injūriā afficitur.   _____ afficit.

E.   Give the Latin equivalent.

1. The daughter is called Lucia, but the son is called Publius.
2. The slave carries water; water is carried by the slave.
3. The son moves the rock; the rock is moved by the son.
4. The sister is moved by joy; joy moves the sister.

5. Father praises the household; the household is praised by father.
6. The soldier wounds his enemy; the enemy is wounded by the soldier.
7. The enemy is wounded by the sword on this day.
8. The soldier courageously (with courage) carries on the combat by force.

IV   PATTERN PRACTICE SIX

A.   Change the active sentence to passive.

1. Māter fīlium laudat.   Ā mātre fīlius laudātur.
2. Māter fīliam laudat.   Ā mātre fīlia laudātur.
3. Māter opus laudat.   Ā mātre opus laudātur.
4. Auctor opus laudat.   Ab auctōre opus laudātur.

5. Auctōrem opus dēlectat.   Auctor opere dēlectātur.
6. Auctōrem pictūra dēlectat.   Auctor pictūrā dēlectātur.
7. Auctōrem nōmen dēlectat.   Auctor nōmine dēlectātur.
8. Servum nōmen dēlectat.   Servus nōmine dēlectātur.

9. Mittit pater servum.   Mittitur ā patre servus.
10. Mittit pater frātrem.   Mittitur ā patre frāter.
11. Mittit soror frātrem.   Mittitur ā sorōre frāter.
12. Mittit frāter sorōrem.   Mittitur ā frātre soror.

B. Give the sentence in Latin.

1. Father calls his daughter.	Fīliam pater vocat.
2. The daughter is called by her father.	Fīlia ā patre vocātur.
3. The son is calling his father.	Fīlius patrem vocat.
4. The father is being called by his son.	Ā fīliō pater vocātur.
5. The son hears his *father*.	Audit fīlius patrem.
6. *Father* is heard by his son.	Audītur ā fīliō pater.
7. The *uproar* is heard by the son.	Audītur ā fīliō tumultus.
8. The brother hears the *uproar*.	Tumultum frāter audit.
9. The uproar does not scare her brother.	Tumultus frātrem nōn terret.
10. Her brother is not frightened by the uproar.	Tumultū frāter nōn terrētur.
11. The young man is not frightened by danger.	Perīculō juvenis nōn terrētur.
12. The young man is not overcome by danger.	Perīculō juvenis nōn vincitur.
13. Danger is never overcome without (undergoing) danger.	Numquam perīculum sine perīculō vincitur.
14. Pretense is defeated by truth.	Vēritāte imitātiō vincitur.
15. Truth defeats pretense.	Vincit imitātiōnem vēritās.

V   OPTIONAL READING

Ignis nōn extinguitur igne.   — in Binder   Vēritās et virtūs   — Motto (Pittsburgh)
Quī capit[1] capitur.   — Anon.   Sine diē   — Legal phrase

VI   WORD STUDY

1. Give English adjectives from: fīlius, mūrus, pater.

2. What is the closest English derivative (in spelling) from: imitātiō, fāmilia, longus? What spelling changes occur?

3. "Peril" has come from *perīculum* with considerable modification.

4. Relate to Latin sources: portable, vocation, movable, terrify, accept, verity, munitions, ammunition.

5. Give an English noun related to *frāter*, one to *soror*.

6. *Mittit* has many English derivatives. As a final letter, the second -*t*- is lost, otherwise it is kept: remi*t*, remi*tt*ance; commi*t*, commi*tt*ed; admi*t*, admi*tt*ed; intermi*tt*ent, transmi*t*. Show the force of the stem *mitt* in each of these words.

7. What Latin adjective stems do "latitude" and "longitude" contain?

8. What does "bonus" mean in English? "boon" companion?

9. *Accipit* is a compound of *capit* + *ad*. In the compounds *a* becomes *i* (*cap* > *cip*), as in the English derivative "recipient."

---

[1] *Quī*: "he who"; *Quī capit* is subject of *capitur*.

VII   VOCABULARY

Nouns	*Adjectives*	*Function Words*
fāmilia, fāmiliā f.	bonus, bona, bonum	sine + abl.
fīlia, fīliā f.	lātus, lāta, lātum	
injūria, injūriā f.	longus, longa, longum	numquam
Lūcia, Lūciā f.		ā quō (?)
	Verbs	
fīlius, fīliō m.		
Lūcius, Lūciō m.	appellat	
mūrus, mūrō m.	portat	
Pūblius, Pūbliō m.	vocat	
gaudium, gaudiō n.	movet	
perīculum, perīculō n.	terret	
frāter, frātre m.	mittit	
imitātiō, imitātiōne f.	accipit	
māter, mātre f.		
pater, patre m.	mūnit	
soror, sorōre f.		
vēritās, vēritāte f.		

LESSON SEVEN

Virtūte nōn verbīs — Motto
"By courage, not by words"

Facta nōn verba — Common phrase
"Deeds not words"

Purpose: to learn plurals of first and second declension nouns

I PATTERN READING

A. Sample sentences

1. Puella equum spectat.   The girl is watching the horse.
   Puellae equum spectant.   The girls are watching the horse.
   Puella equōs spectat.   The girl watches the horses.

2. Puer fābulam nārrat.   The boy is telling a story.
   Puerī fābulam nārrant.   The boys are telling a story.
   Puer fābulās nārrat.   The boy tells stories.

3. Fābula ab auctōre scrībitur. The story is written by an author.
   Fābulae ab auctōre scrībuntur. Stories are written by an author.

4. Librī ā puerīs puellīsque leguntur. Books are read by boys and girls.
   Puerī librōs legunt.   The boys are reading books.

5. Saxa juvenis cōnspicit.   The youth catches sight of the rocks.
   Saxa ā juvene cōnspiciuntur. The rocks are noticed by the youth.

6. Philosophī perīculīs nōn terrentur. Philosophers are not frightened by dangers.

7. Eō annō geritur bellum.   A war is being fought this year.

8. Multum dīcit.   He says much.
   Multa verba dīcuntur.   Many words are spoken.

9. In terrā manet animal.   The animal stays on the ground.

10. Oppidum mūrō portāque mūnītur. The town is strengthened (fortified) by a wall and gate.

11. Oppida relinquuntur post bellum. The towns are abandoned after the war.

B. Practice sentences (You should be able to identify the structure of each plural noun.)

1. Puer puellam videt.   3. Puerī puellās vident.

2. Puerī pueļļam vident.   4. Puellae cōnspiciuntur.

5. Puellae ā puerīs cōnspiciuntur.

6. Puella puerōs cōnspicit.

7. Sine injūriā mūrum mūnit vir.

8. Ā virō mūrus mūnītur.

9. Ā virīs mūrī mūniuntur.

10. Saxīs mūrī mūniuntur.

11. Virī oppidum mūrō mūniunt.

12. Virī oppida mūrīs mūniunt.

13. Oppidum portam habet in mūrō.

14. Oppida portās habent in mūrīs.

15. Fēmina in viā ante aedificium stat.

16. Fēminae in viā ante aedificium stant.

17. Fēminae in viīs ambulant.

18. Fēminae cum amīcīs ambulant.

19. Verba dēlectant philosophōs.

20. Virtūte et verbīs dēlectātur philosophus.

21. Facta ab auctōre dīcuntur.

22. Fābulae ab auctōre nārrantur.

23. Nārratne auctor fābulās?

24. Scrībitne auctor librum?

25. Ab auctōre librī scrībuntur.

26. Fīlius librōs legit.

27. Fīliae librōs habent.

28. In terrā bella geruntur.

29. Per annōs multa bella geruntur.

30. Virī ad bellum prōcēdunt et fāmiliās amīcōsque relinquunt.

C.   Questions on structure

1. What is the signal for the third person plural active verb?
2. What is the signal for the third person plural passive verb?
3. What are the nominative plural signals for the first two declensions?
4. What are the accusative plural signals for the first two declensions?
5. What is the ablative plural signal for the first two declensions?

See Form Chart, page 75 and Appendix B, pages 188-89 and 197.[1]

II   EXERCISES

A.   Change the first noun in each sentence from singular to plural. (Remember that, if the noun you change is the subject, the verb must also be changed to agree.) Give the meaning of the sentence.

1. Pictūra virum dēlectat.
2. Terra virum dēlectat.
3. Silva virum dēlectat.

4. Lupus cum studiō currit.
5. Puer cum studiō currit.
6. Equus cum studiō currit.

7. Perīculum nōn manet.
8. Aedificium nōn manet.
9. Verbum nōn manet.

10. Viam frāter videt.
11. Puellam frāter videt.
12. Fēminam frāter videt.

13. Laudatne librum soror?
14. Laudatne equum soror?
15. Laudatne agnum soror?

16. Oppidum mīles capit.
17. Cōnsilium mīles capit.
18. Saxum mīles capit.

19. Cōnspiciuntur in silvā lupī.
20. Cōnspiciuntur in harēnā lupī.

21. Gladiō juvenis vulnerātur.
22. Ā virō juvenis vulnerātur.

23. Verbō māter nōn dēlectātur.
24. Bellō māter nōn dēlectātur.

[1] The following verbs with singular forms ending in *-it* have plural forms in *-iunt*: accipiunt, capiunt, cōnspiciunt, faciunt, fodiunt; also: audiunt, mūniunt, veniunt. All others you have used in *-it* have plurals in *-unt*.

B.   Metaphrase the following:

1. Virōs puer . . . . t.
2. Equī virum . . . . nt.
3. Fīliās amīcī . . . . nt.
4. Annum agricolae . . . . nt.
5. Aedificia senex . . . . t.

6. Silvīs . . . . tur soror.
7. Ā lupō . . . . ntur agnī.
8. Cum gaudiō . . . . nt fīliae librōs.
9. Cum amīcīs fēminae oppida . . . . nt.
10. Philosophōs nōn . . . . nt barbae.

C.   Give the Latin equivalent.

1. The son is called by his sister.
2. The wall is being built by father.
3. Danger does not frighten the soldier.
4. The soldier carries on the combat courageously (with courage).
5. The combat is carried on with the sword.

6. The soldier chases (his) enemy away without injury.
7. The gladiator is overcome by (his) opponent.
8. He is not overcome without danger.
9. A brother is sent to the city by Lucius.
10. With effort the field is spaded up (dug up with a spade).

III   PATTERN PRACTICE SEVEN

1. The woman is calling a friend.   Fēmina amīcum vocat.
2. The women are calling a friend.   Fēminae amīcum vocant.
3. The women are calling their friends.   Fēminae amīcōs vocant.
4. Friends are calling the women.   Amīcī fēminās vocant.
5. Friends are called by the women.   Amīcī ā fēminīs vocantur.
6. The women are called by friends.   Fēminae ab amīcīs vocantur.

7. The *man* is sending the slave into the town.   Servum in oppidum mittit vir.
8. The *man* is sending the slaves into the town.   Servōs in oppidum mittit vir.
9. The *men* send the slaves into the town.   Servōs in oppidum mittunt virī.
10. The *men* send the slaves into the towns.   Servōs in oppida mittunt virī.
11. The slaves are being sent into the towns.   Servī in oppida mittuntur.
12. The slaves are sent by the men.   Servī ā virīs mittuntur.
13. The slaves are sent through the gates.   Servī per portās mittuntur.

14. The boy hears the *word*.   Verbum puer audit.
15. The boys hear the *words*.   Verba puerī audiunt.
16. The words are heard by the boys.   Verba ā puerīs audiuntur.
17. They are delighted by the words and deeds.   Verbīs factīsque dēlectantur.
18. Deeds are told in words.   Verbīs facta dīcuntur.

19. The *author* speaks.   Verba dīcit auctor.
20. The *author* tells stories.   Fābulās nārrat auctor.
21. Deeds are told in stories.   Facta in fābulīs nārrantur.
22. Stories are related in books.   In librīs fābulae nārrantur.
23. The books are written by an author.   Librī ab auctōre scrībuntur.
24. Books are read by boys and girls.   Librī ā puerīs puellīsque leguntur.
25. The boys read the *books* throughout the year.   Librōs puerī legunt per annum.

26. *The war* is carried on throughout the land.   Per terram geritur bellum.
27. *The wars* are fought on land.   In terrā geruntur bella.
28. Men carry on wars in their lands.   In terrīs virī bella gerunt.

29. During wars men leave their families behind.   In bellīs virī fāmiliās relinquunt.
30. During wars farmers leave their fields behind.   In bellīs agricolae agrōs relinquunt.

IV   OPTIONAL READING

Virtūte et armīs — Motto (Mississippi)   Post proelia, praemia —Motto
Cōnsiliō et animīs — Motto   Ex librīs — Bookplate inscription
                                                     (followed by name of owner)

V   WORD STUDY

1. While some Latin words come into English with no change in spelling (*animal*), there are more which drop the Latin declension ending and add either nothing or silent "-e," (*tumultus*, "tumult"; *pictūra*, "picture.") Many others, of course, add completely new suffixes. What words in this lesson are treated in this way?

2. *Cum*, when used as a prefix, has a variety of forms in both English and Latin. It may appear as *co-*, *col-*, *com-*, *con-*, *cor-*: *co*operate, *col*laborate, *com*mit, *con*vert, *cor*respond. Find ten other words using a form of *cum* as a prefix. (This prefix may mean "with," "together," or make the meaning of the word stronger.)

3. Give the Latin source and meaning of: fable, fabulous, library, narrative, diction, legible, conspicuous, annual, terrace, terrain, relinquish.

4. Notice that two Latin words go into the making of the compound derivative "belligerent." What sort of person is "belligerent" by nature?

5. How many different prefixes (from prepositions) can you find used in derivatives of *scrībit*, "-scribe" words?

6. "Remain," coming into English through French, is derived from *manet*. Similarly words in "-tain" come from *tenet*: con*tain*, etc.

7. What three parts can you distinguish in the word "perennial"? What spelling modification is made in the "-enn-" part?

8. *Dē-* is used as a prefix with both of its prepositional meanings "from" and "about." What does it mean in these derivatives: deport, deter, detain, describe, descend?

VI   VOCABULARY

Nouns

fābula, fābulā f.	bellum, bellō n.	dīcit, dīcunt
porta, portā f.	factum, factō n.	legit, legunt
terra, terrā f.	verbum, verbō n.	relinquit, relinquunt
		scrībit, scrībunt
annus, annō m.	*Verbs*	cōnspicit, cōnspiciunt
liber, librō m.	nārrat, nārrant	(est) sunt
	manet, manent	

LESSON EIGHT

Fugiunt diēs. — Ovid	"The days slip away."
Tempus fugit. — Common phrase	"Time flies."
Quot hominēs tot sententiae. — Terence	"There are as many opinions as men."

Purpose: to learn the plurals of third, fourth, and fifth declension nouns

I   PATTERN READING

A.   Sample sentences

1.	Mīlitēs flūmina vident.	The soldiers see the rivers.
2.	Flūmina mīlitēs dēlectant.	Rivers please the soldiers.
3.	Hominēs flūminibus dēlectantur.	Men are pleased by the rivers.
4.	Ab hominibus flūmina amantur.	Rivers are liked by men.
5.	Manūs servus in aquā pōnit; in aquā pōnuntur manūs.	The slave puts his hands in the water; his hands are put into the water.
6.	Manibus labōrat servus.	The slave works with his hands.
7.	Fugiunt diēs; fēminae in oppidō diēs agunt.	Days slip away; women spend their days in town.
8.	Virī rēs afficiunt.	Men affect (influence) affairs.
9.	Et patrēs et mātrēs dē rēbus rogant.	Both fathers and mothers ask about the matters.
10.	Mātrēs fīliōs fīliāsque monent.	Mothers advise their sons and daughters.

B.   Practice questions and answers (Be able to identify the structure of the plural forms.)

1.	Quis corpus videt?	Homō corpus videt.
2.	Quī corpus vident?	Hominēs corpus vident.
3.	Quās rēs vident hominēs?	Corpora vident hominēs.
4.	Videnturne corpora?	Videntur corpora.
5.	Quis dolōre nōn afficitur?	Juvenis dolōre nōn afficitur.
6.	Quī dolōre nōn afficiuntur?	Juvenēs dolōre nōn afficiuntur.
7.	Quae ab animālī terrentur?	Puellae ab animālī terrentur.
8.	Ā quibus puellae terrentur?	Ab animālibus puellae terrentur.
9.	Quis diēs in urbe agit?	Pater diēs in urbe agit.
10.	Quī in urbe diēs agunt?	Patrēs in urbe diēs agunt.
11.	Ā quibus diēs in urbibus aguntur?	Ā patribus diēs in urbibus aguntur.
12.	Ubi diēs aguntur?	In urbibus diēs aguntur.
13.	Quam diū in urbibus manent patrēs?	Diēs in urbibus manent patrēs.
14.	Quandō in urbibus manent patrēs?	Eīs diēbus in urbibus manent patrēs.
15.	Quibuscum diēs agunt patrēs?	Cum amīcīs diēs agunt patrēs.

71

16. Unde amīcī veniunt?   Ab urbibus amīcī veniunt.
17. Quō amīcī veniunt?   Ad aedificia amīcī veniunt.
18. Quās rēs lavat fīlia?   Manūs lavat fīlia.
19. Quae animālia lavat fīlia?   Canēs lavat fīlia.
20. Quibus rēbus lavat fīlia canēs?   Manibus lavat fīlia canēs.

21. Quid fugit?   Tempus fugit.
22. Quae rēs fugiunt?   Diēs fugiunt.
23. Quōs pater verbīs monet?   Frātrēs pater verbīs monet.
24. Quās māter verbīs monet?   Sorōrēs māter verbīs monet.

C. Questions on structure

1. What do you observe about the nominative and accusative plural forms of III, IV, and V declension nouns?
2. What ending is common to all accusative plurals (five declensions) except neuters?
3. What is the ending common to all neuter nominative and accusative plurals?
4. What are the two possible ablative plural endings?
5. What vowel is most common in the first declension? the fourth? the fifth?

See Appendix B, page 189 and Form Chart, page 75.

II   EXERCISES

A. Turn to the picture on page 46 and answer these questions.

1. Quī sunt mīlitēs?   6. Quandō pūgnant gladiātōrēs?
2. Ubi sunt gladiātōrēs?   7. Quī spectant?
3. Quās rēs gladiātōrēs tenent?   8. Quōs vident?
4. Quibus rēbus gladiātōrēs pūgnant?   9. Quō īnstrūmentō prōcēdunt servī?
5. Quō modō gladiātōrēs rem gerunt? 10. Unde prōcēdunt spectātōrēs?

B. Change the first noun in the sentence to plural form and make any other necessary changes.

1. Juvenis ā cane tenētur.   11. Flūmen agnus nōn amat.
2. Facitne homō vestem?   12. Mīlitem vulnerat hostis.
3. Hiems dēlectat amīcum.   13. Gladiātōrem cōnsilium afficit.
4. Agnus ā lupō nōn capitur.   14. Opus vir legit.
5. Vincitur perīculum virtūte.   15. Videtne manum puella?

6. Mūrus ab homine mūnītur.   16. Ab auctōre opus scrībitur.
7. Caput ab homine cōnspicitur.   17. Aestāte mīles vincit.
8. Terretne puellam canis?   18. Rē pater nōn afficitur.
9. Per urbem viātor ambulat.   19. Manū vestem lavat.
10. Imitātiōnem puer amat.   20. Rogātur ā patre sententia.

C. Metaphrase the following:

1. Nōmina puerōs . . . . nt.   5. Diēs fēmina . . . . t.
2. Manus fīlia . . . . t.   6. Montēs ā viātōre . . . . ntur.
3. Canēs virī . . . . nt.   7. Tempora sententiās . . . . nt.
4. Canēs virōs . . . . nt.   8. Flūminibus animālia . . . . ntur.

9. Pater nōmine . . . . tur.   11. Tumultum mīlitēs . . . . nt.
10. Auctōrēs mentem . . . . nt.   12. Fontēs ab animālibus . . . . ntur.

D. Make up ten sentences on the model of *Quot hominēs tot sententiae*. (Example: *Quot pueri tot puellae*.)

E. Turn to Exercise D, page 49; change at least one noun in each sentence to plural form. Make any other necessary changes.

F. Give the Latin equivalent.

1. The slaves are walking on the road through the gate.
2. The walls are being abandoned by the men because the danger is at hand.
3. Men and women are reading the books.
4. Are the girls frightened by the dog?
5. Mother tells stories about (*dē*) courage and effort.
6. The farmers are friends; they are coming across the fields.
7. The old man is talking (making words) with pleasure.
8. In summer boys run out of the buildings into the streets.
9. Wars on land are never carried on without suffering.
10. (His) daughters are walking toward (their) father.

III   PATTERN PRACTICE EIGHT

Change the first noun in each sentence to plural form.

First, the nominative

1. Auctor nōmen rogat.	Auctōrēs nōmen rogant.
2. Juvenis nōmen rogat.	Juvenēs nōmen rogant.
3. Senex nōmen rogat.	Senēs nōmen rogant.
4. Urbs ā virō laudātur.	Urbēs ā virō laudantur.
5. Māter ā virō laudātur.	Mātrēs ā virō laudantur.
6. Virtūs ā virō laudātur.	Virtūtēs ā virō laudantur.
7. Animal gladiō vulnerātur.	Animālia gladiō vulnerantur.
8. Caput gladiō vulnerātur.	Capita gladiō vulnerantur.
9. Corpus gladiō vulnerātur.	Corpora gladiō vulnerantur.

Next, the accusative

10. Hominem bellum afficit.	Hominēs bellum afficit.
11. Mīlitem bellum afficit.	Mīlitēs bellum afficit.
12. Gladiātōrem bellum afficit.	Gladiātōrēs bellum afficit.
13. Arborem senex videt.	Arborēs senex videt.
14. Urbem senex videt.	Urbēs senex videt.
15. Manum senex videt.	Manūs senex videt.
16. Corpus puerī spectant.	Corpora puerī spectant.
17. Flūmen puerī spectant.	Flūmina puerī spectant.
18. Animal puerī spectant.	Animālia puerī spectant.

Next, the ablative

19. Cum juvene ambulat mīles.   Cum juvenibus ambulat mīles.
20. Cum sene ambulat mīles.   Cum senibus ambulat mīles.
21. Cum viātōre ambulat mīles.   Cum viātōribus ambulat mīles.

22. Ab urbe prōcēdit viātor.   Ab urbibus prōcēdit viātor.
23. Aestāte prōcēdit viātor.   Aestātibus prōcēdit viātor.
24. Ab arbore prōcēdit viātor.   Ab arboribus prōcēdit viātor.

25. Nōmine auctor dēlectātur.   Nōminibus auctor dēlectātur.
26. Opere auctor dēlectātur.   Operibus auctor dēlectātur.
27. Flūmine auctor dēlectātur.   Flūminibus auctor dēlectātur.

IV   OPTIONAL READING

Lēgēs sine mōribus vānae. — Horace
per capita — Common phrase
Tot sunt errōrēs quot habet nātūra colōrēs. — Medieval
Sed fugit intereā, fugit irreparābile tempus. — Vergil

V   WORD STUDY

1. The Latin suffix *-tiō, -tion-* (English "-tion") is used to form nouns from verbs. Explain: audition, imitation, narration, elaboration, transportation.

2. Another of the prefixes which appear in a variety of forms is *ad*. (This change is called "assimilation," a word which itself illustrates the process it names (ad + simila + tion.) Among the possible forms of *ad* are: *ac-, af-, al-, an-, ap-, as-, at-*. Explain the meaning of the prefix in: accept, affect, allocate, announce, apportion, assimilate, attract.

3. There are many words in English which come from *tempus*: for example, temporary, contemporary, extemporaneous. Explain the relationship in meaning to *tempus*.

4. From what Latin words in the vocabulary of this lesson are these English words derived: sentence, admonition, exponent, fugitive, interrogative? What prefixes are used?

5. How do *quot* and *tot* differ from other adjectives you have seen? From words closely related to them come English "quota" and "total."

6. Have you ever done a "rebus" puzzle? Of what does such a puzzle consist?

VI   VOCABULARY

Nouns	*Verbs*	*Adjectives*
sententia, sententiā f.	amat, amant	quot
	rogat, rogant	tot
homō, homine m.		
	monet, monent	*Function Words*
tempus, tempore n.		
	pōnit, pōnunt	quī, quōs (?)
		quae, quās (?)
	afficit, afficiunt	quae, quae (?)
	fugit, fugiunt	quibus (?)
		quibuscum (?)
		et . . . . . . et

VII   FORM CHART[1]

A.   Nouns, three cases singular and plural

Singular	I	II	II (n)	III	III (n)	III (n.i)
Nom.	puell*a*	amīc*us*	sax*um*	mīles	corpus	animal
Acc.	puell*am*	amīc*um*	sax*um*	mīlit*em*	corpus	animal
Abl.	puell*ā*	amīc*ō*	sax*ō*	mīlit*e*	corpor*e*	animāl*ī*

Plural						
Nom.	puell*ae*	amīc*ī*	sax*a*	mīlit*ēs*	corpor*a*	animāl*ia*
Acc.	puell*ās*	amīc*ōs*	sax*a*	mīlit*ēs*	corpor*a*	animāl*ia*
Abl.	puell*īs*	amīc*īs*	sax*īs*	mīlit*ibus*	corpor*ibus*	animāl*ibus*

Singular	IV	V	V
Nom.	man*us*	di*ēs*	r*ēs*
Acc.	man*um*	di*em*	r*em*
Abl.	man*ū*	di*ē*	r*ē*

Plural			
Nom.	man*ūs*	di*ēs*	r*ēs*
Acc.	man*ūs*	di*ēs*	r*ēs*
Abl.	man*ibus*	di*ēbus*	r*ēbus*

B.   Verbs, third person, present tense

Active	I	II	III	III (i)	IV
Singular	port*at*	terr*et*	pōn*it*	cap*it*	aud*it*
Plural	port*ant*	terr*ent*	pōn*unt*	cap*iunt*	aud*iunt*

Passive					
Singular	port*ātur*	terr*ētur*	pōn*itur*	cap*itur*	aud*ītur*
Plural	port*antur*	terr*entur*	pōn*untur*	cap*iuntur*	aud*iuntur*

[1] See Appendix B, pages 188-89.

LESSON NINE, Part I

Ā cane nōn magnō saepe tenētur aper. — Ovid

"A boar (wild hog) is often held at bay by a small dog."

Ā fonte pūrō pūra dēfluit aqua. — Anon.

"Pure water comes from a pure spring."

Nōbilitat stultum vestis honesta virum.
—Medieval

"An honorable garment ennobles a stupid man."

In pulchrā veste sapiēns nōn vīvit honestē.
—Medieval

"A wise man does not live properly in handsome clothes."

Purpose: to learn adjectives of first-second declension form

I PATTERN READING

A. Sample sentences

1. Puer canem magnum spectat.   The boy sees a big dog.
    Puer canem spectat magnum.   The boy sees a *big* dog.
    Magnum puer canem spectat.   The boy sees a *big* dog.

2. Via magna ā puerō spectātur.   The great road is seen by the boy.
3. Magnā sub arbore puer sedet sōlus.   The boy sits under a big tree alone.

4. Inter arborēs magnās puer animal spectat.   The boy sees an animal among the large trees.

5. Magnum animal puer malus nōn terret.   The bad boy does not scare the big animal.

6. In flūminibus magnīs sunt saxa.   There are rocks in the large rivers.
7. In flūminibus magna sunt saxa.   There are large rocks in the rivers.

8. Amīcus est puer.   The boy is friendly.

9. Amīcus laetō cum puerō ambulat.   A friend walks with the happy boy.
   Amicus laetus cum puerō ambulat.   His happy friend walks with the boy.

10. Amīcī laetīs cum puerīs ambulant.   Friends are walking with the happy boys.

11. Fīlius meus bonus est; fīliī tuī   My son is good; yours are bad.
    sunt malī.

12. Sententiae nostrae et vestrae ā   Our statements and yours are heard by the
    puerīs audiuntur.   boys.

13. Sententiās suās puerī scrībunt.   The boys write their own opinions.

14. Viātor nūllam aquam habet.   The traveler has no water.

B.   Be able to read these sentences and answer the questions on them.

1. Ā fonte pūrō pūra dēfluit aqua.
       Quid dēfluit?   Aqua dēfluit.
       Quālis est aqua?   Pūra est aqua.
       Unde dēfluit?   Ā fonte dēfluit.
       Quālī ā fonte dēfluit aqua?   Pūrō ā fonte dēfluit aqua.
       Quālis est fōns?   Pūrus est fōns.

2. Nōbilitat stultum vestis honesta virum.
       Quid nōbilitat?   Vestis nōbilitat.
       Quālis vestis nōbilitat?   Honesta vestis nōbilitat.
       Quem nōbilitat vestis?   Virum nōbilitat vestis.
       Quālem virum nōbilitat?   Stultum virum nōbilitat.
       Quid agit vestis honesta?   Stultum virum nōbilitat vestis honesta.

3. Ā cane nōn magnō tenētur aper.
       Quis tenētur?   Aper tenētur.
       Ā quō tenētur?   Ā cane nōn magnō tenētur.
       Quis aprum tenet?   Canis nōn magnus aprum tenet.
       Estne canis magnus?   Canis nōn magnus sed parvus est.

4. In pulchrā veste sapiēns nōn vīvit honestē.
       Quis vīvit?   Sapiēns vīvit.
       Ubi vīvit?   In pulchrā veste vīvit.
       Quālī in veste nōn vīvit honestē?   Pulchrā in veste nōn vīvit honestē.
       Quālis est vestis?   Pulchra est vestis.

5. Lupī mentēs malās pulchrōs ad agnōs vertunt.
       Quī mentēs vertunt?   Lupī mentēs vertunt.
       Quālēs mentēs vertunt?   Mentēs malās vertunt.
       Quō mentēs vertunt lupī?   Ad agnōs mentēs vertunt lupī.
       Quālēs ad agnōs?   Pulchrōs ad agnōs.
       Quālēs sunt agnī?   Pulchrī sunt agnī.
       Quālēs sunt mentēs?   Malae sunt mentēs.

6. Multae sententiae bonae in librīs Rōmānīs leguntur.
       Quae leguntur?   Sententiae leguntur.
       Quālēs sententiae leguntur?   Sententiae bonae leguntur.
       Quot sententiae leguntur?   Multae sententiae leguntur.
       Ubi leguntur?   In librīs Rōmānīs leguntur.
       Quālēs sunt librī?   Librī sunt Rōmānī.
       Quid Rōmānī legunt?   Rōmānī sententiās bonās legunt.

C.   Questions on structure

1.   What is the difference between the position of adjectives in Latin and in English?

2.   How do you know what noun an adjective goes with in Latin?

3.   How does the gender of the noun affect the form of the adjective? It is in the form of adjectives modifying the noun—and pronouns referring to the noun—that the gender of nouns becomes apparent and important. For a review of genders see the list of nouns on page 85.

4.   What else about the noun affects the form of the adjective?

5.   When are noun and adjective endings alike? When different?

See Appendix B, pages 195-96.

II   FORM CHART

Adjectives of I-II Declension

Singular

	M.	F.	N.	M.	F.	N.
Nom.	magnus	magna	magnum	pulcher	pulchra	pulchrum
Acc.	magnum	magnam	magnum	pulchrum	pulchram	pulchrum
Abl.	magnō	magnā	magnō	pulchrō	pulchrā	pulchrō

Plural

	M.	F.	N.	M.	F.	N.
Nom.	magnī	magnae	magna	pulchrī	pulchrae	pulchra
Acc.	magnōs	magnās	magna	pulchrōs	pulchrās	pulchra
Abl.	magnīs	magnīs	magnīs	pulchrīs	pulchrīs	pulchrīs

Like *magnus*: bonus, honestus, laetus, lātus, longus, malus, meus, multus, parvus, pūrus, Rōmānus, stultus, suus, tuus.

nūllus and *sōlus*, in these three cases.

amīcus is an adjective, though often used as a noun.

all ordinals (*prīmus, secundus*, etc.); see Introduction.

Like *pulcher*: noster, vester

III   EXERCISES

A.   Add the adjective indicated, in the form which will modify the first noun in each sentence.

magnus

1. Canis ante aedificium sedet.
2. Manū rem portat servus.
3. In harēnīs cōnsilia capiuntur.
4. Opus auctōrēs scrībunt.
5. Studium amat vir.

6.   Mīlitēs gladiīs vulnerantur.
7.   Cum gaudiō frāter accipitur.
8.   Relinquuntne portās virī?
9.   Dēlectāturne fonte puella?
10. Animālia servī pellunt.

bonus or *multus*

11. Rogant hominēs sententiās.
12. Opera laudantur ab auctōre.
13. Ā servō aqua portātur.
14. Nōmine juvenis appellātur.
15. Ad urbēs prōcēdunt viātōrēs.

16. Ab urbibus viātōrēs ambulant.
17. Urbēs nōn sunt in pictūrīs.
18. Virtūtem monent philosophī.
19. Gladiātor in terrā manet.
20. Virōs facta dēlectant.

B. Repeat the sentences in A adding one of these adjectives to modify the *second* noun: parvus, bonus, honestus, meus.

C. Metaphrase

1. Mīles magnam virtūtem . . . .
    Mīles magnus virtūtem . . . .
    Mīles magnā cum virtūte . . . .
    Mīles magnus cum virtūte . . . . . .

4. Fōns pūrus aquam . . . .
    Fōns pūram aquam . . . .
    In fonte pūra aqua . . . .
    In fonte pūrō aqua . . . .

2. Manūs meae saxum . . . .
    Manibus meīs saxa . . . .
    Manū meā saxa . . . .

5. Juvenēs pulchrī arborēs . . . .
    Juvenēs pulchrās arborēs . . . .
    Ā juvenibus pulchrīs arborēs . . . .

3. Facta bona vir . . . .
    Facta bonus vir . . . .
    Factum bonum ā virō . . . . .
    Factum bonō ā virō . . . . . .

6. Viātor nūllus urbem . . . .
    Viātor nūllam urbem . . . .
    Viātōrem nūllum urbs . . . .

D. Give in three cases singular and plural.

fīlius meus   fēmina sōla   manus longa
cōnsilium tuum   canis noster   nōmen Rōmānum

LESSON NINE, Part II

In omnī rē vincit imitātiōnem vēritās.
    —Cicero

"In everything truth wins over imitation."

Fortēs[1] *Fortūna adjuvat.* — Terence

"Fortune favors the brave."

Nēmō malus fēlīx. — Juvenal

"No bad person is fortunate."

Omnibus in rēbus gravis est inceptiō prīma. —Proverb

"In all things it is the first start which is hard."

Purpose: to learn adjectives of the third declension

I   PATTERN READING

A.   Sample sentences

1. Bene facit sapiēns rem omnem. — A wise person does everything well.
2. Facilis imitātiō est. — Imitation is easy.
3. Opus difficile nēminem dēlectat. — A difficult piece of work pleases nobody.
4. Nēmō opere difficilī dēlectātur. — Nobody is pleased by a difficult piece of work.
5. Opera difficilia nēminem dēlectant. — Hard tasks delight no one.

6. Equus celer est. — The horse is fast.
7. Pedibus celeribus equus currit. — The horse runs swiftly (with swift feet).
8. Hominēs malī virōs fortēs et fidēlēs nōn amant. — Bad people do not like brave, faithful heroes.

B.   Read these sentences and be able to answer the questions on them.

1. Opus difficile nēminem dēlectat.
    Quid nēminem dēlectat? — Opus nēminem dēlectat.
    Quāle opus nēminem dēlectat? — Difficile opus nēminem dēlectat.
    Quem dēlectat opus? — Nēminem dēlectat opus.
    Quō īnstrūmentō dēlectātur nēmō? — Opere difficilī dēlectātur nēmō.

2. Operibus facilibus dēlectātur stultus.
    Quis dēlectātur? — Stultus dēlectātur.
    Quō īnstrūmentō dēlectātur. — Opere dēlectātur.
    Quālī opere dēlectātur. — Facilī opere dēlectātur.
    Quāle est opus? — Facile est opus.

3. Celeribus pedibus juvenis Rōmānus currit.
    Quis currit? — Juvenis currit.
    Quālis est juvenis? — Rōmānus est juvenis.
    Quō īnstrūmentō currit? — Celeribus pedibus currit.
    Quālis est pēs? — Celer est pēs.

---

[1] Many adjectives are used alone in sentences as if they were nouns. If there is no noun for an adjective to modify, it is used in this way.

4. In omnī rē vincit imitātiōnem vēritās.

       Quid vincit imitātiōnem?   Vēritās vincit imitātiōnem.

       Ubi vincit?   In omnī rē vincit.

       Quid vincitur?   Imitātiō vincitur.

       Quō īnstrūmentō imitātiō   Vēritāte imitātiō vincitur.
          vincitur?

5. Omnibus in rēbus gravis est inceptiō prīma.

       Quid grave est?   Prīma inceptiō gravis est.

       Quālis est inceptiō prīma?   Gravis est inceptiō prīma.

       Ubi est inceptiō gravis?   In rēbus est inceptiō gravis.

       Quot in rēbus est gravis?   Omnibus in rēbus est gravis.

       Quālēs sunt rēs?   Gravēs sunt rēs.

6. Fortēs Fortūna adjuvat.

       Quis adjuvat?   Fortūna adjuvat.

       Quōs adjuvat?   Fortēs adjuvat.

       Quālēs sunt hominēs?   Fortēs sunt hominēs.

7. Nēmō malus fēlīx.

       Quālis nōn est fēlīx?   Malus nōn est fēlīx.

       Quālis nōn est homō malus?   Nōn fēlīx est homō malus.

       Quālis fēlīx est?   Bonus fēlīx est.

C.   Questions on structure

    1. In which case do the endings of third declension adjectives differ from those of the third declension nouns?

    2. What neuter noun is most like the neuter adjectives of this declension?

    3. Is there any way of distinguishing masculine from feminine forms in the third declension?

See Appendix B, pages 195-96.

II FORM CHART

Adjectives of III Declension

Singular		M.	F.	N.	M.	F.	N.
	Nom.	facilis	facilis	facile	fēlīx	fēlīx	fēlīx
	Acc.	facilem	facilem	facile	fēlīcem	fēlīcem	fēlīx
	Abl.	facilī	facilī	facilī	fēlīcī	fēlīcī	fēlīcī
Plural	Nom.	facilēs	facilēs	facilia	fēlīcēs	fēlīcēs	fēlīcia
	Acc.	facilēs	facilēs	facilia	fēlīcēs	fēlīcēs	fēlīcia
	Abl.	facilibus	facilibus	facilibus	fēlīcibus	fēlīcibus	fēlīcibus

Like *facilis*: difficilis, fidēlis, fortis, gravis, omnis, quālis, trīstis; *senex* and *juvenis* are adjectives of this type, also.

Like *fēlīx*: sapiēns (sapient-)

"Three ending adjective": celer (m.), celeris (f.), celere (n.); otherwise like *facilis*. (in nominative)

III   EXERCISES

A.   Add the adjective indicated, in the form which will modify the first noun in the sentence.

omnis   *fortis* or *gravis*

1. Mīles gladiō pūgnat.
2. Māter verbīs fīliās monet.
3. Ad aprum canis mentem vertit.
4. Sententiam cum studiō rogat senex.
5. In rē juvenis vincit.

6. Ā gladiātōre animal vincitur.
7. Capit vir gladium.
8. Bellum geritur cum dolōre.
9. Caput manū tenet puella.
10. Pālā fodit agricola saepe.

B.   Change all the first nouns with modifying adjectives to plural. Make any other necessary changes.

C.   Repeat the sentences using *sapiēns* or *fidēlis* with the second noun in 1-5, *magnus* or *parvus* with the second noun in 6-10.

D.   Metaphrase the following:

1. Frāter sōlus aestāte omnī . . . .
    Frāter sōla aestāte omnis . . . .
    Frātrum sōlum aestās omnis . . . .

2. Inceptiō prīma gravis in rēbus . . . . . .
    Inceptiō prīma gravibus in rēbus . . . .
    Inceptiō prīmīs in rēbus . . . .

3. Philosophus sapiēns fēminam . . . . . .
    Philosophum sapientem fēmina . . . . .
    Philosophus sapientem fēminam . . . .

4. Vir fortis fidēlem amīcum . . . .
    Vir fortem fidēlis amīcum . . . .
    Virī fortēs ab amīcīs fidēlibus . . . .
    Virī fortibus ab amīcīs fidēlēs . . . . . .

5. Māter nostra gaudium . . . .
    Māter nostrum gaudium . . . .
    Mātrem nostram gaudium . . . .
    Māter nostrō gaudiō . . . .

E.   Decline in three cases singular and plural.

tumultus malus	tempus omne	fābula difficilis	aper fortis
quālis hostis	homō sapiēns	verbum grave	rēs pulchra

F.   Give the Latin equivalent.

1. Soldiers carry on wars near cities.
2. War is waged by soldiers with courage.
3. Young men like deeds, not words.
4. Animals have feet, not hands.
5. The boys are walking to the city through the gates.

6. Between the river and the mountains are the fields and forests.
7. Men work enthusiastically with their hands.
8. In the winters men spend their days in town.
9. Behind the walls stand trees; among the trees stands a fountain.
10. In the books there are pictures, but my brother reads the stories with effort.

G.   Turn to page 60, then to page 72, exercise B; rewrite the sentences in the paragraph and exercise adding suitable adjectives.

IV PATTERN PRACTICE NINE

1.	A man looks at the girl.	Vir puellam spectat.
2.	Every man looks at the girl.	Vir omnis puellam spectat.
3.	The man looks at every girl.	Vir omnem puellam spectat.
4.	The man looks at all the girls.	Vir omnēs puellās spectat.
5.	The man looks at a beautiful girl.	Vir puellam pulchram spectat.
6.	The man looks at beautiful girls.	Vir puellās pulchrās spectat.
7.	Beautiful girls are watched.	Puellae pulchrae spectantur.
8.	The girls are watched by every man.	Puellae ā virō omnī spectantur.
9.	A sword wounds the body.	Gladius corpus vulnerat.
10.	My sword wounds the body.	Gladius meus corpus vulnerat.
11.	A sword wounds my body.	Gladius meum corpus vulnerat.
12.	The sword *does wound* a heavy body.	Vulnerat gladius grave corpus:
13.	A heavy sword *does wound* the body.	Vulnerat gladius gravis corpus.
14.	Heavy swords *wound* the body.	Vulnerant gladiī gravēs corpus.
15.	Swords *wound* heavy bodies.	Vulnerant gladiī gravia corpora.
16.	The bodies *are wounded* by heavy swords.	Vulnerantur gladiīs gravibus corpora.
17.	The youth remains in the city.	Juvenis in urbe manet.
18.	The Roman youth remains in the city.	Juvenis Rōmānus in urbe manet.
19.	The youth stays in the Roman city.	Juvenis Rōmānā in urbe manet.
20.	The Roman youths stay in the city.	Juvenēs Rōmānī in urbe manent.
21.	The youths stay in the Roman cities.	Juvenēs Rōmānīs in urbibus manent.
22.	In many things truth wins.	Multīs in rēbus vincit vēritās.
23.	In all things truth wins.	Omnibus in rēbus vincit vēritās.
24.	In every thing truth wins.	In omnī rē vincit vēritās.

V. OPTIONAL READING

Pauca sed bona   — Common phrase
Virum bonum nātūra, nōn ordō facit. — Publilius Syrus
In sōlō Deō salūs. — Motto
Nōn semper aurem facilem habet fēlīcitās. — Publilius Syrus

VI   WORD STUDY

1. Notice the difference between the meaning of *honestus* (honorable) and the derivative "honest."

2. A number of Latin nouns are formed from adjectives by the addition of the suffix *-tās*, English "-ity" or "-ty." What adjectives appear in: celerity, facility, fidelity, difficulty, felicity, purity, gravity, quality? What is probably the form of the Latin noun from which each of these words is derived?

3. Use these English words in sentences: fortitude, omnipotent, stultify, malice, nullify, solitude.

VII   VOCABULARY

Nouns

fortūna, fortūnā f

aper, aprō m.

inceptiō, inceptiōne f.

nēmō, nēminem m.
   (abl., use *nūllus*)

Function Word

   saepe

Verbs

adjuvat, adjuvant

vīvit, vīvunt

Adjectives

honestus, honesta, honestum
malus, mala, malum
meus, mea, meum
noster, nostra, nostrum

nūllus, nūlla, nūllum
pulcher, pulchra, pulchrum
pūrus, pūra, pūrum
sōlus, sōla, sōlum

stultus, stulta, stultum
suus, sua, suum
tuus, tua, tuum
vester, vestra, vestrum

(Review ordinals, Introduction
 page 24.)

celer, celeris, celere
difficilis, difficile
facilis, facile
fēlīx, (fēlīcī)
fidēlis, fidēle

fortis, forte
gravis, grave
omnis, omne
quālis, quāle
sapiēns, (sapientī)

REVIEW LIST OF NOUNS

I

agricola, agricolā m.
aqua, aquā f.
barba, barbā f.
fābula, fābulā f.
fāmilia, fāmiliā f.

fēmina, fēminā f.
fīlia, fīliā f.
fortūna, fortūnā f.
harēna, harēnā f.

hōra, hōrā f.
injūria, injūriā f.
Lūcia, Lūciā f.
pāla, pālā f.
pictūra, pictūrā f.
porta, portā f.

puella, puellā f.
Rōma, Rōmā f.
sententia, sententiā f.
silva, silvā f.
terra, terrā f.
via, viā f.

II

ager, agrō m.
agnus, agnō m.
amīcus, amīcō m.*
animus, animō m.
annus, annō m.

aper, aprō m.
equus, equō m.
fīlius, fīliō m.
gladius, gladiō m.

Jūlius, Jūliō m.
liber, librō m.
Lūcius, Lūciō m.
lupus, lupō m.
Mārcus, Mārcō m.

mūrus, mūrō m.
philosophus,
      philosophō m.
Pūblius, Pūbliō m.
puer, puerō m.
servus, servō m.
vir, virō m.

II (n.)

aedificium, aedificiō n.
bellum, bellō n.
cōnsilium, cōnsiliō n.
factum, factō n.
gaudium, gaudiō n.

oppidum, oppidō n.
perīculum, perīculō n.
saxum, saxō n.
studium, studiō n.
verbum, verbō n.

III

aestās, aestāte f.
arbor, arbore f.
hiems, hieme f.
imitātiō, imitātiōne f.
inceptiō, inceptiōne f.
māter, mātre f.

mēns, mente f.
soror, sorōre f.
urbs, urbe f.
vēritās, vēritāte f.
vestis, veste f.
virtūs, virtūte f.

auctor, auctōre m.
canis, cane m. (f.)
dolor, dolōre m.
fōns, fonte m.
frāter, frātre m.
gladiātor, gladiātōre m.

homō, homine m.
hostis, hoste m.
juvenis, juvene m.*
labor, labōre m.
mīles, mīlite m.
mōns, monte m.

nēmō, nēminem m.
pater, patre m.
pēs, pede m.
senex, sene m.*
spectātor, spectātōre m.
viātor, viātōre m.

III (n.)

caput, capite n.
corpus, corpore n.
flūmen, flūmine n.

nomen, nōmine n.
opus, opere n.
tempus, tempore n.

animal, animālī n.
   (special *i* type)

IV

manus, manū f.
tumultus, tumultū m.

V

diēs, diē m. (f.)
rēs, rē f.
spēs, spē f. (sg. only)

*Adjective often used as noun.

SECOND REVIEW

Rem, nōn spem, quaerit amīcus.
   —in *Carmina dē figūrīs*

"A friend wants the real thing, not hope (a promise)."

Parva levēs capiunt animōs. — Ovid

"Trifles capture frivolous minds."

I   VOCABULARY AND MODEL SENTENCE REVIEW

A.   Review the nouns listed on the preceding page. Pay particular attention to genders and to the classification or declension to which they belong. Try to recall several different meanings you have used, especially for such words as: terra, studium, imitātiō, dolor, rēs.

B.   Make the following substitutions, additions, and transformations in the model sentence: *Rem, nōn spem, quaerit amīcus.*

    1. Substitute three suitable words for *spem*.
    2. Substitute three suitable words for *rem*.
    3. Substitute three suitable words for *amīcus*.
    4. Substitute three suitable words for both *amīcus* and *spem*.
    5. Substitute three suitable words for each of *amīcus*, *rem*, and *spem*.

    6. Substitute three suitable words for *quaerit*.
    7. Use no word of the original except *nōn*.
    8. Add four different modifiers to *amīcus*.
    9. Add three different modifiers to *rem*, to *spem*.
  10. Transform the nominative into an ablative and make the other needed changes.

     (Example: substitution for *rem* and *spem*: *Pecūniam*, nōn spem, quaerit amīcus; Rem, nōn *verba*, quaerit amīcus.)

II   STRUCTURE REVIEW

    1. What letters signal the passive voice in third person verbs?
    2. When the passive is used, how is the doer of the action indicated in Latin?
    3. What is true of endings in the neuter plural of all nouns?
    4. In what ways do adjectives agree with nouns?
    5. What are predicate adjectives? With what nouns do they agree?
    6. What types or classes of adjectives are there in Latin?
    7. What classes or conjugations of verbs can be distinguished by the vowel variations?

III   FORM REVIEW

A.   Answer the questions, using the noun in parentheses.

1. (pāla)
   Quid juvenis tenet?
   Quid juvenem adjuvat?
   Quō īnstrūmentō juvenis fodit?

2. (puellae)
   Quae multum dīcunt?
   Quās spectant juvenēs?
   Quibuscum juvenēs ambulant?

3. (agnus)
   Quis lupum fugit?
   Quem lupus quaerit?
   Ā quō lupus fugitur?

4. (lupī)
   Quī agnōs quaerunt?
   Quōs agnī fugiunt?
   Ā quibus agnī quaeruntur?

5. (cōnsilium)
   Quid gladiātor capit?
   Quid gladiātōrem afficit?
   Quō īnstrūmentō rēs afficitur?

6. (verba)
   Quae rēs audiuntur?
   Quās rēs fīlia audit?
   Quibus rēbus fīlia afficitur?

7. (hiems)
   Quid hominēs fugit?
   Quid ab hominibus fugitur?
   Quandō multī hominēs nōn sunt
      fēlīcēs?

8. (urbēs)
   Quās rēs hominēs laudant?
   Quae rēs ab hominibus laudantur?
   Ubi manent hominēs?

9. (flūmen)
   Quid spectātor videt?
   Ubi stat spectātor?
   Unde ambulat spectātor?

10. (nōmina)
    Quae rēs saepe laudantur?
    Quās rēs virī laudant?
    Quibus rēbus virī appellantur?

11. (tumultus)
    Quid senēs nōn amant?
    Quid ā senibus nōn amātur?
    Quō īnstrūmentō senex pellitur?

12. (manūs)
    Quae rēs canem tenent?
    Quās rēs canis fugit?
    Quibus rēbus canis tenētur?

13. (spēs)
    Quid stultus nōn habet?
    Quid juvenem afficit?
    Quō modō mīles pūgnat?

14. (diēs)
    Quae rēs virōs dēlectant?
    Quandō virī dēlectantur?
    Quās rēs virī amant?

15. (omnis terra)
    Quid viātor amat?
    Quō viātor prōcēdit?
    Ubi viātor ambulat?

16. (animī fortēs)
    Quās rēs mīlitēs habent?
    Quae rēs mīlitēs adjuvant?
    Quō modō sapientēs vīvunt?

17. (perīculum omne)
    Quid vincitur?
    Quid virtūs vincit?
    Ubi mīles fortis est?

18. (fontēs pūrī)
    Quae rēs dēfluunt?
    Ā quibus rēbus aqua dēfluit?
    Quae rēs vident fēminae?

19. (capita longa)
    Quās rēs lupī habent?
    Quae rēs agnum terrent?
    In quibus rēbus sunt injūriae?

20. (liber facilis)
    Quid puer parvus legit?
    Quid puerum parvum dēlectat?
    Ubi sunt pictūrae?

B.   Identify the word each adjective modifies. How is the meaning changed within each group of sentences?

1. a. Stultus lupus mentem vertit ad agnum.
   b. Stultam lupus mentem vertit ad agnum.
   c. Stultum lupus mentem vertit ad agnum.

2. a. Ā cane nōn magnō saepe tenētur aper.
   b. Ā cane nōn magnus saepe tenētur aper.
   c. Canis nōn magnus saepe tenet aprum.
   d. Canem nōn magnum saepe tenet aper.
   e. Canem nōn magnus saepe tenet aper.

3. a. Mīles fortis fidēlem puellam amat.
   b. Mīles fortem fidēlis puellam amat.
   c. Mīlitem fortem fidēlis puella amat.
   d. Mīlitem fortis fidēlem puella amat.

4. a. Parva levēs capiunt animōs.
   b. Parva levēs capiunt animī.
   c. Parvī levia capiunt animī.
   d. Parvōs levia capiunt animōs.

C.   Change all nouns from singular to plural, making any other necessary changes of verbs and modifiers.

1. Manus ā puerō lavātur.
2. Rēx urbem vestram cupit.
3. Laudatne auctor opus difficile?
4. Frāter tuus est amīcus meus.
5. Numquam perīculum sine perīculō vincitur.
6. Omnī in rē gravis est inceptiō.
7. Vulneratne gladiātor hostem gladiō?
8. In flūmen magnum nōn currit aper.
9. In pictūrā senex saepe longam barbam gerit.
10. Eō (pl. Eīs) annō homō multum (pl. add *verba*) dīcit dē rē.

D.   Change each sentence from active to passive.

1. Quaeritne sapiēns bonum?
2. Servus Rōmānus injūriam accipit.
3. Viātor viam facilem spectat.
4. Fortēs Fortūna adjuvat.
5. Agricolam magna animālia nōn dēlectant.
6. Mīles fortis hostēs nōn vulnerat.
7. Parvās puellās tumultus terret.
8. Auctor Rōmānus causam bonam laudat.
9. Stultī rēs malās laudant.
10. Nūllus puer canem fidēlem terret.

E.   Decline (give the case forms, singular and plural) in three cases.

nōmen meum   porta omnis   rēs gravis   quāle oppidum
annus bonus   frāter noster   manus mea   animal celere

F.   Give the Latin equivalent.

1. Pure water is carried from the spring by the slave alone.
2. Beautiful women are praised by many Roman authors.
3. No one wants a long and serious war in our land.
4. Our soldiers are brave and faithful at all times.
5. Your brother is moving heavy stones; he is strong and quick.
6. My sisters are often sent to town too.
7. The father leaves his happy household behind reluctantly.
8. A Roman city is often fortified by thick (wide) walls.
9. A little girl is frightened away from the forest by a large animal.
10. Roman soldiers never leave their swords behind on the ground but fight bravely in war.
11. The statements are good and wise; much is said in little.
12. Our sons win by their courage, not by words.

IV OPTIONAL ORAL PRACTICE ON NOUNS AND ADJECTIVES

As soon as the word is announced, give the singular forms; wait for the check; then give the plural forms. These will also be checked; then the next word will be announced.

PUELLA (I)

puella	puellae
puellam	puellās
puellā	puellīs

VERBUM

verbum	verba
verbum	verba
verbō	verbīs

CORPUS

corpus	corpora
corpus	corpora
corpore	corporibus

SERVUS (II)

servus	servī
servum	servōs
servō	servīs

GLADIUS

gladius	gladiī
gladium	gladiōs
gladiō	gladiīs

FĀBULA

fābula	fābulae
fābulam	fābulās
fābulā	fābulīs

PUER

puer	puerī
puerum	puerōs
puerō	puerīs

MĪLES

mīles	mīlitēs
mīlitem	mīlitēs
mīlite	mīlitibus

VIR

vir	virī
virum	virōs
virō	virīs

SAXUM

saxum	saxa
saxum	saxa
saxō	saxīs

URBS PULCHRA

urbs pulchra	urbēs pulchrae
urbem pulchram	urbēs pulchrās
urbe pulchrā	urbibus pulchrīs

CANIS (III)

canis	canēs
canem	canēs
cane	canibus

PĒS MEUS

pēs meus	pedēs meī
pedem meum	pedēs meōs
pede meō	pedibus meīs

HOMŌ

homō	hominēs
hominem	hominēs
homine	hominibus

MAGNUM CAPUT

magnum caput	magna capita
magnum caput	magna capita
magnō capite	magnīs capitibus

FLŪMEN

flūmen	flūmina
flūmen	flūmina
flūmine	flūminibus

BELLUM GRAVE

bellum grave	bella gravia
bellum grave	bella gravia
bellō gravī	bellīs gravibus

MANUS (IV)

manus	manūs
manum	manūs
manū	manibus

VIA FACILIS

via facilis	viae facilēs
viam facilem	viās facilēs
viā facilī	viīs facilibus

DIĒS (V)

diēs	diēs
diem	diēs
diē	diēbus

OMNIS MŪRUS

omnis mūrus	omnēs mūrī
omnem mūrum	omnēs mūrōs
omnī mūrō	omnibus mūrīs

V WORD STUDY REVIEW

A. Give three examples of each of the following types of English derivatives:

1. Latin words which have come into English unchanged in spelling
2. Words from which the ending of a Latin declension or conjugation has been dropped
3. Words from which the Latin ending has been dropped and final "-e" added

B. Give two English words using each of the following noun-forming suffixes. Use Latin stems that you have studied.

   1. -tion (*-tiō*)   2. -ty (*-tās*)   3. -tude (*-tūdō*)

VI OPTIONAL READING

Ibi semper est victōria ubi concordia est. — Publilius Syrus
Ubi . . . est thēsaurus tuus, ibi est cor tuum. — N. T. (Matthew)
Prudēns cum cūrā vīvit, stultus sine cūrā. — Medieval
Ars longa, vīta brevis   — Hippocrates (translation)

Common phrases

     bonā fidē   alma māter
     dē factō   homō sapiēns

VII VOCABULARY

Nouns	*Adjective*	*Verb*
animus, animō m.	levis, leve	quaerit, quaerunt
spēs, spē f.		

LESSON TEN

Semper fidēlis — Motto (U. S. Marines)	"Always faithful"
Fortiter, fidēliter, fēlīciter — Motto	"Bravely, faithfully, fortunately"
Pulchrē, bene, rēctē — Horace	"Beautifully, well, correctly"

Purpose: to learn to read a connected story

Optional work: formation of adverbs

I   MĪLES, ĪNFĀNS, CANIS

parva casa

silva

arborēs

serpēns mala

saxum ingēns

mīles fortis   īnfāns   canis fidēlis

1.	Ubi est casa?	In silvā est casa.
2.	Quis in casā est?	Īnfāns parvus in casā est.
3.	Estne īnfāns sōlus?	Nōn est sōlus; canis fidēlis cum īnfante manet.
4.	Cūr est īnfāns tūtus?	Est tūtus quod canis fidēlis adest.
5.	Ubi stat mīles?	Ante casam stat mīles.

6. Quālis est mīles?   Fortis est mīles.
7. Quid agit mīles?   Ā casā prōcēdit mīles.
8. Habetne mīles gladium?   Habet.
9. Estne mīles vēnātor?   Vēnātor bonus est; gladiō animālia occīdit.
10. Quod animal in silvā est?   Serpēns in silvā est.

11. Quid in silvā stat?   Saxum ingēns in silvā stat et arborēs stant.
12. Quid canis omnis saepe agit?   Canis omnis saepe lātrat.
13. Quid īnfantēs saepe agunt?   Īnfantēs saepe clāmant.

II   CANIS FIDĒLIS

Prīma fābula dē[1] mīlite et puerō et cane nārrātur. Mīles casam nōn magnam in silvā tenet ubi parvō cum fīliō manet. Pater Rūfus cum īnfante vīvit sōlus - māter mortua[2] est. Nūllus alius[3] homō, sed canis fidēlis, vēnātor bonus, semper adest. Diem dē diē nōn multās hōrās abest pater.

Sed magnum bellum geritur et eō[4] tempore omnēs mīlitēs ā rēge convocantur.[5] Rūfus, quod īnfantem habet, ad bellum prōcēdere[6] nōn cupit, sed in animō habet ad rēgem prōcēdere et honestē[7] rem narrāre. Quōcum īnfāns relinquitur? Cum cane fidēlī pater fīlium relinquit. Canis nōn procul ā puerō sedet, et mīles ex casā prōcēdit.

Ecce! Magna serpēns adest et ad īnfantem statim venit. Puer terrētur clāmatque. Currit canis in ingentem serpentem; bene et fortiter[7] pūgnat. Animal malum occīdit et in ōre igitur sanguinem habet multum. Post bonum factum, ante casam sedet animal fidēle; tandem mīlitem audit, ad Rūfum currit laetē; multum lātrat. Canem et sanguinem in ōre videt pater. Putat igitur, "Fīlius īnfāns mortuus est!" Statim canem gladiō occīdit.

Deinde in casam venit pater et puerum tūtum serpentemque mortuam cōnspicit. Magnō cum dolōre afficitur quod canem fidēlem sine causā occīdit.

Notā bene

1. *dē*: may mean "about"
2. *mortuus -a -um*: "dead"
3. *alius*: "other"
4. *eō*: form of "this," "that"
5. *convocat*: *con + vocat*, "call together," "assemble"

6. Forms ending in *-re* are infinitives. The English meaning is "to go," "to tell," etc.
7. For formation of adverbs see page 94.

Respondē Latīnē

1. Ubi est casa?
2. Quis in casā manet?
3. Cūr pater est sōlus homō in casā?
4. Quis cum patre vīvit?
5. Cūr pater casam relinquere cupit?

6. Cūr pūgnāre nōn cupit mīles?
7. Quōcum īnfāns relinquitur?
8. Quid in casam venit?
9. Quid facit puer īnfāns?
10. Quid agit canis?

11. Quid canis in ōre habet?
12. Ubi sedet canis?
13. Quālis est canis semper?
14. Ubi est puer?
15. Quem audit canis?

16. Quid videt pater?
17. Quid agit pater?
18. Quid in casa videt?
19. Quō modō pater afficitur?
20. Cūr mīles canem occīdit?

III WORD STUDY

1. Form an English adjective ending in "-al" from the Latin noun *rēx* and one from *ōs*.

2. Explain the relationship of these derivatives in meaning to the Latin source word: cupidity, tutor, homicide, reputation, curiosity, rectify.

3. Note the change of *clāmat* to give English "exclaim." What other words come from *clāmat*?

4. Look up in a dictionary the meaning of "sanguine" and "sanguinary."

5. If a hospital nurse sees "stat" beside a doctor's orders for a patient, she will get the order carried out *statim*, immediately.

6. What is an "omnibus"? a "bus"? What is the source of these words?

7. The prefix *in-* is another which appears in assimilated forms in both Latin and English: *im-*, *il-*, *ir-*. Note the prefixes in these English words: inspect, impel, illuminate, irrigate.

IV VOCABULARY[1]

Nouns	*Verbs*	*Function Words*	*Adjectives*
casa, casā f.	clāmat, clāmant	cūr	rēctus, rēcta, rēctum
causa, causā f.	putat, putant	sī	tūtus, tūta, tūtum
Rūfus, Rūfō m.	occīdit, occīdunt		ingēns (ingentī)
īnfāns, īnfante m.	cupit, cupiunt	deinde	
rēx, rēge m.		igitur	
sanguīs, sanguine f.	abest, absunt	semper	
serpēns, serpente f.	adest, adsunt	statim	
ōs, ōre n.		tandem	
		ecce	

[1]Words listed in the vocabularies are those occurring in the lesson which recur sufficiently to deserve special attention. Those new in the lesson but not listed recur infrequently in the material you are likely to read. If they are not clear from the context, consult your teacher or the dictionary at the back of the book.

V OPTIONAL WORK ON ADVERBS

A.   Formation of adverbs

1. "Pulchrē, bene, rēctē"
From this quotation (disregarding the irregular form *bene* from *bonus*) tell how adverbs are formed from I-II declension adjectives.

2. "Fortiter, fidēliter, fēlīciter"
How are adverbs formed from III declension adjectives?

Answer these "if" questions with the appropriate adverb. (Example: Sī vir *honestus* est, quō modō agit? *Honestē* agit.)

a. Sī puer *laetus* est, quō modō labōrat? _____ labōrat.
b. Sī fēmina *fidēlis* est, quō modō virum amat? _____ amat.
c. Sī mīles *fortis* est, quō modō pūgnat? _____ pūgnat.
d. Sī vir *stultus* est, quō modō agit? _____ agit.
e. Sī homō *fēlīx* est, quō modō vincit? _____ vincit.

f. Sī philosophus *gravis* est, quō modō legit? _____ legit.
g. Sī puella *bona* est, quō modō vestem lavat? _____ lavat.
h. Sī servus *malus* est, quō modō puellās terret? _____ terret.
i. Sī pēs *celer* est, quō modō puer currit? _____ currit.
j. Sī pater *rēctus* est, quō modō rem gerit? _____ rem gerit.

LESSON ELEVEN

Certa mittimus dum incerta petimus.
— Plautus

"We lose sure things while seeking uncertain ones."

Purpose: to learn the present tense of verbs of all conjugations

I TABERNA

1. Ubi sunt hominēs?	In tabernā sunt hominēs.
2. Quid agunt?	Vīnum bibunt.
3. Quis vīnum portat?	Servus vīnum portat.
4. Ā quō vīnum portātur?	Ā servō vīnum portātur.
5. Cūr ūnus sōlus sedet?	Sōlus sedet quod laetus nōn est.
6. Cūr nōn laetus est?	Ēbrius est; iterum iterumque bibit.
7. Quid agit ēbrius?	Clāmat ēbrius.
8. Quid manū agit?	Manū mēnsam pulsat.
9. Quid agit vir cum duōbus amīcīs?	Vir rīdet quod ēbrium audit.
10. Quot mīlitēs in tabernā adsunt?	Duo mīlitēs adsunt.
11. Prīmus mīles sedet. Quid agit?	Pecūniam in mēnsam jacit.
12. Cūr pecūniam jacit?	Pecūniam prō vīnō solvit.
13. Secundus mīles stat. Quid agit?	Vīnum accipit et grātiās agit.

II   PATTERN READING

A.   Sample sentences

1. Librum portō.	I am carrying a book.
2. Librum portās.	You are carrying a book.
3. Ego librum portō;	*I* carry a book;
tū gladium portās.	*you* carry a sword.
4. Librōs portāmus.	We carry our books.
5. Librōs portātis.	You-all[1] carry your books.
6. Nōs librōs portāmus;	*We* carry our books;
vōs gladiōs portātis.	*you-all* carry swords.
7. Sapiēns librum portat;	A wise man carries a book;
mīlitēs gladiōs portant.	soldiers carry swords.
8. Nunc magnā vōce dīcis.	Now you are speaking in a loud voice.
9. Linguam audītis vestram.	You-all hear your *own* language (tongue).
10. Montem oculīs nostrīs vidēmus.	We see the mountain with our eyes.
11. Surgō et prōcēdō.	I get up and go along.

B.[2]   Be able to answer the questions by supplying the separate pronoun to identify the person of the verb.

1. Auctor opus laudat.

Opus laudō.	Quis opus laudat?	Ego opus laudō.
Opus laudās.	Quis opus laudat?	Tū opus laudās.
Opus laudat.	Quis opus laudat?	Auctor opus laudat.
Opus laudāmus.	Quis opus laudat?	Nōs opus laudāmus.
Opus laudātis.	Quis opus laudat?	Vōs opus laudātis.
Opus laudant.	Quis opus laudat?	Auctorēs opus laudant.

2. Stultus in terrā sedet.

In terrā sedent.	Quis in terrā sedet?	Stultī in terrā sedent.
In terrā sedeō.	Quis in terrā sedet?	Ego in terrā sedeō.
In terrā sedēmus.	Quis in terrā sedet?	Nōs in terrā sedēmus.
In terrā sedēs.	Quis in terrā sedet?	Tū in terrā sedēs.
In terrā sedētis.	Quis in terrā sedet?	Vōs in terrā sedētis.
In terrā sedet.	Quis in terrā sedet?	Stultus in terrā sedet.

3. Sapiēns vīvit fēlīciter.

Vīvunt fēlīciter.	Quis vīvit fēlīciter?	Sapientēs vīvunt fēlīciter.
Vīvimus fēlīciter.	Quis vīvit fēlīciter?	Nōs vīvimus fēlīciter.
Vīvō fēlīciter.	Quis vīvit fēlīciter?	Ego vīvō fēlīciter.
Vīvitis fēlīciter.	Quis vīvit fēlīciter?	Vōs vīvitis fēlīciter.
Vīvis fēlīciter.	Quis vīvit fēlīciter?	Tū vīvis fēlīciter.
Vīvit fēlīciter.	Quis vīvit fēlīciter?	Sapiēns vīvit fēlīciter.

[1] This is not the same as the regional, colloquial phrase, for in the South "You-all" can refer to one person. This is a device to distinguish rapidly between "you" sg. and "you" pl.

[2] This exercise lends itself well to taping for oral practice.

4. Senex facta cupit.

Facta cupimus.	Quis facta cupit?	Nōs facta cupimus.
Facta cupiunt.	Quis facta cupit?	Senēs facta cupiunt.
Facta cupis.	Quis facta cupit?	Tū facta cupis.
Facta cupit.	Quis facta cupit?	Senex facta cupit.
Facta cupitis.	Quis facta cupit?	Vōs facta cupitis.
Facta cupiō.	Quis facta cupit?	Ego facta cupiō.

5. Puella pedibus venit.

Pedibus veniō.	Quis pedibus venit?	Ego pedibus veniō.
Pedibus venītis.	Quis pedibus venit?	Vōs pedibus venītis.
Pedibus venit.	Quis pedibus venit?	Puella pedibus venit.
Pedibus venīmus.	Quis pedibus venit?	Nōs pedibus venīmus.
Pedibus veniunt.	Quis pedibus venit?	Puellae pedibus veniunt.
Pedibus venīs.	Quis pedibus venit?	Tū pedibus venīs.

C. Questions on structure

1. List the signals contained in the verb for: I, you, we, you-all, he, they.

2. Compare the second person singular of the verbs; what vowel is found in each type? How many classes of verbs are there?

3. How can you tell to which class or group a verb belongs?

4. What forms are somewhat irregular?

See Appendix B, page 199; Form Chart, page 100; also verb list, page 112 to determine classification of all verbs studied to that point.

III EXERCISES

A. Answer the question for each person indicated by the noun or pronoun.
   (Example: Quis venit? Puella.   Puella venit.
   Ego.   Veniō.
   Puellae. Puellae veniunt.
   Vōs.   Venītis. etc.)

1. Quis multum clāmat?   Spectātor. Ego. Tū. Vōs. Nōs. Spectātōrēs.

2. Quis cum īnfante sedet?   Canis. Ego. Tū. Vōs. Nōs. Canēs.

3. Quis saepe librum legit?   Tū. Sapiēns. Ego. Sapientēs. Vōs. Nōs.

4. Quis venit in urbem?   Viātor. Viātōrēs. Ego. Tū. Nōs. Vōs.

5. Quis patrem vocat?   Ego. Tū. Fīlia. Nōs. Vōs. Fīliae.

6. Quis statim fugit?   Hostis. Tū. Nōs. Vōs. Hostēs. Ego.

7. Quis incerta petit?   Juvenis. Tū. Juvenēs. Vōs. Nōs. Ego.

8. Quis perīculum vincit?   Ego. Nōs. Tū. Vōs. Gladiātor. Gladiātōrēs.

9. Quis equum terret?   Servus. Servī. Nōs. Ego. Vōs. Tū.

10. Quis est in urbe?   Vōs. Nōs. Tū. Senex. Ego. Senēs.

B.   Give in all persons of the present tense (with no pronoun subject).

1. Saxum tenet.
2. Aestāte labōrat.
3. Dē causā putat.
4. Librum pōnit.
5. Verba audit.
6. Vestem facit.

C.   Give the Latin equivalent.

1. I myself want the truth about the man.
2. You-all see the river at a distance.
3. *We* like good books always.
4. They are standing across the street near the gate.
5. You turn your attention to study with reluctance.

IV PATTERN PRACTICE TEN[1]

1. I walk to the town.
2. You-all walk to the town.

Ad oppidum ambulō.
Ad oppidum ambulātis.

3. You are walking to the town.
4. They walk to the town.

Ad oppidum ambulās.
Ad oppidum ambulant.

5. We walk to the town.
6. He is walking to the town.

Ad oppidum ambulāmus.
Ad oppidum ambulat.

7. You-all see the gate.
8. I see the gate.

Portam vidētis.
Portam videō.

9. We see the gate.
10. You see the gate.

Portam vidēmus.
Portam vidēs.

11. They see the gate.
12. He sees the gate.

Portam vident.
Portam videt.

13. A stupid person loses sure things.
14. Stupid people lose sure things.

Stultus certa mittit.
Stultī certa mittunt.

15. *I* lose sure things.
16. *We* lose sure things.

Ego certa mittō.
Nōs certa mittimus.

17. *You-all* lose sure things.
18. *You* lose sure things.

Vōs certa mittitis.
Tū certa mittis.

19. You catch sight of the river.
20. We catch sight of the river.

Flūmen cōnspicis.
Flūmen cōnspicimus.

21. They catch sight of the river.
22. You-all catch sight of the river.

Flūmen cōnspiciunt.
Flūmen cōnspicitis.

23. He catches sight of the river.
24. I catch sight of the river.

Flūmen cōnspicit.
Flūmen cōnspiciō.

25. You-all are building a long wall.
26. He is building a long wall.

Mūrum longum mūnītis.
Mūrum longum mūnit.

27. We are building a long wall.
28. I am building a long wall.

Mūrum longum mūnīmus.
Mūrum longum mūniō.

29. They are building a long wall.
30. You are building a long wall.

Mūrum longum mūniunt.
Mūrum longum mūnīs.

[1] Be able to give this practice from Latin to English also.

V IN TABERNĀ

In tabernam pedibus incertīs venit ēbrius.[1] Oculī volvuntur, lingua balbūtit.[2] Nōs eum[3]
vidēmus et rīdēmus omnēs. Sed ad mēnsam ambulat, eam[3] manū pulsat, magnā vōce:

"Pecūniam habeō magnam," inquit. "Puer, vīnum portā."[4]

"Vīnum pōnitur; deinde clāmat ēbrius:

"Sōlus bibere nōn cupiō.[5] Quandō ego bibō, omnēs bibunt. Portāte[4] vīnum et omnēs
bibite!"

Vīnum celeriter ā servīs portātur. Omnēs magnō cum gaudiō bibimus et grātiās agimus:

"Grātiās nōn cupiō. Cupiō vīnum. Et sī bibō, omnēs bibunt!"

Iterum vīnum pōnitur et omnēs laetī bibimus. Nunc magnus in tabernā tumultus est.
Ēbrium maximē amāmus omnēs. Eum manū capimus et grātiās agimus. Deinde nūllum vīnum
adest, et ēbrius iterum clāmat:

"Sī dī mē amant,[6] bibere[5] sōlus nōn cupiō. Et quandō bibō, omnēs bibite!"

Nunc, quod magnus est tumultus, nēmō in tabernā verba audīre potest.[7] Tandem ēbrius
surgit et pecūniam in mēnsam jacit.

"Pecūniam," inquit, "cupiō[5] solvere prō vīnō meō. Et quandō ego solvō, omnēs
solvunt!"

Notā bene

1. *ēbrius -a -um* (adj.): one who has already patronized the shop too long or too well
2. *balbutit*: "babbles"
3. *eum*: "him"; *eam*: "it" (see form table, page 105)
4. forms like *portā*, *portāte*, and *bibite* signal a command: "bring," "drink," (see
   page 120)
5. *cupiō*: patterns with forms in -*re*, infinitives; see Lesson Thirteen.
6. *Sī dī mē amant*: "if the gods love me" = "by heaven."
7. *potest*: "can," "is able"; (followed by infinitive in -*re* like *cupiō*.

Respondē Latīnē

1. Quō modō ambulat ēbrius?
2. Quid cupit ēbrius in tabernā?
3. Quid agunt aliī in tabernā?
4. Quō ambulat?
5. Habetne ēbrius pecūniam?
6. Quid nōn cupit ēbrius?
7. Quid clāmat?
8. Quid servus agit?
9. Quid omnēs agunt?
10. Suntne omnēs laetī?
11. Cūr magnus tumultus est?
12. Cūr ēbrius pecūniam jacit?
13. Quid tandem agunt omnēs?

VI OPTIONAL READING

Ego sum rēx Rōmānus et suprā grammaticam. — reputedly said by Sigismund I
Elephantum ex muscā facis. — Proverb
Prō bonō pūblicō — Common phrase
Prō tem(pore) — Common phrase

VII WORD STUDY

1. Roman wealth was, in early times, reckoned by cattle (*pecus*), and was called *pecūnia*. Even after coined money was used, the same term was kept.

2. Give the Latin source and meaning of: bilingual, oculist, vocal, revolve, pulsate, dissolve, ridicule, reiterate, gratitude, compete.

3. Give an English derivative from: taberna, vīnum, surgō, ego, bibō, certus.

4. The preposition *prō* is used in Latin and in English as a prefix, with the meaning "before," "ahead," "in front of," "in return for," "in behalf of," etc. Explain the meaning of: propeller, proclamation, provide, project, proponent.

VIII VOCABULARY

Nouns	*Pronouns*	*Verbs*[1]
grātia, grātiā f.	ego, nōs	pulsō, pulsāre
lingua, lingua f.	tū, vōs	
mēnsa, mēnsā f.	is, ea, id	rīdeō, rīdēre
pecūnia, pecūniā f.		bibō, bibere
taberna, tabernā f.	*Function Words*	petō, petere
oculus, oculō m.	prō + abl.	solvō, solvere
		surgō, surgere
vīnum, vīnō n.	dum	volvō, volvere
vōx, vōce f.	iterum	jaciō, jacere
	maximē	inquam, inquis,[2]
Adjectives	nunc	inquit, inquiunt
certus, certa, certum		
incertus, incerta, incertum		

IX FORM CHART

present tense active of verbs

portō, portāre (I)

portō	portāmus
portās	portātis
portat	portant

agō, agere (III)

agō	agimus
agis	agitis
agit	agunt

audiō, audīre (IV)

audiō	audīmus
audīs	audītis
audit	audiunt

habeō, habēre (II)

habeō	habēmus
habēs	habētis
habet	habent

capiō, capere (III-i)

capiō	capimus
capis	capitis
capit	capiunt

sum, esse

sum	sumus
es	estis
est	sunt

---

[1] Hereafter verbs will be listed as they are here to conform to the listing in standard dictionaries. For the complete list, by conjugation, of the verbs studied so far, see page 112.

[2] This verb is defective; that is, it has only a few forms of which these are among the most common.

LESSON TWELVE

Tempore fēlīcī multī numerantur amīcī.
  — Medieval

"In good times many count themselves as friends."

Amīcus certus in rē incertā cernitur.
  — Ennius (quoted in Cicero)

"A reliable friend is proven in an uncertain situation." (cf. our proverb, "A friend in need is a friend indeed.")

Omnia mūtantur, nōs et mūtāmur in illīs.
  — Borbonius (?)

"All things are changed and we too are changed with them."

Purpose: to learn all the persons of the present tense passive

I   PATTERN READING

A.   Sample sentences

1. Verbīs movētur. — He is moved by the words.
2. Verbīs movēris. — You are moved by the words.
3. Ad urbem mittor. — I am being sent to the city.
4. Numerantur amīcī; numerāmur amīcī. — Friends are counted; we are counted as friends.
5. Ā nōbīs audīminī. — You-all are heard by us.
6. Asinus ab eō mediā in viā dūcitur. — A donkey is led in the middle of the road by him.
7. Pater in asinō vehitur. — The father is carried (transported) on the donkey.
8. Tē dūcō; mē dūcis. — I lead you; you lead me.
9. Ā mē dūceris; ā tē dūcor. — You are led by me; I am led by you.
10. Nōs dūcitis; vōs dūcimus. — You-all lead us; we lead you.
11. Multum sciō; multum nesciō. — (There is) much I know; much I do not know.

B.[1]   Be able to repeat these sentences rapidly, supplying the pronoun which shows the person of the verb.

1. Fēmina ab auctōre laudātur.
   Ab auctōre laudor.
   Ab auctōre laudāris.
   Ab auctōre laudātur.
   Ab auctōre laudāmur.
   Ab auctōre laudāminī.
   Ab auctōre laudantur.

2. Is post casam vidētur.
   Post casam videor.
   Post casam vidēmur.
   Post casam videntur.
   Post casam vidēris.
   Post casam vidētur.
   Post casam vidēmur.

---

[1] This exercise lends itself well to rapid oral practice on tape.

3. In asinō vehitur.	4. Mīles cum dolōre afficitur.	5. Ā rēge audītur.
In asinō vehor.	Cum dolōre afficitur.	Ā rēge audior.
In asinō vehiminī.	Cum dolōre afficeris.	Ā rēge audītur.
In asinō vehimur.	Cum dolōre afficior.	Ā rēge audiuntur.
In asinō vehitur.	Cum dolōre afficiuntur.	Ā rēge audīmur.
In asinō veheris.	Cum dolōre afficiminī.	Ā rēge audīminī.
In asinō vehuntur.	Cum dolōre afficimur.	Ā rēge audīris.

C. Questions on structure

1. List the signals for the passive forms.
2. What letter is found in all but one of these endings?
3. Compare the active and passive forms of the second person singular of the III conjugation. What is the difference?
4. Observe the forms of the personal pronouns in three cases, page 105.

II EXERCISES

A. Answer the question in the person indicated.

1. Quis ab omnibus amātur? Ego. Tū. Nōs. Vōs. Īnfāns. Īnfantēs.
2. Quis multōs amīcōs numerat? Fēlīx. Tū. Ego. Fēlīcēs. Nōs. Vōs.
3. Quis ā mātre monētur? Tū. Frāter. Ego. Vōs. Nōs. Frātrēs.
4. Quis dolōre movētur? Fīlia. Fīliae. Vōs. Nōs. Ego. Tū.
5. Quis amīcum cernit? Vōs. Tū. Nōs. Ego. Virī. Vir.
6. Quis ā puerō dūcitur? Asinus. Asinī. Ego. Tū. Nōs. Vōs.
7. Quis cum gaudiō accipitur? Ego. Puer. Nōs. Tū. Puerī. Vōs.
8. Quis trāns montēs mittitur? Puella. Nōs. Ego. Vōs. Puellae. Tū.
9. Quis ad silvam venit? Aper. Aprī. Tū. Vōs. Ego. Nōs.
10. Quis laetē audītur? Ego. Tū. Senex. Senēs. Nōs. Vōs.

B. Change these sentences to the equivalent passive form.

1. Servus mēnsam pulsat.
   Mēns___ ā serv___ pulsā___.
2. Servī vīnum portant.
   Ā serv___ vīn___ portā___.
3. Amīcum cernimus.
   Amīc___ ā nō___ cerni___.
4. Oculōs vertis.
   Ocul___ ā t___ vert___.
5. Multum sciō.
   Mult___ ā m___ sci___.
6. Eum adjuvō.
   Ā m___ adjuvā___.
7. Eās adjuvātis.
   Ā vō___ adjuvā___.
8. Mē pater vocat.
   Ā patr___ voc___.
9. Nōs mātrēs vocant.
   Ā mātr___ vocā___.
10. Vōs fīlius videt.
    Ā fīli___ vide___.
11. Nōs mūtat tempus.
    Temp___ mūtā___.
12. Tē adjuvat Fortūna.
    Ā Fortūn___ adjuvā___.
13. Mē vidēs.
    Ā t___ vide___.
14. Tē vincō.
    Ā m___ vinc___.
15. Vōs relinquimus.
    Ā nō___ relinqui___.

C. Conjugate (give all six forms of) the present tense, active and passive, of these verbs:

1. numerāre   2. terrēre   3. pōnere   4. jacere   5. mūnīre

D.   Give the Latin equivalent.

1. I am washing my hands.
2. Do you hear the uproar?
3. We do not run in the city.
4. You-all are honorable men.
5. He does not tell good stories.

6. You are standing near the building.
7. Kings build great cities.
8. You-all did not pay (the money).
9. We get up and go out of the shop.
10. I laugh at the matter.

E.   Use the form charts on pages 100 and 105 as a paradigm practice for rapid memorization of the present tense forms, active and passive. (Optional)

III   PATTERN PRACTICE ELEVEN

1. I am frightened by the wolf.   Ā lupō terreor.
2. We are frightened by the wolf.   Ā lupō terrēmur.

3. You are frightened by the wolf.   Ā lupō terrēris.
4. You-all are frightened by the wolf. Ā lupō terrēminī.

5. He is frightened by the wolf.   Ā lupō terrētur.
6. They are frightened by the wolf.   Ā lupō terrentur.

7. The language pleases me.   Lingua mē dēlectat.
8. I am pleased by the language.   Linguā dēlector.

9. The language pleases us.   Lingua nōs dēlectat.
10. We are pleased by the language.   Linguā dēlectāmur.

11. The language pleases you-all.   Lingua vōs dēlectat.
12. You-all are pleased by the language. Linguā dēlectāminī.

13. The language pleases them.   Lingua eōs dēlectat.
14. They are pleased by the language.   Linguā dēlectantur.

15. The boy is chasing me away.   Puer mē pellit.
16. I am chased by the boy.   Ā puerō pellor.

17. The boy is chasing us away.   Puer nōs pellit.
18. We are chased by the boy.   Ā puerō pellimur.

19. The boy is chasing you away.   Puer tē pellit.
20. You are chased by the boy.   Ā puerō pelleris.

21. The boy chases them away.   Puer eōs pellit.
22. They are chased by the boy.   Ā puerō pelluntur.

23. The boy chases you-all away.   Puer vōs pellit.
24. You-all are chased by the boy.   Ā puerō pelliminī.

25. You are heard by people.   Audīris ab hominibus.
26. They are heard by people.   Audiuntur ab hominibus.

27. I am heard by people.   Audior ab hominibus.
28. You-all are heard by people.   Audīminī ab hominibus.

29. He is heard by people.   Audītur ab hominibus.
30. We are heard by people.   Audīmur ab hominibus.

IV   LĒCTIO

1. Dum spīrō,[1] spērō. — Motto
2. Auribus teneō lupum. — Terence
3. Amīcitiam[2] trahit amor. — Motto
4. Omnia vincit Amor. — Vergil
5. Verba movent, exempla trahunt. — Anon.
6. Nihil rēctē sine exemplō docētur aut discitur. — Columella
7. In vīlī veste nēmō tractātur[3] honestē. — Medieval
8. Amphora[4] sub veste numquam portātur honestē. — Medieval
9. Hōrās nōn numerō nisī serēnās.[5] — Inscription on sun dial
10. Trahimur omnēs studiō laudis.[6] — Cicero
11. Vulpēs nōn capitur mūneribus. — Medieval
12. Sapienta[2] vīnō obumbrātur.[7] — Pliny, the Elder (adapted)
13. In vīnō vēritās.[8] — Plutarch (translation)
14. Hominēs, dum docent, discunt. — Seneca
15. Sī valēs bene est, ego quoque valeō.[9] — from Roman Letters

Notā bene

1. *spīrō, spīrāre:* "breathe." What is a similar English saying?
2. *amīcitia:* state of being an *amīcus;* similarly, *sapientia:* quality possessed by someone who is *sapiēns*
3. *tractō -āre:* "treat"
4. *amphora:* a pottery jar for wine, oil, or water
5. *serēnus -a -um:* cf. derivative

6. *laudis:* genitive case of *laus:* "of (for) praise"
7. *obumbrō -āre:* "overshadow," "obscure"
8. Frequently the verb *est* is omitted in brief remarks such as this.
9. This opening phrase of Roman letters was so common that it was often abbreviated S V B E E Q V

V   WORD STUDY

1. Give the Latin source of each of these derivatives, noting familiar prefixes and suffixes also. Show how the English word is related in meaning to the Latin source: enumerate, vehicle, remuneration, annihilate, docile, mutation, aural, commute, subtrahend, disciple, science, medium, vilify.

2. There are many derivatives from *dūcō, dūcere:* e.g., "induce," "reduce." Give at least three other English derivatives, using familiar prefixes and the stem form "-duce."

3. How are these derivatives related in meaning to *valeō, valēre:* valid, value, prevail, equivalent?

4. From the verb *cernere* come a number of interesting words: discern, discreet, secret, and secrete. Check with a good dictionary to see how words of such varied meanings come from one basic stem.

5. There are some prefixes found in Latin and English which are not similar to prepositions; they are called inseparable prefixes. Among them are:

   re-, back, again   *dis-*, apart from, differently, not
   se-, apart from, away from   *in-*, not

6. Degrees from colleges are awarded to high ranking students as *magnā cum laude* or *cum laude.*

VI VOCABULARY

Nouns	*Adjectives*	*Verbs*
amīcitia, amīcitiā f.	medius, media, medium	mūtō, mūtāre
asinus, asinō m.	vīlis, vīle	numerō, numerāre
exemplum, exemplō n.		spērō, spērāre
	Function Words	doceō, docēre
amor, amōre m.	aut	valeō, valēre
auris, aure f.	nisī	
laus, laude f.		cernō, cernere
vulpēs, vulpe f.	quoque	discō, discere
		dūcō, dūcere
mūnus, mūnere n.		trahō, trahere
nihil, nihilō n.		vehō, vehere
(lacks most other forms)		
		nesciō, nescīre
		sciō, scīre

VII FORM CHART

A. Personal Pronouns

	First Person			Second Person	
	Singular	Plural		Singular	Plural
Nom.	ego	nōs		tū	vōs
Acc.	mē	nōs		tē	vōs
Abl.	mē	nōbīs		tē	vōbīs

There is no proper third person pronoun. Forms of such words as *is* are used at times.

	Singular			Plural		
	M.	F.	N.	M.	F.	N.
Nom.	is	ea	id	eī	eae	ea
Acc.	eum	eam	id	eōs	eās	ea
Abl.	eō	eā	eō	eīs	eīs	eīs

B. Verbs: present tense passive

I *portō, portāre*

portor	portāmur
portāris	portāminī
portātur	portantur

II *habeō, habēre*

habeor	habēmur
habēris	habēminī
habētur	habentur

III *agō, agere*

agor	agimur
ageris	agiminī
agitur	aguntur

III-1 *capiō, capere*

capior	capimur
caperis	capiminī
capitur	capiuntur

IV *audiō, audīre*

audior	audīmur
audīris	audīminī
audītur	audiuntur

LESSON THIRTEEN

Praeterita mūtāre nōn possumus. — Cicero   "We cannot change the past."

Potest ex casā magnus vir exīre. —Seneca   "A great man can come from a humble home.'

Purpose: to learn the complementary infinitive, possum, and volō

I   VIĀTŌRĒS

1. **Quī** adsunt?	Asinus, fēmina, agricola, viātōrēs adsunt.
2. Ubi fēmina est?	In asinō fēmina est; in asinō vehitur.
3. Quālis est fēmina?	Fessa et senex est fēmina.
4. Quis barbam gerit?	Agricola barbam gerit.
5. Quō īnstrūmentō omnēs virī prōcēdunt?	Pedibus prōcēdunt omnēs.
6. Unde viātōrēs veniunt?	Dē montibus viātōrēs veniunt; dēscendunt.
7. Quō accēdunt viātōrēs?	Ad urbem accēdunt.
8. Quot viātōrēs adsunt?	Trēs viātōrēs adsunt.
9. Quid agit agricola?	Asinum dūcit agricola.

106

10. Quī ab urbe prōcēdunt?   Asinus, fēmina, agricola ab urbe prōcēdunt; viam ascendunt.

11. Quōcum prōcēdit agricola?   Cum fēminā in asinō prōcēdit agricola.

12. Quō prōcēdit agricola?   Ad montēs prōcēdit.

13. Quid fēmina gerit?   Vestem longam gerit.

14. Quem asinus vehit?   Fēminam fessam asinus vehit.

II   PATTERN READING

A.   Sample sentences

1. Servus pecūniam cupit.   The slave wants money.
   Servus pecūniam habēre cupit.   The slave wants to have the money.
   Servus pecūniam solvī cupit.   The slave wants the money to be paid.

2. Homō pecūniam accipī vult.   The person wishes the money to be taken.
   Hominēs labōrāre volunt.   Men are willing to work.

3. Pecūniam dēbēs.   You owe money.
   Pecūniam solvere dēbēs.   You ought to pay the money.

4. Spectāre possum tēcum.   I can watch with you.
   Spectārī possumus vōbiscum.   We can be watched with you-all.

5. Vidērī nōn possunt.   They can't be seen.
   Audīrī nōn potes.   You cannot be heard.

B.   Practice sentences

1. Auctor opus laudat.   Quid auctor cupit?   Auctor opus laudāre cupit.
2. Amīcī numerantur.   Quid amīcī cupiunt?   Amīcī numerārī cupiunt.
3. Ad urbem accēdimus.   Quid cupimus?   Ad urbem accēdere cupimus.

4. Ab amīcīs videor.   Quid cupiō?   Ab amīcīs vidērī cupiō.
5. Pater fortis est.   Quid pater vult?   Pater fortis esse vult.
6. Patrēs fortēs sunt.   Quid patrēs volunt?   Patrēs fortēs esse volunt.

7. Ab amīcīs audior.   Quid volō?   Ab amīcīs audīrī volō.
8. Ab amīcīs audīris.   Quid vīs?   Ab amīcīs audīrī vīs.
9. Ab amīcīs audīmur.   Quid volumus?   Ab amīcīs audīrī volumus.

10. Vestis virum facit.   Quid vestis potest?   Vestis virum facere potest.
11. Perīculum vincitur.   Quid perīculum potest?   Perīculum vincī potest.
12. Certa mittuntur.   Quid certa possunt?   Certa mittī possunt.

13. Perīculum saepe vincō.   Quid possum?   Perīculum saepe vincere possum.
14. Servī ad mēnsam prōcēdunt.   Quid servī possunt?   Servī ad mēnsam prōcēdere possunt.
15. Vincit vēritās.   Quid vēritās agere dēbet?   Vincere vēritās dēbet.

16. Pecūnia solvitur.   Quid agī dēbet?   Pecūnia solvī dēbet.
17. Certa petimus.   Quid agere dēbēmus?   Certa petere dēbēmus.
18. Multa discis.   Quid agere dēbēs?   Multa discere dēbēs.

C.   Questions on structure

1. What forms pattern with *possum, dēbeō, volō*?
2. How is the present passive infinitive formed in each conjugation?
3. What final letter do all present passive infinitives have in common?
4. How are the forms of *possum* related to those of *sum*?
5. Which forms of *volō* are irregular?

See Form Chart, page 111-12, and Appendix B, page 184, in Part II.

III   EXERCISES

A.   Answer the question in the person and number of the verb that is asked by the noun or pronoun.

1. Quis honestus est?   Ego.   Nōs.   Tū.   Vōs.   Amīcus.   Amīcī.
2. Quis virtūtem spērat?   Ego.   Nōs.   Tū.   Vōs.   Philosophus.   Philosophī.
3. Quis vincī potest?   Hostēs.   Vōs.   Nōs.   Hostis.   Tū.   Ego.
4. Quis fortiter vīvere vult?   Ego.   Vir.   Tū.   Nōs.   Virī.   Vōs.
5. Quis cōnsilium capī cupit? Gladiātor.   Gladiātōrēs.   Nōs.   Vōs.   Ego.   Tū.

B.   Supply the proper form of an infinitive, choosing verbs from the list:

accipiō	currō	habeō	maneō	teneō	vincō
amō	dēlectō	laudō	mittō	vertō	vīvō
capiō	fugiō	legō	pūgnō	videō	vocō

1. Mūnus mīles _____ e dēbet.
2. Gladiō vir perīculum _____ e vult.
3. Lupus mentem ad agnum _____ e potest.
4. In aedificiō patrēs _____ e volunt.
5. Vulpēs celeriter _____ e potest.

6. Fortiter _____ e dēbētis.
7. Fābulā fīlius _____ ī cupit.
8. _____ ī cupiō.
9. Ā rēge servī _____ ī volunt.
10. Imitātiō saepe _____ ī potest.

C.   Change the verb of the sentence to a complementary infinitive, completing the new verb indicated. Keep the subject now used (this will determine the form of *cupiō, dēbeō*, etc.) and the voice (this will determine whether the infinitive is active or passive). Cf. Practice sentences, page 107.

(Example: *cupiō*   Vir pecūniam habet.   *Vir pecūniam habēre cupit.*
          dēbeō   Nōn laudāminī.   *Laudārī nōn dēbētis.*   )

cupiō   *volō*

1. Gladiātor cōnsilium capit.   5. Philosophus sapienter vīvit.
2. Rēgēs laudem accipiunt.   6. Spem quaerimus.
3. Ab amīcīs nōn laudor.   7. Cōnspiciminī nōbīscum.
4. Adjuvāmur vōbīscum.   8. In rē incertā cernor.

dēbeō

9. Manus manum lavat.
10. Verba scīs.
11. Mūrī mūniuntur.
12. Sententiam auribus vestrīs audītis.

possum

13. Philosophum nōn facit barba.
14. Bene docēmur.
15. Praeterita nōn mūtāmus.
16. Ē casīs magnī virī veniunt.

D. Give the Latin equivalent.

1. We are taught by difficult situations.
2. I form a plan on the road.
3. You-all are avoided by the fox.
4. I am drawn by good example.
5. A great gift is sought by the king.
6. We are being hit with stones.
7. You-all are transported on donkeys.
8. If you are well, I am happy.
9. We are being destroyed by our enemies.
10. All things are conquered by love and courage.

IV   PATTERN PRACTICE TWELVE

1. I am telling a good story. Fābulam bonam nārrō.
2. I want to tell a story. Fābulam nārrāre cupiō.
3. I ought to tell a story. Fābulam nārrāre dēbeō.
4. I can tell a story. Fābulam nārrāre possum.

5. The man is pleased by the story. Fābulā homō dēlectātur.
6. The man can be pleased by the story. Fābulā homō dēlectārī potest.
7. The man ought to be pleased by the story. Fābulā homō dēlectārī dēbet.
8. The man is willing to be pleased by the story. Fābulā homō dēlectārī vult.

9. You are moved by my words. Verbīs meīs movēris.
10. You ought to be moved by the words. Verbīs movērī dēbēs.
11. You wish to be moved by words. Verbīs movērī vīs.
12. You can be moved by words. Verbīs movērī potes.

13. You-all hear my words. Verba mea audītis.
14. You-all can hear the words. Verba audīre potestis.
15. You-all want to hear the words. Verba audīre cupitis.
16. You-all ought to hear the words. Verba audīre dēbētis.

17. Examples should attract. Exempla trahere dēbent.
18. Examples can attract. Exempla trahere possunt.
19. We ought to be led by examples. Exemplīs trahī dēbēmus.
20. We can be led by examples. Exemplīs trahī possumus.
21. We are willing to be led by examples. Exemplīs trahī volumus.

22. We often seek risks. Saepe incerta petimus.
23. We want to seek risks. Incerta petere cupimus.
24. We can seek risks. Incerta petere possumus.

25. Many are counted as friends. Multī numerantur amīcī.
26. Many ought to be counted as friends. Multī numerārī dēbent amīcī.
27. Many can be counted as friends. Multī numerārī possunt amīcī.
28. Many wish to be counted as friends. Multī numerārī volunt amīcī.

V   DĒ PARVŌ ASINŌ

Fābulam nārrāre cupiō nōtam.

Senex, nōmine Titus et fīlius, nōmine Decimus, parvō cum asinō in viā prōcēdunt. Mox duae puellae eōs cōnspiciunt. Ūna, "Quam stultī," inquit, "sunt hominēs! Ecce! Habent asinum, sed pedibus prōcēdunt, nōn in animālī vehuntur. Trēs asinī, nōn ūnus, prōcēdunt!"

Titus, quandō eam audit, fīlium jubet in asinum ascendere et prōcēdunt, fīlius in asinō, pedibus pater.

Deinde eōs vident trēs senēs. Ūnus prō omnibus, "Quam¹ mōrēs mūtantur!" inquit. "Ubi est pīetās in patrēs?"

Dolōre afficitur Decimus, et patrem in asinum ascendere cōgit. Fīlius dēscendit, prōcēditque pedibus.

Dūcit deinde eōs via ad flūmen, ubi fēminae sub arboribus sedent. Accūsant fēminae duae ūnā vōce patrem, quod parvum fīlium tantum labōrem sustinēre cōgit.

Titus vult facere id quod² omnēs probant. "Tū mēcum in asinō sedēre dēbēs." Eīs verbīs fīlium ascendere in asinum cōgit.

Mox autem viātor dē montibus venit quī³ murmurat.⁴ "Asinus tam parvus est. Cūr in asinō vehiminī? Hominēs estis fortēs et ambulāre potestis. Etiam animal portāre potestis!"

Verbīs afficiuntur et Titus et Decimus. Ambo⁵ dēscendunt et parvum animal portant duo⁵ hominēs. Omnēs in viā rīdent quod hominēs tam stultī sunt. Tandem pater, "Nihil," inquit, "facere possumus quod ab omnibus probātur. Nunc id facimus quod² nōs probāmus."

Asinum igitur dēpōnunt⁶ et omnēs magnō cum gaudiō pedibus prōcēdunt.

Notā bene

1. *quam*: "how"
2. *id quod*: "that which," "what"
3. *quī*: "who"
4. *murmurat*: the sound says the meaning of the word
5. *ambo, duo*: have irregular forms
6. *dē + pōnō*: *dē*, "down" + *pōnō*

Respondē Latīnē

1. Quālis est fābula?
2. Quī in viā prōcēdunt?
3. Quī sunt trēs asinī?
4. Quid putat puella?
5. Quid agunt pater et fīlius?
6. Quid putant senēs dē fīliō?
7. Quid deinde agitur?
8. Ubi sunt fēminae?
9. Quid eae putant?
10. Quid agunt et Titus et Decimus?
11. Quid putat viātor?
12. Quid portant hominēs?
13. Cūr omnēs in viā rīdent?
14. Quid tandem agunt? Quō modō?
15. Quid pater putat?

VI OPTIONAL READING

Nēmō . . . . omnia potest scīre. — Varro
Labōrāre est ōrāre. — Motto (Benedictine monks)
Effugere nōn potes necessitātēs, potes vincere. — Seneca
O tempora! O mōrēs! — Cicero
Deus vult! — Battle cry of the First Crusade

VII WORD STUDY

1. There are several words in this vocabulary which come into English minus the Latin ending or with final "e" added. List at least five of them.

2. What does the "debit" side of an account book list? What other English word comes from the same source with slightly different spelling?

3. Show the Latin source and meaning of: mutation, accede, cogent, posse, voluntary, piety, annihilate, probation, sustain, notable.

4. Your customs are your "mores." Your "morals" are your customary forms of behavior.

5. *Sub* appears as a prefix in *sus + tineō*. Make a list of ten words in English using other assimilated forms of this prefix: sub-, suc-, sus-, suf-, sug-, sup-, sur-.

VIII VOCABULARY

Nouns	*Verbs*	*Irregular*
mōs, mōre m.	accūsō, accūsāre	aiō (defective): lacks many
pīetās, pīetāte f.	probō, probāre	forms
Decimus, Decimō m.	dēbeō, dēbēre	possum, posse
Titus, Titō m.	jubeō, jubēre	volō, velle
	sustineō, sustinēre	
Adjectives	accēdō, accēdere	*Function Words*
fessus, fessa, fessum	ascendō, ascendere	autem
nōtus, nōta, nōtum	cōgō, cōgere	mox
praeteritus, praeterita, praeteritum	dēpōnō, dēpōnere	quam
tantus, tanta, tantum	dēscendō, dēscendere	tam

IX FORM CHART

A. Present infinitives, active and passive

I	conjugation	portāre	portārī
II	conjugation	vidēre	vidērī
III	conjugation	agere	agī
III-i	conjugation	accipere	accipī
IV	conjugation	audīre	audīrī

B. Present tense of two irregular verbs

possum, posse		*volō, velle*	
possum	possumus	volō	volumus
potes	potestis	vīs	vultis
potest	possunt	vult	volunt

VERB REVIEW LIST

Classified by conjugations

I

accūsō, accūsāre
adjuvō, adjuvāre
ambulō, ambulāre
amō, amāre
appellō, appellāre

clāmō, clāmāre
dēlectō, dēlectāre
labōrō, labōrāre
laudō, laudāre
lavō, lavāre

mūtō, mūtāre
nārrō, nārrāre
natō, natāre
numerō, numerāre
portō, portāre

probō, probāre
pūgnō, pūgnāre
pulsō, pulsāre
putō, putāre
rogō, rogāre

spectō, spectāre
spērō, spērāre
stō, stāre
vocō, vocāre
vulnerō, vulnerāre

II

dēbeō, dēbēre
doceō, docēre
habeō, habēre
jubeō, jubēre
maneō, manēre

II (cont'd)

moneō, monēre
moveō, movēre
rīdeō, rīdēre
sedeō, sedēre
sustineō, sustinēre

teneō, tenēre
terreō, terrēre
timeō, timēre
valeō, valēre
videō, vidēre

III

accēdō, accēdere
agō, agere
ascendō, ascendere
bibō, bibere
cernō, cernere

cōgō, cōgere
currō, currere
dēscendō, dēscendere
dīcō, dīcere
discō, discere

dūcō, dūcere
fluō, fluere
gerō, gerere
legō, legere
mittō, mittere

occīdō, occīdere
pellō, pellere
petō, petere
pōnō, pōnere
dēpōnō, dēpōnere
prōcēdō, prōcēdere

III (cont'd)

quaerō, quaerere
relinquō, relinquere
scrībō, scrībere
solvō, solvere
surgō, surgere

trahō, trahere
vehō, vehere
vertō, vertere
vincō, vincere
vīvō, vīvere
volvō, volvere

III (i)

accipiō, accipere
afficiō, afficere
capiō, capere
cōnspiciō, cōnspicere
cupiō, cupere

faciō, facere
fodiō, fodere
fugiō, fugere
jaciō, jacere

IV

audiō, audīre
mūniō, mūnīre
nesciō, nescīre
sciō, scīre
veniō, venīre

Irregular

aiō (defective)
inquam
sum, esse
absum, abesse
adsum, adesse
possum, posse
volō, velle

THIRD REVIEW

Saepe malum petitur, saepe bonum fugitur.
— Anon.

"Often the evil is sought after, often the good is avoided."

Stultī timent fortūnam, sapientēs ferunt.
— Publilius Syrus

"The stupid fear luck, the wise endure it."

Est certum praesēns, sed sunt incerta futūra.
— Medieval

"The present is certain, things to come are uncertain."

I   VOCABULARY, MODEL SENTENCE, AND STORY REVIEW

A.   Review and learn accurately the classification by conjugation of all verbs studied so far. They are listed on the opposite page.

B.   Rewrite quotations as follows:

1. Rewrite three sentences on page 104 changing the person of the verb.
2. Rewrite two other sentences on page 104 changing from active to passive or passive to active.
3. Rewrite the three model sentences of this review, making substitutions for two words in each.

C.   With or without the help of a tape recording, practice reading one story (page 92, page 99, or page 110) aloud so you can read it fluently, with correct grouping of words into meaningful phrases.

II   STRUCTURE REVIEW

1. List the personal endings for the present tense active; for the present tense passive. (These endings are used repeatedly for other tenses also.)

2. What is the characteristic vowel or vowel pattern of verbs of each conjugation? What is the one exception to the general rule that the vowel pattern is the same for active and passive forms?

3. What is the ending of present infinitives active? What are the two possible endings for the present infinitive passive?

4. List the verbs you have studied which can be completed by the infinitive.

III   FORM REVIEW

A.   Change the sentence from active to passive, expressing the same idea.

1. Stultī semper timent fortūnam.
2. Omnia verba mē afficiunt.
3. Fēminae tē accūsant in viā.
4. Agrōs vestrōs pālīs foditis.
5. Parvum animal nōs hominēs vehit.
6. In nūllā rē vōs probant viātōrēs.
7. Tē in asinum ascendere cōgit pater.
8. Oculōs volvō et corpus videō.
9. Mē jubet pater per montēs prōcēdere.
10. Futūra incerta mē terrent.

B.   Change these sentences from passive to active form, expressing the same idea.

1. Īnfāns ā patre relinquitur.
2. Ā fēminīs viātōrēs cōnspiciuntur.
3. Auribus oculīsque multa ā nōbīs discuntur.
4. Eō diē grātiae ab omnibus in tabernā aguntur.
5. Amor ā vōbīs semper quaeritur.

6. Praesentia certa ā nōbīs mittuntur.
7. Laus incerta ā tē petitur.
8. Saepe trahimur exemplīs bonīs.
9. Mūneribus pulchrīs numquam capior.
10. Ā mē sōlō magna pecūnia nōn solvitur.

C.   Give three cases, singular and plural, of:

animus levis	lingua facilis	tempus praeteritum
auris tūta	magnum ōs	mōs noster

D.   Turn to the story of the donkey, page 110, and pick out these items:

1. five noun-adjective combinations
2. three predicate adjectives
3. two substantive uses of adjectives

Explain the form of the adjective in each example.

E.   Give the Latin equivalent.

1. The loyal father ought to go to the king quickly.
2. Soldiers cannot remain with us.
3. Rufus is not coming into the little cottage.
4. The baby is helped by the faithful dog.
5. We are saddened (affected with sadness) by the story.

6. I can walk with you; I do not want to be transported by a tired animal.
7. You-all are ordered to go to the town again.
8. Are you being blamed about the matter?
9. Can we change the past or the future?
10. The men are compelled to carry the donkey.
11. I hope (for) good fortune; I wish to avoid evil.

IV   WORD STUDY REVIEW

A.   Give three English words, each using a different assimilated form of the prefix *ad-*; three more, each using a different form of *con-*; two others, each using a form of *in-*; two, each using a form of *sub-*.

B.   List all preposition prefixes you have studied up to this time; list also the inseparable prefixes you have studied.   Using this list and the verbs on page 112, see how many derivatives you can find containing these prefixes.

V   OPTIONAL READING

Vēritās numquam perit.   — Seneca

Nihil sub sōle novum.   — Ecclesiastices

Ignis aurum probat, miseria fortēs virōs.   — Seneca

Oculī sunt in amōre ducēs.   — Propertius

Nēmō in amōre videt.   — Propertius

Caecī ducem quaerunt; nōs sine duce errāmus.   — Seneca

Fēlēs amat piscēs sed aquās intrāre recūsat.   — Medieval

Difficile est trīstī fingere mente jocum.   — Tibullus

Humilis nec altē cadere nec graviter potest.   — Publilius Syrus

Nōn ministrārī sed ministrāre — N. T. (used as motto of Wellesley College)

Common phrases

inter nōs   terra firma

i.e. (id est)

VI   VOCABULARY

Adjectives	*Verb*
futūrus, futūra, futūrum	timeō, timēre
praesēns (praesentī)	

LESSON FOURTEEN

Rēs est magna tacēre. — Anon.

"It is an important thing to know when to be silent."

Purpose: to read an adaptation of a well-known fable

Optional work: imperative and vocative

I   CORVUS

fenestra   penna

cibus   carō   ōs   corvus

1. Quis in fenestrā stat?   Corvus in fenestrā stat.
2. Quid rapit corvus?   Cibum rapit corvus.
3. Ā quō cibus rapitur?   Ā corvō cibus rapitur.
4. Quid cibus est?   Carō est.
5. Unde carnem corvus rapit?   Dē fenestrā carnem rapit.

116

6. Num¹ vidētis multās fenestrās?   Nōn multās fenestrās sed ūnam tantum
                                        fenestram vidēmus.

7. Quot pedēs habet corvus?   Duōs pedēs habet.

8. Quot ōra habet corvus?   Ūnum ōs habet.

9. Quot pennās habet corvus?   Multās pennās habet.

II   CORVUS ET VULPĒS

corvus

rāmus

arbor

vulpēs

1. Quō corvus carnem fert?²
   Altam in arborem carnem fert.

2. Quō modō carnem fert?
   Cum celeritāte carnem fert.

3. Quō īnstrūmentō carnem fert?
   Ōre carnem fert.

4. Ubi sedet corvus?
   In rāmō sedet.

5. Cūr in rāmō sedet?
   Quod cibum cōnficere cupit.

6. Quālēs pennās corvus habet?
   Pulchrās pennās habet.

7. Potestne canere corvus?   Canere nōn potest.

8. Cūr canere nōn potest?   Quod vōcem dulcem nōn habet.

9. Num potest vulpēs canere?   Neque vulpēs neque corvus canere potest.

10. Habetne vulpēs multōs dentēs?   Itā, multī et avidī dentēs in ōre sunt.

11. Ostenditne vulpēs dentēs?   Dentēs vidēre nōn possumus.

¹ *Num* is used when a negative answer is expected.
² See page **119** for forms of *ferō*.

III   DĒ VULPE ET CORVŌ

Dē fenestrā cibum rapit corvus. Quod cibum cōnficere cupit, carnem in arborem fert,[1] altō sedet in rāmō. Vulpēs eum videt; deinde sīc magnā vōce incipit:

"Quam pulchrae, corve,[2] sunt tuae pennae! Et quam pulchram etiam est ōs! Tē vērō maximē amō. Ei![3] Num vōcem pulchram et dulcem habēs? Ego miser sum quod tū canere nōn potes. Cūr vōcem dulcem nōn habēs?"

At corvus stultus, quod vult vōcem ostendere, mittit ex ōre cibum quem[4] cum celeritāte avidīs rapit dentibus perfida vulpēs. Profert corvus carmen; carnem vulpēs aufert.

Sī cupis quoque verbīs perfidīs laudārī, accipe[5] tālem[6] fortūnam tuam.

Notā bene

1. forms of the irregular verb *ferō* appear on the next page. They should be learned. Many compounds of this verb, with its general meaning of "carry" "bear" are found. *proferō*: "bring forth," and *auferō*: "take away."

2. *corve*: vocative form, see page 120 (addressing a person or personified creature)
3. *Ei*! exclamation of sorrow or dismay
4. *quem*: (acc. of *quī*, "who") "whom"
5. For imperative forms, see page 120.
6. *tālem . . . tuam*: "such" (as is related here) . . . "as yours"

Respondē Latīnē

1. Unde corvus cibum rapit?
2. Quō corvus carnem fert?
3. Cūr altō sedet in rāmō?
4. Quō modō vulpēs incipit?
5. Dē ōre quid ait vulpēs?
6. Habetne vōcem pulchram corvus?
7. Estne vulpēs miser?

8. Cūr corvus ex ōre cibum mittit?
9. Quid agit perfida vulpēs?
10. Nōnne[1] est corvus stultus?
11. Cūr corvus stultus est?
12. Cūr vulpēs perfida est?
13. Sī verbīs perfidīs laudāris, quid accipere dēbēs?
14. Cūr est magna rēs tacēre?

---

[1] *Nōnne* is used when an affirmative answer is expected.

IV WORD STUDY

1. *Carmen* became the name of a singer as well as the word for a song or poem; from this came the title of an opera "Carmen."

2. From what Latin word is "pen" derived? Explain the connection.

3. What do "carnivorous" animals eat? What is an "incipient" infection? What quality is meant by "perfidy"? What are the "ramifications" of an idea? What kind of agreement is "tacit"?

4. There are many English derivatives from *ferō, ferre*: for example, infer (inferred), inference; interfere, etc. Give fifteen other examples.

5. Give English derivatives from: dēns, altus, avidus, miser, minimē.

V VOCABULARY

Nouns

fenestra, fenestrā f.
penna, pennā f.

cibus, cibō m.
corvus, corvō m.
rāmus, rāmō m.

carō, carne f.
celeritās, celeritāte f.
dēns, dente m.

carmen, carmine n.

Adjectives

altus, alta, altum
avidus, avida, avidum
miser, misera, miserum
perfidus, perfida, perfidum

dulcis, dulce
tālis, tāle

Verbs

taceō, tacēre

canō, canere
ostendō, ostendere

cōnficiō, cōnficere
incipiō, incipere
rapiō, rapere

ferō, ferre

Function Words

minimē
sīc
tantum
vērō

at
neque (nec) . . .
      neque (nec)

nōnne (?)
num (?)

VI FORM CHART

A. Present tense of *ferō, ferre*

Active		Passive	
ferō	ferimus	feror	ferimur
fers	fertis	ferris	feriminī
fert	ferunt	fertur	feruntur

B. Imperative forms (optional work)

The simple base of the verb is used in giving a command to one person, *-te* is added to give the command to more than one.

I	(portāre)	portā	portāte
II	(sedēre)	sedē	sedēte
III	(mittere)	mitte	mittite
III-i	(capere)	cape	capite
IV	(audīre)	audī	audīte

C. Vocative Case forms (optional work)

The form of nouns used in addressing a person is like the nominative except in the II declension singular: *amīcus > amīce; Lūcius > Lūcī;* etc.

LESSON FIFTEEN

Vēnī, vīdī, vīcī. — Caesar (quoted by Suetonius)

"I came, I saw, I conquered."

Prīmus in orbe deōs fēcit timor. — Statius

"Fear first created gods in the world."

Purpose: to learn the perfect tense active

I   RĀNAE IN AQUĀ

1.	Quae animālia in pictūrā sunt?	Animālia sunt rānae.
2.	Ubi sunt rānae?	Aut in aquā aut in terrā sunt rānae. In aquā lātā et in terrā habitant.
3.	Quid agunt rānae?	Et nātant et saliunt. Clāmōrem magnum etiam faciunt. Silentium nōn est.
4.	Ubi sedent?	In foliīs sedent.
5.	Num habent rānae rēgem?	Neque habent neque petunt. Animālia lībera sunt.
6.	Timentne rānae eō tempore?	Nōn timent. Laetae sunt. Timor eās nōn tenet.
7.	Quandō timent rānae?	Quandō hominēs magnum sonum faciunt.
8.	Quid agunt?	Sub aquā manent.
9.	Possuntne cōnspicī?	Nōn jam cōnspicī possunt.

II PATTERN READING

A.   Sample sentences

1. Verba nunc scrībō;   I am writing the words now;
   verba tunc scrīpsī.   I wrote the words then.
2. Verba scrībis;   You write words;
   verba scrīpsistī.   you wrote words.
3. Nunc verba scrībit;   He is now writing the words;
   tunc verba scrīpsit.   He wrote the words then.

4. Verba scrībimus;   We are writing words;
   verba scrīpsimus.   we wrote words.
5. Verba scrībitis;   You-all write words;
   verba scrīpsistis.   you-all wrote words.
6. Verba scrībunt;   They write words;
   verba scrīpsērunt.   they wrote words (they have written).

B.   In this reading the present and perfect tense of each verb are paired. In each group the perfect is formed in a different way. Note how the perfect is formed in each group and give the meanings.

1(a)
spectat/spectāvit
natat/natāvit

cupit/cupīvit
petit/petīvit

2(b)
videt/vīdit
movet/mōvit
vincit/vīcit
relinquit/relīquit

1(b)
dēbet/dēbuit
habet/habuit
tenet/tenuit
terret/terruit

3(a)
accēdit/accessit
prōcēdit/prōcessit
gerit/gessit
jubet/jussit

mittit/mīsit
scrībit/scrīpsit
rīdet/rīsit

2(a)
agit/ēgit
capit/cēpit
facit/fēcit

accipit/accēpit
afficit/affēcit

sedet/sēdit
venit/vēnit

3(b)
dīcit/dīxit
dūcit/dūxit
vehit/vēxit

4
currit/cucurrit
pellit/pepulit

5
solvit/solvit
vertit/vertit
respondet/respondit

6 (irregular)
fert/tulit
est/fuit

C.   Be able to answer the question with the correct pronoun to identify the person of the verb. (This may be an oral, taped practice.)

1. Diēs numerāvī.   Quis numerāvit?   Ego diēs numerāvī.
   Diēs numerāvistī.   Quis numerāvit?   Tū diēs numerāvistī.
   Diēs numerāvit.   Quis numerāvit?   Is diēs numerāvit.
   Diēs numerāvimus.   Quis numerāvit?   Nōs diēs numerāvimus.
   Diēs numerāvistis.   Quis numerāvit?   Vōs diēs numerāvistis.
   Diēs numerāvērunt.   Quis numerāvit?   Eī diēs numerāvērunt.

2. Tunc fortūnam timuī.   Quis timuit?   Ego tunc fortūnam timuī.
   Tunc fortūnam timuimus.   Quis timuit?   Nōs tunc fortūnam timuimus.
   Tunc fortūnam timuistī.   Quis timuit?   Tū tunc fortūnam timuistī.
   Tunc fortūnam timuistis.   Quis timuit?   Vōs tunc fortūnam timuistis.
   Tunc fortūnam timuit.   Quis timuit?   Is tunc fortūnam timuit.
   Tunc fortūnam timuērunt.   Quis timuit?   Eī tunc fortūnam timuērunt.

3. Sine timōre vīximus.   Quis vīxit?   Nōs sine timōre vīximus.
   Sine timōre vīxī.   Quis vīxit?   Ego sine timōre vīxī.
   Sine timōre vīxērunt.   Quis vīxit?   Eī sine timōre vīxērunt.
   Sine timōre vīxit.   Quis vīxit?   Is sine timōre vīxit.
   Sine timōre vīxistis.   Quis vīxit?   Vōs sine timōre vīxistis.
   Sine timōre vīxistī.   Quis vīxit?   Tū sine timōre vīxistī.

4. Vēnī, vīdī, vīcī.   Quis vēnit, vīdit, vīcit?
                                   Ego vēnī, vīdī, vīcī.

   Vēnistī, vīdistī, vīcistī.   Quis vēnit, vīdit, vīcit?
                                   Tū vēnistī, vīdistī, vīcistī.

   Vēnimus, vīdimus, vīcimus. Quis vēnit, vīdit, vīcit?
                                   Nōs vēnimus, vīdimus, vīcimus.

   Vēnistis, vīdistis, vīcistis. Quis vēnit, vīdit, vīcit?
                                   Vōs vēnistis, vīdistis, vīcistis.

   Vēnit, vīdit, vīcit.   Quis vēnit, vīdit, vīcit?
                                   Caesar vēnit, vīdit, vīcit.

   Vēnērunt, vīdērunt, vīcērunt. Quis vēnit, vīdit, vīcit?
                                   Eī vēnērunt, vīdērunt, vīcērunt.

5. Cēpit tunc cōnsilium.   Quis cēpit?   Is cēpit tunc cōnsilium.
   Cēpistis tunc cōnsilium.   Quis cēpit?   Vōs cēpistis tunc cōnsilium.
   Cēpimus tunc cōnsilium.   Quis cēpit?   Nōs cēpimus tunc cōnsilium.
   Cēpistī tunc cōnsilium.   Quis cēpit?   Tū cēpistī tunc cōnsilium.
   Cēpērunt tunc cōnsilium.   Quis cēpit?   Eī cēpērunt tunc cōnsilium.
   Cēpī tunc cōnsilium.   Quis cēpit?   Ego cēpī tunc cōnsilium.

D.   Questions on structure

1. What endings are signals of the perfect tense (active) for verbs of all conjugations?
2. In what ways are these similar to the endings of the present tense?
3. Name six of the ways in which the stems of verbs may be changed in forming the base for the perfect tense.
4. Is there any set rule by which the shifts in the perfect stem can be predicted?
5. What patterns of stem change predominate in the first conjugation verbs? second? fourth?

Principal parts of all verbs you have studied are given on pages 134-35. The third part gives the perfect active stem for each verb. Consult this list until you have mastered these parts. Also see Appendix C in Part II under each conjugation.

III   EXERCISES

A.   Answer the question in the person indicated. (Do not use separate pronouns in your answer.)

1.   Quis in aquā tunc natāvit?   Ego. Tū. Rāna. Nōs. Vōs. Rānae.
2.   Quis in aquā nunc natat?   Ego. Tū. Rāna. Nōs. Vōs. Rānae.
3.   Quis in foliō sedet?   Rāna. Ego. Tū. Rānae. Nōs. Vōs.
4.   Quis celeriter cucurrit?   Tū. Egō. Juvenis. Vōs. Nōs. Juvenēs.
5.   Quis malum petīvit?   Homō. Tū. Ego. Hominēs. Vōs. Nōs.
6.   Quis certa mīsit?   Vōs. Puerī. Nōs. Tū. Ego. Puer.
7.   Quis cibum dēposuit?   Fēminae. Nōs. Vōs. Fēmina. Ego. Tū.
8.   Quis tumultum audīvit?   Ego. Nōs. Tū. Vōs. Senex. Senēs.
9.   Quis carnem rapit?   Corvus. Tū. Vōs. Corvī. Ego. Nōs.
10. Quis in agrō stetit?   Asinus. Asinī. Tū. Nōs. Vōs. Ego.

B.   Change each verb to the present tense in the same person and number.

1.   Philosophus barbam gessit.   6.   Tāle carmen cecinimus.
2.   Mīles hostem occīdit.   7.   Laborāvistis diū.
3.   Tantum labōrem sustinuistī.   8.   Hominēs ē casā prōcessērunt.
4.   Omnēs bene pūgnāvērunt.   9.   Inter arborēs sonum audīvī.
5.   Omnia relīquī tēcum.   10.   Cum labōre aedificium cōnfēcimus.

C.   Change each verb to the perfect tense in the same person and number.

1.   Vestis virum facit.   6.   Opus laudās.
2.   Tot diēs fugiunt.   7.   Manus manum lavat.
3.   Gladiātōrēs in harēnā cōnsilium   8.   Praeterita mūtāre nōn possumus.
     capiunt.   9.   Pulchrē, bene, rēctē scrībis.
4.   Amīcum certum in rē incertā cernō. 10.   Fortēs adjuvō fidēliter.
5.   Rem, nōn spem, quaeritis.

D.   Conjugate the verb in the entire perfect tense active.

1.   Nōmen clāmō.   4.   Agnōs dūcō.
2.   Fontem inveniō.   5.   Sapienter taceō.
3.   Piētātem ostendere cupiō.

E.   Give the Latin equivalent.

1.   A lamb never wants to be chased by a wolf.
2.   All eyes ought to be turned onto the books.
3.   You can hear many tongues (languages) in the city (of) Rome.
4.   No one ought to pound the table with his fist (hand).
5.   They ought never to throw stones at travelers.
6.   But I cannot be defeated by danger.
7.   Your brother wants to go up into the mountains in the winter with his son.
8.   Are you willing to fight? You (all) can wound your enemies with your swords.
9.   He makes (compels) the farmer (to) get up on the donkey.
10. The father orders his son to dig the field with a spade.

F.   Learn the third principal part of all the verbs used in this lesson. (Optional. It is possible to combine learning all four parts at one time.)

IV   PATTERN PRACTICE THIRTEEN

Change the verb from present to perfect. Be able to reverse the process also.

1.	Ad fenestram ambulō.	Ad fenestram ambulāvī.
2.	Pecūniam dēbēs.	Pecūniam dēbuistī.
3.	Nihil accipit.	Nihil accēpit.
4.	Pedibus prōcēdimus.	Pedibus prōcessimus.
5.	Oculōs habent.	Oculōs habuērunt.
6.	Grātiās agō.	Grātiās ēgī.
7.	Id scīs.	Id scīvistī.
8.	Rēgem dēlectat.	Rēgem dēlectāvit.
9.	Deōs facit timor.	Deōs fēcit timor.
10.	Ad oppidum venīmus.	Ad oppidum vēnimus.
11.	Fidēlēs estis.	Fidēlēs fuistis.
12.	Venīre nōn possunt.	Venīre nōn potuērunt.
13.	Per annōs manēmus.	Per annōs mānsimus.
14.	In flūmen currunt.	In flūmen cucurrērunt.
15.	Carnem portās.	Carnem portāvistī.
16.	Librōs legitis.	Librōs lēgistis.
17.	Multum dīcō.	Multum dīxī.
18.	Rīdēre volō.	Rīdēre voluī.
19.	Eōs tenētis.	Eōs tenuistis.
20.	Bellum gerit.	Bellum gessit.
21.	Ūnam hōram spectant.	Ūnam hōram spectāvērunt.
22.	Canēs pellimus.	Canēs pepulimus.
23.	Urbem relinquis.	Urbem relīquistī.
24.	Inter arborēs stō.	Inter arborēs stetī.
25.	Aquam petunt.	Aquam petīvērunt.
26.	Saxa jacitis.	Saxa jēcistis.

V   RĀNAE RĒGEM PETUNT

Rānae in lātīs aquīs habitāvērunt; līberae sed nōn laetae fuērunt. Magnō clāmōre ā Jove[1] petīvērunt rēgem.

"Rēx," inquiunt, "nostrōs animōs vī[2] retinēre potest."

Juppiter rīsit et rāmum in aquam jēcit, quī[3] magnō sonō rānās terruit. Eae in aquam saluērunt et sub foliīs nātāvērunt; rāmus diū in aquā mānsit. Tandem ūna ē rānīs silentiō

prōtulit[4] ex aquā caput, atque suum rēgem spectāvit. Deinde aliās rānās vocāvit. Omnēs

timōrem dēposuērunt et magnā cum celeritāte adnātāvērunt.[5] Deinde in rāmum ascendērunt.

Maximē īrātae autem erant[6] quod nūllum rēgem sed tantum habuērunt rāmum. Statim

maledīxērunt.[7] Ad Jovem igitur prōcessērunt et rēgem petīvērunt alium.

"Rēgem ad nōs mīsistī, sed is inūtilis est," inquiunt, "nisī nostrōs animōs retinēre potest

Eum dēpōnere et alium rēgem apud nōs habēre cupimus."

At mox ad rānās ingentem horribilemque mīsit deus serpentem quae[3] eās dente avidō

rapere incēpit singulās. Aquam relinquere cupīvērunt mīserae, sed frūstrā; vōcem etiam

timor tenuit. Tandem rānam fortem ad Jovem mīsērunt:

"Fer[8] auxilium!" petīvit rāna, "Ā rēge quem[3] mīsistī occīdimur. Rēgem nōn jam

apud nōs cupimus."

Respondit deus: "Quod nōluistis[9] fortūnam ferre bonam, nunc malam perferte."[10]

Notā bene

1. *Juppiter, Jovem, Jove*: chief Roman god, "Jupiter."
2. *vī*, abl. of noun *vīs*: "force," "power"
3. *quī, quae*, "who," "which"; *quem*: "whom," "which"
4. *prōtulit*: from *prōferō*
5. *adnātāvērunt*: *ad* + *nātō*
6. *erant*: "were"
7. *maledīxērunt*: *male* + *dīcō*; evil speaking involves such things as slandering or cursing.
8. *fer*: irregular imperative of *ferō*, "bring." (Used to a god, it indicates a desperate kind of plea.)
9. *nōlō, nōlle, nōluī* = *nōn* + *volō*
10. *perferte*: irregular plural imperative of *perferō*: "endure"

Respondē Latīnē

1. Quālēs sunt rānae?
2. Cūr rānae rēgem tunc petīvērunt?
3. Quid ēgit Juppiter?
4. Timuēruntne rānae rāmum?
5. Amāvēruntne rānae rāmum?
6. Quid deinde cūpivērunt? Cūr?
7. Quid mīsit Juppiter?
8. Timuēruntne rānae rēgem?
9. Cūr auxilium ā Jove petivērunt?
10. Quam diū rānae rēgem malum tūlerunt?
11. Fēcitne timor prīmōs rēgēs in orbe?

VI   OPTIONAL READING

Deus dedit. Deus abstulit. — Book of Job
Nēminem pecūnia dīvitem fēcit. — Seneca
Nōn ego sum stultus ut ante fuī. — Ovid
Ōtium et rēgēs . . . et beātās perdidit urbēs. — Catullus

After this lesson the supplementary story *Jūstā dē Causā*, Appendix A, page 185, may be
read.

VII   WORD STUDY

1. Notice the difference between the Latin spelling of *Juppiter* and the English spelling, "Jupiter."

2. From what Latin words do these derivatives come: deity, orbit, terrain, foliage, retain, irate?

3. There are only occasional examples of derivatives from Latin adverbs. What English word is based on *frūstrā*?

4. Give English derivatives from: silentium, timor, auxilium, clāmor, līber, habitō.

5. What words in this lesson come into English almost unchanged?

6. How does Latin *singulī* differ in meaning from English "singular"?

7. The abbreviation *et al.* (*et aliī*) means "and others."

8. To what Latin noun are "consonant" and "resonant" as well as "sound" related?

VIII   VOCABULARY

Nouns

rāna, rānā f.

deus, deō m.
sonus, sonō m.

auxilium, auxiliō n.
folium, foliō n.
silentium, silentiō n.

clāmor, clāmōre m.
Juppiter, Jove m.
orbis, orbe m.
timor, timōre m.

Adjectives

īrātus, īrāta, īrātum
līber, lībera, līberum
singulī, singulae, singula

horribilis, horribile
inūtilis, inūtile

Irregular

alius, alia, aliud

Verbs

habitō, habitāre, habitāvī,
    habitātus

retineō, retinēre, retinuī
    retentus

saliō, salīre, saluī, saltus

Function Words

diū
enim
frūstrā
jam, nōn jam
tunc

apud + acc.

LESSON SIXTEEN

Nihil est . . . simul et inventum et perfectum. "Nothing has been discovered and perfected
— Cicero at the same time."

Purpose: to learn the perfect tense passive

I VĪLLA RŌMĀNA

1. Estne in pictūrā aedificium ā
   parte sinistrā?

   Ā parte sinistrā aedificium est. Vīlla est.

2. Nōnne sunt arborēs ā parte
   dextrā?

   Ā parte dextrā sunt arborēs atque vīnea
   pulchra.

3. Unde senex in asinō vehitur?

   Ab urbe proximā vehitur.

4. Quid in urbe ēgit?

   Inter alia, magnam lucernam accēpit.

5. Ā quō lucerna portātur?

   Ā servō portātur.

6. Quandō lucerna accenditur?

   Nocte lucerna accenditur.

7. Habetne senex magnam pecūniam?

   Senex vītam rūsticam ēgit; sed labōre gravī
   dīves factus est et magnam pecūniam habet.

8. Dīvesne etiam juvenis est?

   Nōn dīves est; pauper est.

9. Quid agunt juvenēs?

   Juvenēs in vīneā fodiunt.

10. Ubi sunt fīnēs?

    Sunt procul ā vīllā post vīneam ad montēs.

11. Ubi sunt puellae?

    Sub arboribus sunt; in umbrā sedent.

12. Quālēs puellae sunt?

    Sunt pulchrae sed, nisī labōrant, pigrae sunt.

II PATTERN READING

A. Sample sentences

1.	Nihil dīcō; nihil ā mē dīcitur.	I say nothing; nothing is said on my part.
2.	Nihil dīxī; nihil ā mē dictum est.	I said nothing; nothing was said (has been said) on my part.
3.	Mīles captus est. Urbs capta est. Oppidum captum est.	The soldier was captured. A city was captured. A town was captured.
4.	Mātrēs amātae sunt. Patrēs amātī sunt. Exempla amāta sunt.	Their mothers were loved. Their fathers were loved. Their examples were admired.
5.	Tumultū nōn territus sum.	I was not frightened by the uproar.
6.	Ab hominibus spectātī estis.	You-all were watched by the people.

B. Practice sentences

1. Puer fortis est.
2. Puer fortis laudātus est.

3. Puella fēlīx est.
4. Puella fēlīx laudāta est.

5. Animal fidēle est.
6. Animal fidēle laudātum est.

7. Sunt multī mīlitēs.
8. Multī mīlitēs numerātī sunt.

9. Sunt pulchrae sorōrēs.
10. Sorōrēs pulchrae spectātae sunt.

11. Sunt multa carmina.
12. Multa carmina scrīpta sunt.

13. Soror clāmat, "Missa sum ad urbem."

14. Soror frātrem rogāvit, "Nōnne tū missus es?"

15. Animālia ingentia videntur.
16. Animālia ingentia vīsa sunt.

17. Nārrantur multae fābulae.
18. Nārrātae sunt multae fābulae.

19. Ā mātre docta sum, quod fīlia sum.
20. Ā patre doctus es quod fīlius es.

21. Ab juvenibus vōs puellae vocātae estis.
22. Ā puellīs vocātī sumus nōs juvenēs.

23. Magnās vōcēs audīvimus.
24. Ā nōbīs magnae vōcēs audītae sunt.

25. Puer malus magnum saxum jēcit.
26. Ā puerō malō magnum saxum jactum est.

27. Hominēs bona cōnsilia accēpērunt.
28. Bona cōnsilia ab hominibus accepta sunt.

29. Tunc rānās terruistis.
30. Ā vōbīs rānae tunc territae sunt.

C. Questions on structure

1. What two verb elements are combined to form the compound tense which is used as the perfect passive?
2. What endings may the first part (participle) of this form have?
3. What do these endings resemble?
4. What determines the choice of ending?
5. How is the person of the verb shown?
6. What are two fairly common patterns of ending for the fourth or perfect passive (participle) stem of the verb?

Use the chart of principal parts of verbs on page 134 until they have been learned thoroughly. Also see Appendix B, page 201.

III FORM CHART

Perfect Passive (sample verb)

captus (capta, captum) sum	captī (captae, capta) sumus
captus (capta, captum) es	captī (captae, capta) estis
captus (capta, captum) est	captī (captae, capta) sunt

A. Change the verb to the perfect tense.

1. Opus ab auctōre laudātur.
2. Imitātiō vēritāte vincitur.
3. Rēs, nōn spēs, quaeritur.
4. Certa mittuntur.
5. Multī numerantur amīcī.
6. Amīcus certus cernitur.
7. Fortēs adjuvantur.
8. Saepe bonum fugitur.
9. Rēs gladiō geritur.
10. Exemplīs trahimur.
11. Perīculō numquam vincor.
12. Nōs mūtāmur.
13. Nōn sine exemplō docēris.
14. Nōn capiminī mūneribus.
15. Mentēs ad studia vertuntur.

B. Change the sentence from active to passive, expressing the same idea.

1. Cibum rapuit corvus.
2. Carnem in arborem tulit.
3. Fābulam incēpit auctor.
4. Pennās laudāvit vulpēs.
5. Dentēs vulpēs ostendit.
6. Tē maximē amāvī.
7. Mē maximē amāvistī.
8. Omnēs nōs nōn probāvērunt.
9. Fēminae vōs accūsāvērunt.
10. Pater fīlium prōcēdere jussit.

C. Conjugate the verb.

1. Multum nescīvī.
2. In viā stetī.
3. Bene cecinī.
4. (Mīles) nōn victus sum.
5. (Fīlia) ā mātre amāta sum.
6. (Juvenis) ab amīcīs acceptus sum.
7. (Fēmina) dolōre mōta sum.

D. Give the Latin equivalent.

1. The water flowed again in summer.
2. We ran swiftly into the forest.
3. You-all lived in such a great city.
4. She soon began to show off her voice.
5. Then they could not hear the story.
6. The greedy fox has taken the food.
7. You have always counted many friends.
8. The slave put the food on the table.
9. I led the soldiers into the city today.
10. Men often wished silence.

E. Learn the principal parts of all verbs used in this lesson and Lesson 15. An optional practice is given with the Fourth Review. It may now be used in part.

IV   PATTERN PRACTICE FOURTEEN

Change the verb from present to perfect tense. Be able to reverse the process also.

1.	Puellam vocat.	Puellam vocāvit.
2.	Puella vocātur.	Puella vocāta est.
3.	Saxa movet.	Saxa mōvit.
4.	Saxa moventur.	Saxa mōta sunt.
5.	Mūrus mūnītur.	Mūrus mūnītus est.
6.	Mūrum mūnītis.	Mūrum mūnīvistis.
7.	Hominēs mittō.	Hominēs mīsī.
8.	Ab hominibus mitteris.	Ab hominibus missus es.
9.	Vīnum pōnō.	Vīnum posuī.
10.	Vīnum pōnitur.	Vīnum positum est.
11.	Capita vulnerantur.	Capita vulnerāta sunt.
12.	Ab auctōre audīminī.	Ab auctōre audītī estis.
13.	Ab equīs pellimur.	Ab equīs pulsī sumus.
14.	Nihil invenītur.	Nihil inventum est.
15.	Ab hoste cogor.	Ab hoste coāctus sum.
16.	Fēminae cōnspiciuntur.	Fēminae cōnspectae sunt.
17.	Bella geruntur.	Bella gesta sunt.
18.	Ā sene dūcimur.	Ā sene ductī sumus.
19.	Mīlitēs nōn terrentur.	Mīlitēs nōn territī sunt.
20.	Vīllam ostendis.	Vīllam ostendistī.
21.	Mūnus accipere possumus.	Mūnus accipere potuimus.
22.	Venīre jubēminī.	Venīre jussī estis.
23.	Amīcī absunt.	Amīcī āfuērunt.
24.	Amīcus cernor.	Amīcus crētus sum.
25.	Ab omnibus probāris.	Ab omnibus probātus es.
26.	Cibus rapitur.	Cibus raptus est.
27.	Corvī cibum rapiunt.	Corvī cibum rapuērunt.

V   VĪNEA PECŪNIŌSA

Agricola Rōmānus, nōmine Cornēlius, paulō ante mortem suam, in vīllam fīliōs vocāvit. Fīliī eum maximē amābant[1] sed pigrī erant;[2] vītam enim rūsticam agere nōn cupīvērunt. Pater, autem, quod voluit eōs vītam rūsticam agere,[3] incēpit:

"Vīta mea paene perfecta est. Aiunt omnēs: 'Agricola es pauper.' Nihilō minus[4] in vīneā meā latet magna pecūnia. Sī eam quaeritis, dīvitēs esse potestis."

Proximō diē ē vītā discessit Cornēlius. Fīliī, postquam senex sepultus[5] est, rogāvērunt:

"Ubi in vīneā latet pecūnia? Ad vīllam an ad fīnēs posita est? Ā dextrā parte an ā sinistrā?"

"Mente, nōn manibus, labōrāre dēbēmus."

"Tōtam enim vīneam dēfodere[6] nōn cupimus!"

In vīllam igitur ambulāvērunt et sēdērunt. Nox vēnit et lucerna accēnsa est. Sine cibō somnōque tōtam noctem dē pecūniā putāvērunt.

Proximō diē, ūnus[7] ē fīliīs: "Pecūnia," inquit, "ā dextrā parte latet."

"Cūr?" quaesīvērunt aliī.

"Quod ibi umbra maxima[8] est," respōnsum est.[9]

"Quid dē umbrā?" aliī rogā'runt.[10]

"Nihil," inquit prīmus, "sed in umbrā fodere volō. Probātisne?"

"Probāmus!" respondērunt.

"Meā sententiā, inquam, manibus, nōn mentibus nunc labōrāre dēbēmus."

Statim omnēs in vīneam prōcessērunt. Trēs diēs noctēsque labōrā'runt. Nihil invēnērunt; tōta autem vīnea dēfossa est. Nihil inventum est, sed dīvitēs factī sunt fīliī;[11] vīnea enim ūvās[12] dulcēs et magnās tulit.

Notā bene

1. *amābant*: imperfect tense, shows action habitual in past time
2. *erant*: imperfect of *sum*, "they were"
3. *vītam agere*: "to lead a life"
4. *nihilō minus*: "nevertheless"
5. *sepeliō, sepelīre, sepelīvī, sepultus*: "bury"
6. *dēfodere*: *dē + fodere*, "dig up"
7. *ūnus ē*: "one of"
8. *maximus -a -um*: (cf. adverb, *maximē*) "greatest," "most"
9. *respōnsum est*: neuter passive, no personal subject: "the answer was," "they answered"
10. *rogā'runt*: contracted form of *rogāvērunt*
11. *factī sunt*: "became"
12. *ūva, ūvā* f: "grape"

Respondē Latīnē

1. Quis agricola est?
2. Quandō agricola fīliōs vocāvit?
3. Quid pater fīliōs agere cupīvit?
4. Quālēs erant fīliī?
5. Quid dīxit pater dē pecūniā?
6. Quō īnstrūmentō labōrāre voluērunt fīliī?
7. Quō prōcessērunt fīliī?
8. Quam diū putāvērunt fīliī?
9. Ubi proximō diē ūnus fodere voluit?
10. Probāvēruntne aliī?
11. Invēnēruntne fīliī pecūniam?
12. Cūr dīvitēs factī sunt?

VI   OPTIONAL READING

Simul dictum et factum. — Anon.
Ālea jacta est. — Caesar
Quod nōn dedit Fortūna, nōn ēripit. — Seneca
In virtūte posita est vēra fēlīcitās. — Seneca

After this lesson the Supplementary Story *Nāvis*, Appendix A, page 186 may be used.

VII   WORD STUDY

1. List at least five words in this lesson which come into English unchanged, or minus an ending, or with silent "e" added (the simplest changes).

2. Add familiar suffixes to four words in the vocabulary.

3. Give the Latin source and meaning of: vitamin, mortality, nocturne, insomnia, approximate, latent.

4. What does a "somnambulist" do? What by derivation is one of the uses of an "umbrella"?

5. A "village" was so named because often an ancient *vīlla* included on the landowner's estate the dwellings of farm workers and the places where basic necessities were provided, like the blacksmith shop. Such a unit became a self-sufficient "village" in the Middle Ages.

6. From the fact that the left was regarded as unlucky comes our meaning of "sinister."

7. A "peninsula" (*paene + īnsula*) is almost an island, but not quite.

8. Note that some new verbs are merely compounds of ones you have met before, with the same pattern of principal parts.

9. What noun is related to *vīnea*?

10. One of the richest sources of English derivatives from Latin is the fourth (perfect passive) part of the verb. As you learn these new parts, think of derivatives to help your memory of the forms.

VIII   VOCABULARY

Nouns	Verbs	Function Words
lucerna, lucernā f.	lateō, latēre, latuī	ibi
umbra, umbrā f.	respondeō -spondēre -spondī -spōnsus	paene
vīlla, vīllā f.	accendō -cendere -cendī -cēnsus	paulō
vīnea, vīneā f.	discedō -cedere - cessī - cessus	simul
vīta, vītā f.	perficiō -ficere -fēcī -fectus	an
	inveniō -venīre -vēnī -ventus	postquam
Cornēlius, Cornēliō m.		
somnus, somnō m.		

Phrases

ā dextrā parte
ā sinistrā parte

Adjectives

piger, pigra, pigrum
proximus, proxima, proximum
tōtus, tōta, tōtum
dīves (dīvite)
pauper (paupere)

IX   FORM CHART

REVIEW LIST OF PRINCIPAL PARTS OF VERBS

I Conjugation

accūsō, accūsāre, accūsāvī, accūsātus
ambulō, ambulāre, ambulāvī, ambulātus
amō, amāre, amāvī, amātus

following same form pattern:

appellō	mūtō	pulsō
clāmō	nārrō	putō
dēlectō	natō	rogō
habitō	numerō	spectō
labōrō	portō	spērō
laudō	probō	vocō
	pūgnō	vulnerō

adjuvō, adjuvāre, adjūvī, adjūtus
lavō, lavāre, lāvī, lautus (lōtus)
stō, stāre, stetī, status

II Conjugation

dēbeō, dēbēre, dēbuī, dēbitus
doceō, docēre, docuī, doctus
habeō, habēre, habuī, habitus
jubeō, jubēre, jussī, jussus
lateō, latēre, latuī
maneō, manēre, mānsī, mānsus

moneō, monēre, monuī, monitus
moveō, movēre, mōvī, mōtus
respondeō, respondēre, respondī, respōnsus
rīdeō, rīdēre, rīsī, rīsus
sedeō, sedēre, sēdī, sessus
taceō, tacēre, tacuī, tacitus

teneō, tenēre, tenuī, tentus
    retineō, retinēre, retinuī, retentus
    sustineō
terreō, terrēre, terruī, territus
timeō, timēre, timuī
valeō, valēre, valuī, valitus
videō, vidēre, vīdī, vīsus

III Conjugation

accēdō, accēdere, accessī, accessus
    discēdō
    prōcēdō
accendō, accendere, accendī, accēnsus
agō, agere, ēgī, āctus
ascendō, ascendere, ascendī, ascēnsus
bibō, bibere, bībī
canō, canere, cecinī, cantus

cernō, cernere, crēvī, crētus
cōgō, cōgere, coēgī, coāctus
currō, currere, cucurrī, cursus

dēscendō, dēscendere, dēscendī, dēscēnsus
dīcō, dīcere, dīxī, dictus
discō, discere, didicī
dūcō, dūcere, dūxī, ductus
fluō, fluere, flūxī, flūxus
gerō, gerere, gessī, gestus

legō, legere, lēgī, lēctus
mittō, mittere, mīsī, missus
occīdō, occīdere, occīdī, occīsus
ostendō, ostendere, ostendī, ostentus
pellō, pellere, pepulī, pulsus

petō, petere, petīvī, petītus
pōnō, pōnere, posuī, positus
    dēpōnō
quaerō, quaerere, quaesīvī, quaesītus
relinquō, relinquere, relīquī, relictus
scrībō, scrībere, scrīpsī, scrīptus

solvō, solvere, solvī, solūtus
surgō, surgere, surrēxī, surrēctus
trahō, trahere, trāxī, tractus
vehō, vehere, vēxī, vectus

vertō, vertere, vertī, versus
vincō, vincere, vīcī, victus
volvō, volvere, volvī, volūtus
vīvō, vīvere, vīxī, vīctus

III (i) Conjugation

capiō, capere, cēpī, captus
    accipiō, accipere, accēpī, acceptus
    incipiō
cōnspiciō, cōnspicere, cōnspexī, conspectus
cupiō, cupere, cupīvī, cupītus

faciō, facere, fēcī, factus
    afficiō, afficere, affēcī, affectus
    cōnficiō
    perficiō
fodiō, fodere, fōdī, fossus
fugiō, fugere, fūgī, fugitus
jaciō, jacere, jēcī, jactus
rapiō, rapere, rapuī, raptus

IV Conjugation

audiō, audīre, audīvī, audītus
mūniō, mūnīre, mūnīvī, mūnītus
saliō, salīre, saluī, saltus
sciō, scīre, scīvī, scītus
    nesciō
veniō, venīre, vēnī, ventus
    inveniō

Irregular

sum, esse, fuī, futūrus[1]
    absum, abesse, āfuī, āfutūrus
    adsum, adesse, adfuī, adfutūrus
    possum, posse, potuī
ferō, ferre, tulī, lātus
volō, velle, voluī

Defective

aiō
inquam

---

[1] This is a future participle, not perfect passive.

LESSON SEVENTEEN

Stultus stulta loquitur. — Anon.

"A stupid person says stupid things."

Dulce et decōrum est prō patriā morī.
— Horace

"It is a fine and fitting thing to die for one's country."

Purpose: to learn about deponent verbs

I PATTERN READING

A. Sample sentences

1. Stultus stulta dīcit.
   Stultus stulta loquitur.

   A stupid person says stupid things.

2. Rēx dīxit.
   Rēx locūtus est.

   The king has spoken.

3. Stultī fortūnam timent.
   Stultī fortūnam verentur.

   Stupid people fear luck.

4. Fortūnam ferre voluistis.
   Fortūnam patī voluistis.

   You-all were willing to bear your fortune.

5. Omnēs eam mīrantur.
   Omnes eam amant.

   All admire (like) her.

6. Profectī sumus et prōgredimur.

   We have started and are advancing.

7. Ubi nātus es?

   Where were you born?

8. Orior; ortus sum.

   I arise; I arose.

B. Practice sentences

1. Id dīcō; sīc loquor.
2. Id dīcis; sīc loqueris.
3. Id dīcit; sīc loquitur.
4. Id dīcimus; sīc loquimur.
5. Id dīcitis; sīc loquiminī.
6. Id dīcunt; sīc loquuntur.

7. Mīles hostem fessum pellit.
8. Mīles hostem fessum sequitur.
9. Mīlitēs nostrī hostēs pepulērunt.
10. Mīlitēs nostrī hostēs secūtī sunt.
11. Vulpem ingentem timēs.
12. Vulpem ingentem verēris.
13. Vulpēs saepe timuistī.
14. Vulpēs saepe verita es.

15. Ex oppidō tēcum prōcēdō.
16. Ex oppidō tēcum proficīscor.
17. In viā iterum prōgredior.
18. Homō ē vītā jam discessit.
19. Homō jam mortuus est.
20. Hominēs mortuī sunt.
21. Puer tantum vīvit.
22. Puer tunc nātus est.
23. Puer nunc nāscitur.

24. Vōs gladiātōrēs moriminī in harēnā.
25. Vōs multa mūnera mīrāminī.
26. Vōs multa mūnera amātis.

27. Ā mēnsā surgunt omnēs.
28. Ā mēnsā oriuntur omnēs.

29. Ā mēnsā omnēs ortī sunt.
30. Nōs mātrēs multa patimur.
31. Nōs mātrēs multa ferimus.

32. Nōs mātrēs multa passae sumus.
33. Nōs mātrēs multa tulimus.

C.   Questions on structure

   1. In what way do deponent verbs differ from other verbs?
   2. Which deponents in this lesson pattern with objects? Which do not?
   3. What differences are there between the principal parts of deponent verbs and those of regular verbs?
   4. Are deponents found in all conjugations?

   See Appendix B, Part II, page 160.

II   FORM CHART

Deponent Verbs by conjugation

I	mīror, mīrārī, mīrātus	See passive of *portō, portāre*, page 105 and App. C in Part II.
II	vereor, verērī, veritus	See passive of *videō, vidēre*, page 105 and App. C in Part II.
III	loquor, loquī, locūtus	See passive of *agō, agere*, page 105 and App. C in Part II.
III-i	patior, patī, passus	See passive of *capiō, capere*, page 105 and App. C in Part II.
IV	orior, orīrī, ortus	See passive of *audiō, audīre*, page 105 and App. C in Part II.

III   EXERCISES

A.   Change the verb to perfect tense.

   1. Auctōrēs opus mīrantur.
      Opus mirāris.
      Opus mirāmur.
      Opus mīror.

   2. Juvenis dē sanguine rogat.
      Dē sanguine rogāmus.
      Dē sanguine rogātis.
      Dē sanguine rogant.

   3. Senex omnia patitur.
      Omnia patior.
      Omnia patimur.
      Omnia patiminī.

   4. Virum sequitur fēmina.
      Virum sequiminī.
      Virum sequuntur fēminae.
      Virum sequeris.

B.   Change the verb to present tense.

   1. Ā fāmiliā bonā ortus sum.
      Ā fāmiliā bonā ortus es.
      Ā fāmiliā bonā ortī sumus.
      Ā fāmiliā bonā ortī estis.

   2. Ad flūmen servus profectus est.
      Ad flūmen servī profectī sunt.
      Ad flūmen profectus sum.
      Ad flūmen profectī estis.

   3. Cum gaudiō mānsit pater.
      Cum gaudiō mānsistī.
      Cum gaudiō mānsimus.
      Cum gaudiō mānsērunt patrēs.

   4. Bellum verita sum apud nōs.
      Bellum verita es apud nōs.
      Bellum veritae sumus apud nōs.
      Bellum fēminae veritae sunt apud nōs.

C.   Fill in the blanks. Give the reason for the forms you supply.

1. Fīlia dē amīcitiā locūt___ _____.
2. Multī (hominēs) Deum secūt_____ ___.
3. Dē montibus viātōrēs prōgredi_____.
4. Spēs numquam mortu___ _____.
5. Somnus labōrem sequ_____.
6. Aestāte multī agnī nāsc_____.
7. Mediā in viā multum loqu_____ nōn potest.
8. Mortem ver_____ nōn dēbēmus.
9. Nōs paucī hōrā prīmā proficīsc_____.
10. Vōs singulī ort___ _____ in tabernā.

Ḋ.   Complete the verb in both sentences in the pairs. The first is a regular verb, the second a deponent. Compare the meanings of the pair of sentences. (Optional)

1. Vīta misera ā fēminā fer_____.
   Fēmina vītam miseram pat_____.

2. Lupī tunc ā frātribus tuīs puls___ _____.
   Lupōs tunc frātrēs tuī secūt___ _____.

3. Ā spectātōribus equī tim_____.
   Spectātōrēs equōs ver_____.

4. (Ego) ā vōbīs amāt___ _____.
   Vōs mē mīrāt___ _____.

5. Sententiae ā mē dict____ _____.
   (Ego) dē sententiīs meīs locūt___ _____.

E.   Give the Latin equivalent.

1. Help has been sent and our enemies have been held back.
2. Many stones were thrown into the river.
3. Finally the money was found at our home (among us).
4. Then strange sounds were heard in the forest.
5. I (a boy) was scared by the huge animal.
6. Again the lamp was lighted at night.
7. We (women) were called away from the city.
8. You are now sitting in the shade because the work has been completed.
9. Therefore the faithful dog was killed at once by the angry soldier.
10. The sad boy answered without enthusiasm.

IV   PATTERN PRACTICE FIFTEEN

1. They are born in a well-known land.	In terrā nōtā nāscuntur.
2. They were born in a well-known land.	In terrā nōtā nātī sunt.
3. You-all arose from the ground.	Ā terrā ortī estis.
4. You-all arise from the ground.	Ā terrā orīminī.
5. You are setting out for your native land.	Ad patriam proficīsceris.
6. You did set out for your native land.	Ad patriam profectus es.
7. We are willing to fight for our country.	Prō patriā pūgnāre volumus.
8. We are willing to die for our country.	Prō patriā morī volumus.
9. Our father has already died.	Pater noster jam mortuus est.
10. Your father is not dying.	Pater vester nōn moritur.
11. Your mother admires you.	Māter vestra vōs mīrātur.
12. Your mother admired you.	Māter vestra vōs mīrāta est.
13. We have always admired you.	Vōs semper mīrātī sumus.
14. We liked you a great deal.	Vōs multum amāvimus.
15. We often say a great deal.	Saepe multum dīcimus.
16. We often talk a lot.	Saepe multum loquimur.
17. You bear much for us.	Prō nōbīs multum fers.
18. You endure much for us.	Prō nōbīs multum pateris.
19. I chased the animals away quickly.	Animālia celeriter pepulī.
20. I pursued the animals quickly.	Animālia celeriter secūtus sum.
21. The women feared the animals.	Fēminae animālia veritae sunt.
22. The women were afraid of the animals.	Fēminae animālia timuērunt.
23. I am beginning to fear the animals.	Animālia verērī incipiō.
24. I am starting to go to the city.	Ad urbem prōcēdere incipiō.
25. I am setting out for the city.	Proficīscor ad urbem.
26. At the same time you-all are going ahead into the city.	Simul prōgrediminī in urbem.
27. At the same time you-all are going into the city.	Simul prōcēditis in urbem.

V LĒCTIO

1. Duōs quī[1] sequitur leporēs[2] neutrum capit. — Proverb

2. Cūrae levēs loquuntur, ingentēs stupent.[3] — Seneca

3. Virtūs omnī locō[4] nāscitur. — Seneca

4. Rēx numquam moritur. — Legal phrase

5. Vir sapit[5] quī[1] pauca loquitur. — Anon.

6. Multī fāmam, cōnscientiam[6] paucī verentur. — Pliny

7. Ōre plēnō[7] vel bibere vel loquī nec honestum est nec tūtum. — Petrus Alphonsus (?)

8. Tardē sed graviter sapiēns mēns īrāscitur.[8] — Publilius Syrus

9. Lēgem nocēns[9] verētur, fortūnam innocēns. — Publilius Syrus

10. Plērīque Deum vōcibus sequuntur, mōribus autem fugiunt. — Anon.

11. Nēmō prophēta[10] acceptus est in patriā suā. — N.T. (Luke)

12. Prōgredimur quō dūcit quemque[11] voluntās.[12] — Lucretius

13. Laus nova nisī oritur,[13] etiam vetus āmittitur. — Publilius Syrus

14. Glōria . . . virtūtem tamquam umbra sequitur. — Cicero

15. Sequitur vēr hiemem. — Anon.

16. Amīcus vester quī[1] fuit rāna,[14] nunc est rēx. — Petronius

17. Vincit quī patitur. — in Burton

Notā bene

1. *quī*: as frequently in sayings, "he who"
2. *lepus, lepore* m.: "hare"
3. *stupeō, stupēre*: "be stunned," "be silent"
4. The preposition *in* is regularly omitted with the word *locus* when it patterns with an adjective.
5. *sapit = sapiēns est*
6. *cōnscientia*: cf. derivative
7. *plēnus -a -um*: "full"

8. *īrāscor*: become *īrātus*
9. *nocēns*: opposite of *innocēns*, *innocentī*
10. *prophēta*: Greek word (therefore -ā), for meaning cf. derivative
11. *quisque* (acc. *quemque*): "each one"
12. *voluntās*: noun based on *volō*
13. *oritur*: here has a short *i*. This verb has some III conjugation (i) forms.
14. The frog is used here as a symbol of one in a lowly position in life.

VI   WORD STUDY

1. Relate these words to *sequor*: consequence, sequence, consecutive, executive, persecute.
2. Give the meaning of these words related to *loquor*: loquacious, eloquent, soliloquy, elocution.
3. If you "admire" yourself in a "mirror," it is no "miracle," even though all three words come from Latin *mīror*.
4. To what Latin noun is *morior* related?
5. Compounds of the verb *faciō* have the stem *-fic-*; *proficīscor* contains it, with the prefix *pro-* and a verb suffix often used in Latin to indicate something beginning (*sc-*).
6. Give the Latin source and meaning of: progressive, native, compassion, compatible, repatriate, curator, vernal.
7. Give English derivatives from: cūra, fāma, glōria, locus, lēx, tardus, novus.
8. "Neuter" is neither _____ nor _____.
9. What is meant by "paucity," as in "a paucity of players"?
10. The "Orient" is the land of the _____ sun.
11. A "sinecure" is a job *sine cūrā,* requiring little or no effort.

VII   VOCABULARY

Nouns	*Adjectives*	*Verbs*
cūra, cūrā f.	neuter, neutra, neutrum	āmittō -mittere -mīsī -missus
fāma, fāmā f.	novus, nova, novum	*Deponents*
glōria, glōriā f.	paucī, paucae, pauca	
patria, patriā f.	plērīque, plēraeque, plēraque	mīror, mīrārī, mīrātus
	tardus, tarda, tardum	
locus, locō m.		vereor, verērī, veritus
(the pl. is neuter)	vetus	
	(veterī)	loquor, loquī, locūtus
lēx, lēge f.		nāscor, nāscī, nātus
vēr, vēre n.	*Function Words*	proficīscor, proficīscī, profectus
		sequor, sequī, secūtus
	vel . . . vel	
		morior, morī, mortuus
	tamquam	patior, patī, passus
		prōgredior, prōgredī, prōgressus
		orior, orīrī, ortus

FOURTH REVIEW

Dormiunt aliquandō lēgēs, numquam moriuntur.
  — Legal commonplace

"The laws sometimes sleep, but they never die."

Nōn omnēs omnia possumus. — Vergil

"We can't all do everything."

I   VOCABULARY AND MODEL SENTENCE REVIEW

A.   Rewrite each of these model sentences in the following ways: 1) with one addition, 2) with a substitution for one or more words, 3) with one transformation (active to passive, singular to plural, present to perfect or vice versa).

  1. Gladiātor in harēnā capit cōnsilium.
  2. Numquam perīculum sine perīculō vincitur.
  3. Ā fonte pūrō pūra dēfluit aqua.
  4. Omnibus in rēbus gravis est inceptiō prīma.
  5. Potest ex casā magnus vir exīre.

  6. Prīmus in orbe deōs fēcit timor.
  7. Amīcus certus in rē incertā cernitur.
  8. Nōn omnēs omnia possumus.
  9. Nihil est . . . simul et inventum et perfectum.
 10. Dormiunt aliquandō lēgēs, numquam moriuntur.

B.   Be sure that you have learned thoroughly the principal parts of verbs on pages 134-35. Pay attention to the conjugation, as well as to the perfect active and passive stems. Review Practice on Principal Parts may be used, pages 145-46.

II   STRUCTURE REVIEW

  1. What are the four principal parts of a Latin verb?
  2. Why is it essential to know the last three of these?
  3. How is the perfect active tense formed?

  4. What are the personal endings of the perfect active?
  5. What combination of forms is used as the perfect tense passive?
  6. What is a deponent verb?
  7. Can a deponent verb pattern with an object?
  8. How can a deponent be recognized in the listing of vocabulary?

III   FORM REVIEW

A.   Conjugate in the perfect tense active:

       habitāre,   relinquere,   tenēre,   dormīre

B. Conjugate in the perfect tense passive:

> probāre (m. subject),   valēre (m. subject)
> accipere (f. subject),   vehere (f. subject)

C. Conjugate in the present and perfect tenses:

> mīrārī,   verērī,   proficīscī,   orīrī

D. Answer the questions with *tempore praesentī* ("in the present") or *tempore praeteritō* ("in the past"), being sure to match the tense. Preferably do this as a rapid oral practice.

Example:

Quō tempore rānae rēgem petunt?   Tempore praesentī rānae rēgem petunt.
Quō tempore rānae rēgem petīvērunt?   Tempore praeteritō rānae rēgem petīvērunt.

1. Quō tempore rēx ā rānīs petitur?
2. Quō tempore rēx ā rānīs petītus est?
3. Quō tempore folia in aquā natāvērunt?
4. Quō tempore folia in aquā vīsa sunt?
5. Quō tempore folia in aquā sunt?
6. Quō tempore rānae ex aquā surrēxērunt?
7. Quō tempore rānae rēgem nōn habent?
8. Quō tempore rāmus missus est?
9. Quō tempore rāmus in aquā est?
10. Quō tempore in aquā saluērunt?
11. Quō tempore timor ā rānīs dēponitur?
12. Quō tempore serpēns ad flūmen vēnit?
13. Quō tempore rānae ā serpente raptae sunt?
14. Quō tempore rānae fēlīcēs sunt?
15. Quō tempore rāna ad Jovem missa est?
16. Quō tempore rāna ante Jovem est?
17. Quō tempore rānae occīsae sunt?
18. Quō tempore Juppiter respondit?
19. Quō tempore fābula nārrāta est?
20. Quō tempore fābula legitur?

E. Change the verb to perfect tense; explain the use of the noun forms.

1. Pedēs in flūmine pōnit parva puella.
2. Animālia horribilia in silvīs latent; ea maximē vereor.
3. Ab hostibus fortibus gravī in bellō vinciminī.
4. Ā servō bonō aqua ad vīllam statim portātur.
5. Magnās viās, ingentia saxa, arborēs altās cōnspicimus in terrā novā.
6. Canis magnō cum dolōre relinquitur ā puerō.
7. Ad urbem deinde proficīscimur vōbīscum.
8. Saepe patrēs grātiās nōn agunt prō mūneribus vestrīs.
9. Procul ab aedificiō clāmōrēs magnī facile audīrī possunt.
10. Simul dē amīcitiā dīcis et amīcōs magnā cum laude numerās.
11. Cibum in fenestrā videt corvus; eam rapere vult.
12. Carō in arborem jam fertur; arbor alta est.
13. Corvus autem cibum ex ōre mittit in terram.
14. Vulpēs perfidus eum capit dentibus avidīs.
15. Multum vērō rogās, vulpēs, dē vōce dulcī.
16. Nōn carmen mīrātur vulpēs sed carnem amat.

F. Change the verb to the present tense; explain the use of the noun forms.

1. Fābulās nārrāvimus bonās; aut dē amōre, aut dē factīs locūtī sumus.
2. Accēpistīne ā patre magnam pecūniam paulō ante mortem?

3. Suntne per silentium carmina pulchra audīta?
4. Cōnspectī estis ad portās ab hostibus vestrīs.
5. Magnō cum gaudiō vīllam mūnīvistis et vīneam dēfōdistis.

6. Bene dormīvit pater quod fīliī tūtī mānsērunt.
7. Ab hominibus tardīs tempus semper āmissum est.
8. Frātrēs meōs frūstrā secūta sum.
9. Ā fīliā tuā carmen dulce cantum est.
10. Mox pedibus in oppidum vīle vēnērunt mīlitēs Rōmānī.

11. Agricola dīves tunc ē vītā discessit.
12. Quam diū latuit pecūnia in vīneā?
13. Labōrāvistisne mentibus an manibus?
14. Magna pecūnia inventa est quod bene et diū labōrāvērunt frātrēs.
15. Senex voluit facere id quod omnēs probāvērunt.

IV   WORD STUDY REVIEW

A. List all prefixes you have studied, both those formed from prepositions and inseparable prefixes.

B. Use this list of prefixes and the verb review sheet to find derivatives. It should be easy to give at least twenty pairs of English words, one of the pair coming from the present stem of the verb, another from the perfect passive stem. Do not use the same verb twice.

(Example: commit, commission; describe, description)

C. Give at least ten derivatives from *each* of these verbs: capiō, faciō, pōnō, mittō, dūcō (prefixes may be used).

V   OPTIONAL READING

Rōma locūta est; causa fīnīta est. — Anon.
Homō extrā corpus est suum cum īrāscitur. — Publilius Syrus
Lēx videt īrātum; īrātus lēgem nōn videt. — Publilius Syrus

Quī mē amat amat et canem meum. — Anon.
Alta diē sōlō nōn est exstrūcta Corinthus. — Medieval
Fortis cadere, cēdere nōn potest. — Proverb

Nūllum quod tetigit nōn ōrnāvit. — Dr. Johnson's epitaph on Goldsmith
Bonum certāmen certāvī, cursum cōnsummāvī, fidem servāvī. — N. T. (Timothy II)

Common phrases

alter ego	nōn sequitur
alibi	prīmā faciē
alias	in tōtō

VI VOCABULARY

Verb | *Function Word*

dormiō, dormīre, dormīvī, dormītus | aliquandō

VII OPTIONAL ORAL PRACTICE ON PRINCIPAL PARTS

After the verb is announced, give the principal parts. Listen to the check; continue in the same way.

ambulō	ambulō, ambulāre, ambulāvī, ambulātus
accipiō	accipiō, accipere, accēpī, acceptus
agō	agō, agere, ēgī, āctus
dēbeō	dēbeō, dēbēre, debuī, dēbitus
audiō	audiō, audīre, audīvī, audītus
portō	portō, portāre, portāvī, portātus
maneō	maneō, manēre, mānsī, mānsus
sum	sum, esse, fuī, futūrus
stō	stō, stāre, stetī, status
terreō	terreō, terrēre, terruī, territus
currō	currō, currere, cucurrī, cursus
dīcō	dīcō, dīcere, dīxī, dictus
gerō	gerō, gerere, gessī, gestus
jaciō	jaciō, jacere, jecī, jactus
possum	possum, posse, potuī
habeō	habeō, habēre, habuī, habitus
mittō	mittō, mittere, mīsī, missus
relinquō	relinquō, relinquere, relīquī, relictus
moveō	moveō, movēre, mōvī, mōtus
pellō	pellō, pellere, pepulī, pulsus
mūniō	mūniō, mūnīre, mūnīvī, mūnītus
petō	petō, petere, petīvī, petītus
pōnō	pōnō, pōnere, posuī, positus
veniō	veniō, venīre, vēnī, ventus
surgō	surgō, surgere, surrēxī, surrēctus
nārrō	nārrō, nārrāre, nārrāvī, nārrātus
videō	videō, vidēre, vīdī, vīsus
cupiō	cupiō, cupere, cupīvī, cupītus
jubeō	jubeō, jubēre, jussī, jussus
respondeō	respondeō, respondēre, respondī, respōnsus
ferō	ferō, ferre, tulī, lātus
prōcēdō	prōcēdō, prōcēdere, prōcessī, prōcessus
dūcō	dūcō, dūcere, dūxī, ductus
quaerō	quaerō, quaerere, quaesīvī, quaesītus
sciō	sciō, scīre, scīvī, scītus

afficiō	afficiō, afficere, affēcī, affectus
ostendō	ostendō, ostendere, ostendī, ostentus
cōnspiciō	cōnspiciō, cōnspicere, cōnspexī, cōnspectus
trahō	trahō, trahere, trāxī, tractus
scrībō	scrībō, scrībere, scrīpsī, scrīptus
volō	volō, velle, voluī
rogō	rogō, rogāre, rogāvī, rogātus
vehō	vehō, vehere, vēxī, vectus
adjuvō	adjuvō, adjuvāre, adjūvī, adjūtus
solvō	solvō, solvere, solvī, solūtus
cernō	cernō, cernere, crēvī, crētus
faciō	faciō, facere, fēcī, factus
vertō	vertō, vertere, vertī, versus
vincō	vincō, vincere, vīcī, victus
capiō	capiō, capere, cēpī, captus
mīror	mīror, mīrārī, mīrātus
vereor	vereor, verērī, veritus
proficīscor	proficīscor, proficīscī, profectus
prōgredior	prōgredior, prōgredī, prōgressus
orior	orior, orīrī, ortus

LESSON EIGHTEEN

Poēta nāscitur, ōrātor fit. — Anon.   "A poet is born, an orator is made."

Purpose: to increase facility in reading connected Latin and develop a knowledge of Roman writers

Optional work: Locative case; Roman names

I   AUCTŌRĒS RŌMĀNĪ

Saepe in librō nostrō lēgistis et sententiās et nōmina Rōmāna. Nōnne vultis discere aliquid dē auctōribus et librīs Rōmānīs?

Prīmīs aetātibus, dum Rōma rēs pūblica[1] est,[2] multī virī magnī erant[3] ōrātōrēs. Eō tempore virī Rōmānī saepe magistrātūs tenēre cupīvērunt, dē lēgibus et jūdiciīs dīxērunt: vītam pūblicam ēgērunt. Multās ōrātiōnēs,[4] igitur, habuērunt: sed nōs nunc paucās ex eīs[5] habēmus. Etiam eīs aetātibus multa bella gesta sunt. Per bella magna et gravia Rōmānī aliquandō dē aliīs rēbus putāre cupīvērunt. Ad lūdōs, igitur, scaenicōs[6] prōgressī sunt. Aliquae fābulae scaenicae Latīnae apud nōs et lēctae et āctae sunt. Tandem virī Rōmānī antīquī quoque agricolae erant[3]— et nōs hodiē librōs Rōmānōs dē vītā rūsticā habēmus.

Dum rēs pūblica Rōmāna ad fīnem venit, plērīque ōrātōrēs aut verba sua scrīpsērunt aut amanuēnsēs[7] habuērunt quī[8] notās brevēs fēcērunt et omnia dēscrīpsērunt. Tālis ōrātor magnus erat[3] M. Tullius Cicero.[9] Magistrātūs tenuit, habuit ōrātiōnēs; erat quoque philosophus. Multōs librōs suōs dē philosophiā, ōrātiōnēs dē rēbus ́pūblicīs, dē lēgibus, dē jūdiciīs, litterās[10] prīvātās dē rēbus suīs relīquit et multa ex eīs nōs nunc habēmus et legimus. C. Jūlius Caesar[9] scrīpsit dē factīs suīs, maximē dē bellīs. Aliī auctōrēs dē rēbus pūblicīs et dē clārīs bellīs librōs fēcērunt. Paucī poētae etiam carmina[11] fēcērunt: Catullus dē amōre carmina lepida[12] fēcit, aliquis Publīlius, servus Syrus,[13] mīmōs[14] prōtulit. Eō tempore etiam Rōmānī rēs Graecās et pulchrās et dīvitēs amāre et imitārī coepērunt.

Post multa bella cīvīlia Augustus, imperātor bonus, pācem fēcit et omnēs rēs Rōmānās in manūs suās accēpit. Tunc omnēs Rōmānī pācem maximē cupīvērunt et laudāvērunt. Sed dum imperātor rēs pūblicās gerit, nōn jam multī virī ōrātiōnēs habuērunt. Sed tamen aetās clāra est quod tot poētās clārōs habuit. Inter eōs erant[3] trēs poētae maximē notī. In Italiā nātī sunt rūrī;[15] ut multī aliī, juvenēs Rōmam iērunt ubi dē litterīs discere coepērunt. Postquam Rōmae[15] diū doctī sunt, in Graeciam profectī sunt et Athēnīs[15] linguam litterāsque

Graecās didicērunt. Postquam Rōmam rediērunt, Imperātor eōs adjūvit quod per carmina fāma sua magna fīerī potuit. P. Vergilius Maro fēcit magnum carmen *Aenēida*[16] dē virō magnō et veteribus aetātibus. Q. Horātius Flaccus scrīpsit dē vītā rūsticā, dē rēbus suīs, dē hominibus, etiam dē fonte in vīllā rūsticā. Dē deīs et clārīs virīs antīquīs carmen *Metamorphōsēs*[17] fēcit P. Ovidius Nāso; multa quoque dē amōre locūtus est — inter carmina est *Ars Amātōria*.[18] Verba ab Horātiō scrīpta,[19] "Nōn omnis moriar,"[20] dē eīs tribus poētīs vēra sunt. Opus magnum etiam fēcit Titus Līvius; historiam tōtam nārrāvit, fāmam glōriamque Rōmānam ostendit, patriam laudāvit.

Per multōs annōs Rōma Imperātōrēs[21] habuit—aliōs bonōs et honestōs, aliōs malōs et superbōs. Inter superbōs fuit Domitiānus. Eum plērīque auctōrēs nōn amāvērunt. D. Jūnius Juvenālis et dē imperātōre superbō et dē aetāte malā et dē malīs hominibus sine virtūte scrīpsit; pictūram trīstem fēcit. M. Valerius Martiālis, autem, eō tempore in Hispāniā nātus est; quandō juvenis pauper Rōmam vēnit, carmina dulcibus verbīs scrīpsit et ad Imperātōrem mīsit; cupīvit pecūniam, pecūniam accēpit. Sed postquam Domitiānus mortuus est, eum multum accūsāre coepit. Tālem hominem nōs nōn multum laudāmus, sed poētam mīrāmur quod hominēs et facta sua leviter irrīsit[22] carminibus lepidīs.[12] Eā aetāte aliī auctōrēs librōs historicōs, litterās prīvātās etc. scrīpsērunt.[23]

Per aetātēs quae[24] secūtae sunt multī librī Latīnī, sed nōn tam clārī, scrīptī sunt. Multae rēs Christiānae quoque Latīnē scrīptae sunt. Etiam mediīs aetātibus et apud nōs lingua Latīna bene et pulchrē scrīpta est et jam hodiē scrībitur.

Notā bene

1. *rēs pūblica*: "public affair" came to mean the government at Rome and then the form of government, "republic."
2. Present tense always patterns with conjunction *dum*, "while".
3. *erat, erant*: imperfect (past) of *sum*, "was," "were"
4. Words that are obvious from English derivatives or related Latin words, and that do not need to be learned, will not be footnoted or listed in the vocabulary: ōrātiō(n), philosophia, prīvātus, historicus, cīvīlis, rūsticus, etc.

5. *ex eīs*: "of them"
6. *lūdī scaenicī*: "stage plays"
   Plautus and Terence were writers of comedy at this time.
7. *amanuēnsis*: a secretary who is *ā manū* to make shorthand notes (*notās brevēs*), to write down (*dē + scrībere*) one's words
8. *quī, quibus*: forms of "who," "which"
9. Full names of Roman citizens had three parts, the first abbreviated (see Sec. V). For brevity the second or third name only is often used in Latin or English.
10. *littera*: means a letter of the alphabet; in pl., either a "letter" as a communication or "literature," as in our phrase "a man of letters."
11. *carmen*: a "poem" here. Lucretius also wrote poetry-about philosophy and science.
12. *lepidus -a -um*: "charming," "witty"

13. *Syrus -a -um*: "Syrian"
14. *mīmae*: "farces"
15. *rūrī, Rōmae, Athēnīs*: locative case forms (See V also, for omission of prepositions with these words.)
16. *Aenēida*: The *Aeneid*, title of Vergil's great epic on Rome's forefathers.
17. *Metamorphōsēs*: a long poem containing myths and legends involving "Transformations"
18. *Ars Amātōria*: "The Art of Love"
19. *scrīpta*: used as adjective with *verba*, "written"
20. "I shall not perish entirely."
21. *Imperātor*: originally meant a top military commander. Because Augustus retained the title as a sign of authority, it became the title of rulers who followed him and acquired the meaning of "Emperor."
22. *irrīsit*: *in + rīsit*
23. Tacitus and Pliny were among them.
24. *quae*: "which"

II OPTIONAL READING

Catullus: Nūlla potest mulier tantum sē dīcere amātam
vērē, quantam ā mē Lesbia amāta mea es.

Jam vēr ēgelidōs refert teporēs.

Vergil: Labor omnia vincit.

Possunt quia posse videntur.

Arma virumque canō.

Horace: Dum loquimur, fugit invida aetās.

Fortūna . . . trānsmūtat incertōs honōrēs.

Auream quisquis mediocritātem dīligit.

Ovid: Ācta deōs numquam mortālia fallunt.

Crēdula rēs Amor.

Intrā fortūnam dēbet quisque manēre suam.

Martial: Nōn amō tē, Sabidī, nec possum dīcere quā rē.
Hoc tantum possum dīcere: nōn amō tē.

Difficilis, facilis, jūcundus, acerbus es īdem,
Nec tēcum possum vīvere nec sine tē.

Juvenal: Mēns sāna in corpore sānō.

Sī nātūra negat, facit indignātiō versūs.

Nōbilitās sōla est atque ūnīca virtūs.

III WORD STUDY

1. What words in this lesson come into English unchanged or almost unchanged?
2. Give English derivatives from: jūdicium, rūs, imitor, expellō (two stems).
3. Note carefully the distinction in spelling between *aetās* and *aestās*.
   (As a memory helper: there is an "s" in both *s*ummer and ae*s*tās.)

4. See the notes on the reading for the relationship of the Latin *imperātor* to "emperor."
5. What Latin words are these English derivatives related to: pacify, verify, clarify? Define each derivative.
6. In stage directions for Latin plays and early modern ones, the words "exit" and "exeunt" occur frequently. The singular form has continued on as a noun in English.

7. *Littera* is also spelled *lītera,* the form from which our derivatives like "literal," "literature," and "literary" come. Explain the meaning of these derivatives.
8. Our words "Greece," "Greek," and the first part of "Greco-Roman" come from the Roman name for this country and people, not from their own names for their country and people (Hellas, Hellenes).

IV VOCABULARY

Nouns

littera, litterā f.
poēta, poētā m.

jūdicium, jūdiciō n.

aetās, aetāte f.
ars, arte f.
imperātor, imperātōre m.
ōrātor, ōrātōre m.
pāx, pāce f.

rūs, rūre n.

magistrātus, magistrātū m.

Athēnae, Athēnīs f. pl.
Graecia, Graeciā f.
Hispānia, Hispāniā f.
Italia, Italiā f.

Adjectives and Pronouns

antīquus, antīqua, antīquum
clārus, clāra, clārum
Graecus, Graeca, Graecum
Latīnus, Latīna, Latīnum
pūblicus, pūblica, pūblicum
superbus, superba, superbum
vērus, vēra, vērum

aliquis, aliquid

Verbs

imitor, imitārī, imitātus
expellō -pellere -pulī -pulsus

coepī, coeptus

eō, īre, iī, ītus
redeō -īre -iī -itus
fīō, fīerī, factus

Function Words

hodiē

ut

V FORM CHART
Irregular Verbs

fīō, fīerī, factus

Present tense		Perfect tense
fīō	---	factus sum
---	---	etc.
fit	fīunt	

eō, īre, iī, ītus

Present tense		Perfect tense	
eō	īmus	iī	iimus
īs	ītis	īstī	īstis
it	eunt	iit	iērunt

VI   OPTIONAL WORK

A.   Locative Case

A few Latin nouns have a form known as the locative case. In this lesson *rūrī*, *Rōmae*, and *Athēnīs* occur. For further information see Appendix B, page 164, in Part II.

These same words (names of cities and towns, *domus* and *rūs*) are used without place prepositions as follows:

if someone is going to this place, the accusative case is used without a preposition (no *in* or *ad*); *Rōmam*, etc.

if someone is going away from it, the ablative case is used without *ab* or *ex*: *Rōmā*, etc.

(if someone is in the place, the locative form is used (no *in*): *Rōmae*).

B.   Roman Names

The names of Roman citizens, during the Roman republic and early empire, had three parts: the *praenōmen* or "first name," usually abbreviated since there were few of them; the *nōmen*, name of the clan or *gēns*; and the *cognōmen*, family name or special personal designation.

The abbreviations for some of the *praenōmina* are:

A. = Aulus	C. = Gaius	Cn. = Gnaeus	D. = Decimus	L. = Lūcius
M'. = Mānius	M. = Mārcus	P. = Pūblius	Q. = Quīntus	S. = Sextus
T. = Titus	Ti. = Tiberius			

Romans were frequently designated by one rather than by all three parts of the name. The names used in this lesson and the familiar English designations are:

M. Tullius Cicero	Cicero	P. Ovidius Nāso	Ovid
C. Jūlius Caesar	Caesar	T. Līvius	Livy
C. Valerius Catullus	Catullus	D. Jūnius Juvenālis	Juvenal
P. Vergilius Maro	Vergil	M. Valerius Martiālis	Martial
Q. Horātius Flaccus	Horace		

For other information on names—those of women, slaves, adopted sons, and emperors (for example, C. Jūlius Caesar Octāviānus Augustus)—see a good book on Roman life or a classical dictionary.

LESSON NINETEEN

Fortibus est fortūna virīs data. — Ennius   "To brave men fortune has been given."

Deō, Rēgī, Patriae — Motto   "For God, for king, for country."

Purpose: to learn the forms of the dative case and its use as indirect object

I PATTERN READING

A. Sample sentences

1. Homō fīliae pecūniam dat.   The man gives his daughter money.

2. Cui pater verba dīcit? Fīliō.   To whom is the father speaking? To his son.

3. Quibus fēminae fābulās nārrāvērunt? Amīcīs.   To whom did the women tell stories? To their friends.

4. Dux mīlitī castra ostendit.   The leader showed the soldier the camp.

5. Dux exercituī arma dedit.   The general gave weapons to his army.

6. Dux ad exercitum praemia mīsit.   The general sent prizes to his army.

7. Ā duce arma mīlitibus data sunt.   Arms were given the soldiers by their leader.

8. Bellum reī pūblicae tumultum facit.   War creates confusion for the government.

B. Practice sentences

1. Pater nōmen dat.

2. Pater puellae nōmen dat.

3. Cui nōmen dat? Puellae.

4. Ego tibi verbum dīcō.

5. Cui ego verbum dīcō? Tibi.

6. Māter grātiās agit.

7. Māter Deō grātiās agit.

8. Cui grātiās agit? Deō.

9. Mātrēs Rōmānae deīs grātiās agunt.

10. Fortibus virīs praemia dantur.

11. Quibus praemia dantur? Fortibus virīs.

12. Praemia eīs dantur.

13. Pater mihi praemium dat.

14. Imperātor ad ducem praemium mīsit.

15. Dux vōbīs arma dedit.

16. Dux paucīs mīlitibus gladium ostendit.

17. Dux exercituī castra ostendit.

18. Ducēs exercitibus castra ostendērunt.

19. Gladius gladiātōrī miserō ostentus est.

20. Cibus puerō pauperī datus est.

21. Cibus ad puerum pauperem lātus est.

22. Nūllī fīliō mūnus ostendit pater.

23. Poēta clārus carmen ad imperātōrem mīsit.

24. Ōrātōrēs antīquī nōbīs opera nōta relīquērunt.

25. Auxilium hostibus datur.

26. Arma hostibus dantur.

27. Mīlitēs veterēs Deō, Rēgī, Patriae
    pūgnāvērunt.

28. Lucernās fēminīs dō.

29. Nēminī omnia dīcuntur.

30. Omnibus aliquid dīcitur.

C.   Questions on structure

1. List four Latin verbs that pattern with a dative.
2. What two Latin interrogatives are answered by a dative?
3. Why is *exercituī* used in sample sentence 5, but *ad exercitum* in sentence 6?
4. What similarities do you notice between dative case forms and endings of other cases?
5. What similarities are there among dative case forms?

See Appendix B, pages 192-93.

II   FORM CHART

A.   Dative case

	I	II	III	IV	V
Sg.	puell*ae*	puer*ō*	mīlit*ī*	man*uī*	di*ēī*
Pl.	puell*īs*	puer*īs*	mīlit*ibus*	man*ibus*	di*ēbus*

B.   Adjectives have the same endings as nouns, type one using forms of I-II declension, type two using those of III declension. (Note exceptions in C.)

C.   Pronouns and irregular adjectives

	Interrogative	Personal		(Reflexive)		Adjectives
Singular	cui	mihi	tibi	(sibi)	eī	nūllī
Plural	quibus	nōbīs	vōbīs	(sibi)	eīs	nūllīs
						(also ūnī, neutrī
						tōtī, sōlī)

III   EXERCISES

A.   Answer the questions on the pictures.

Quis dat librum?
Cui dat librum?
Quid agit puer?
Quid puella accipit?
Quid datur?
Cui datur?

Quis dat?
Quid dat?
Cui dat?
Quid agit mīles?
Quid agit servus?
Cui mīles pecūniam dat?

B.   Answer all questions in Latin.

1. Frātrī fābulam puer nārrat.

Quis fābulam nārrat?
Cui fābulam nārrat?
Quid puer nārrat?
Quid nārrātur?
Cui nārrātur?
Ā quō nārrātur?

2. Soror mātrī mūnera dat.

Quis dat?
Cui dat?
Quae dat?

3. Ā frātre fābula puerīs nārrātur.

Quid nārrātur?
Quibus nārrātur?
Ā quō nārrātur?
Quis fābulam nārrat?

4. Arborem juvenī puer ostendit.

Quis arborem ostendit?
Cui arborem ostendit?
Quid puer ostendit?
Quid ostenditur?
Cui ostenditur?
Ā quō ostenditur?

5. Virīs fortibus fortūna data est.

Quid datum est?
Quibus fortūna data est?
Quālēs sunt virī?

6. Poētae nōbīs carmina relīquērunt.

Quī relīquērunt?
Quae relīquērunt?
Quibus relīquērunt?

C.   Decline in four cases:

1. Singular only: rēx, exercitus, patria omnis, amīcus noster, ego.

2. Plural only: ōs, māter, vir fortis, bona rēs, nōs.

D.   Give the Latin equivalent.

1. The boy became king immediately after his father died.
2. You-all endured many injustices (injuries) for your country.
3. The orator spoke well at (*ad*) the trial.
4. The Romans admired and, at the same time, imitated the Greeks.
5. Aren't you setting out for Rome soon?
6. How long have you remained in the country?
7. We followed our friends to Athens and began to learn the Greek language.
8. I never feared loud sounds or a tremendous uproar.
9. The soldiers haven't yet advanced into your town, have they?
10. We went across the river to a strange place.

E.   Change these words from dative plural to dative singular.

1. mūneribus vērīs	5. diēbus clārīs	9. terrīs lātīs
2. aetātibus antīquīs	6. manibus nostrīs	10. corvīs stultīs
3. fīliīs fidēlibus	7. urbibus dīvitibus	11. foliīs levibus
4. puellīs superbīs	8. oppidīs vīlibus	12. virīs trīstibus

IV   PATTERN PRACTICE SIXTEEN

1. The man pointed out the boy.	Homō puerum ostendit.
2. The man pointed out the boy to the girl.	Homō puellae puerum ostendit.
3. The man pointed out the girl to the boy.	Homō puellam puerō ostendit.
4. The man pointed out the girls to the boy.	Homō puellās puerō ostendit.
5. The man pointed out the girls to the boys.	Homō puellās puerīs ostendit.
6. The man pointed out the boys to the girls.	Homō puellīs puerōs ostendit.
7. The brother told a story.	Frāter fābulam nārrāvit.
8. The brother told his sister a story.	Frāter sorōrī fābulam nārrāvit.
9. The sister told her brother a story.	Frātrī soror fābulam nārrāvit.
10. The sister told her little brother a story.	Frātrī parvō soror fābulam nārrāvit.
11. The sister told a story for her brothers.	Frātribus soror fābulam nārrāvit.
12. The brothers told a story for their sisters.	Frātrēs sorōribus fābulam nārrāvērunt.
13. The brothers told their little sisters a story.	Frātrēs parvīs sorōribus fābulam narrāvērunt.
14. The *leader* gave money.	Pecūniam dedit dux.
15. The *leader* gave the army money.	Exercituī pecūniam dedit dux.
16. The army didn't give the leader money.	Exercitus pecūniam ducī nōn dedit.
17. The soldiers didn't give the leader prizes.	Mīlitēs praemia ducī nōn dedērunt.
18. The *leaders* gave the soldiers prizes.	Mīlitibus praemia dedērunt ducēs.
19. The *leaders* sent the soldiers prizes.	Praemia ad mīlitēs mīsērunt ducēs.
20. The *leaders* sent letters to the homeland.	Litterās ad patriam mīsērunt ducēs.
21. The *leaders* thanked their country.	Patriae grātiās ēgērunt ducēs.
22. The *leader* thanked God.	Deō grātiās ēgit dux.
23. Thanks were given to God.	Deō sunt āctae grātiae.
24. Thanks were given the good king.	Rēgī bonō sunt āctae grātiae.
25. Good luck was granted the good king.	Rēgī bonō est fortūna data.
26. Good luck has been granted to a brave man.	Fortī est fortūna data virō.
27. Good luck has been given to brave men.	Fortibus est fortūna data virīs.

V   LĒCTIO

1. Dā[1] glōriam Deō. -- Motto

2. Jūstitia omnibus   — Motto (Washington, D. C.)

3. Magistrī puerīs parvīs crustula[2] saepe dant. — Horace

4. Nīl[3] sine magnō vīta labōre dedit mortālibus. -- Horace

5. Inopī[4] beneficium bis dat quī[5] dat celeriter. -- Publilius Syrus

6. Fortūna multīs dat nimis, satis nūllī.[6] — Martial

7. Lūsistī satis, ēdistī satis atque bībistī; tempus abīre[7] tibi est. — Horace

8. Verbum sapientī sat[8] est. — Anon.

9. Sīc semper tyrannīs [9] — Motto (Virginia)

10. Hodiē mihi, crās tibi   — Common epitaph

11. Nōn sibi[10] sed patriae   — Motto (108th Field Artillery)

12. Sex hōrīs dormīre sat[8] est juvenīque senīque; septem
    vix pigrō, nūllī[6] concēdimus octō. —Anon.

13. Bonus vir nēmō est nisī quī bonus est omnibus. — Publilius Syrus

14. Sōl omnibus lūcet.[11] — Petronius

15. Fortī et fidēlī nihil difficile. — Motto

Notā bene

1. *dā*: imperative, see page 120
2. *crustulum*, n.: "cookie"
3. *nīl = nihil*
4. *inops, inopem*: "needy"
5. *quī*: "who," "he who," "one who"
6. *nūllī*: irregular dative

7. *abīre = ab + īre*
8. *sat = satis*
9. *tyrannus -ō* m.: "tyrant"
10. *sibi*: meaning varies according to subject
    to which it refers; here it means "for
    themselves"
11. *lūcet*: what the sun does

VI   WORD STUDY

1. Roman camps, *castra*, were located in conquered territory and became the centers of towns. In this way many city names in England acquired the ending "-caster" or "-chester"; for example, Winchester, Manchester, Chester, Lancaster. These names, of course, were brought from England to the U. S. A.

2. The name of the "dative" case comes from *datus (dō)*. Other derivatives are "data" and "date." Explain the connection in meaning of each to the Latin source.

3. To what Latin words are each of these related: dux, atque, beneficium, abeō, mortālis?

4. What words in this lesson come into English with very slight changes?

5. Give derivatives from: populus, beneficium, magister, satis, sōl. Also from these words used in the reading lesson: tyrannus, crustulum.

6. When you "procrastinate" you don't do it today but you hold off for _____ (or longer).

7. To what Latin words are these derivatives related: edible, illusion, elusive, biennial, bilingual, concession, satisfaction?

VII VOCABULARY

Nouns	*Adjectives*	*Verbs*
jūstitia, jūstitiā f.	mortālis, mortāle	dō, dare, dedī, datus
magister, magistrō m.	(Indeclinable)	concēdō -cēdere -cessī -cessus
populus, populō m.		edō, ēsse, ēdī, ēsus[1]
arma, armīs n. pl.	nimis	lūdō, lūdere, lūsī, lūsus
beneficium, beneficiō n.	satis	abeō -īre -iī -ītus
castra, castrīs n. pl.		
praemium, praemiō n.		*Function Words*
dux, duce m.		bis
sōl, sōle m.		crās
exercitus, exercitū m.		vix
		atque

[1] This verb has some regular and some irregular forms in the present.

LESSON TWENTY

Nīl hominī certum est. — Ovid

Mors omnibus īnstat. — Grave inscription

Frūstrā labōrat quī omnibus placēre studet. — Proverb

"Nothing is certain for human beings."

"Death impends for all."

"He labors in vain who strives to please all."

Purpose: to learn more uses of the dative case

I   POPULUS RŌMĀNUS

1. Quis est vir?	Vir est cīvis Rōmānus; ūnus ex patribus Rōmānīs est.
2. Quī sunt hominēs?	Hominēs sunt cīvēs. Populus est; plēbs est.
3. Quae urbs in pictūrā est?	Rōma est.
4. Ubi est plēbs?	In monte nōn procul ā Rōmā est.
5. Quālis appellātur mōns?	Mōns Sacer appellātur.
6. Quid agit vir?	Vir loquitur. Plēbem monet.
7. Dē quā rē loquitur?	Dē lībertāte, dē rēbus hūmānīs loquitur. Nesciō an dē bellō an dē pāce. Eīs persuādēre cōnātur.
8. Suntne castra in monte?	Castra ibi posita sunt.
9. Quid agunt hominēs?	In omnī parte stant et sedent hominēs.

II   PATTERN READING

A.   Sample sentences

1. Omnēs dēlectāre volumus.   We want to please everybody.
   Omnibus placēre volumus.

2. Mīlitēs ducem adjuvant.   The soldiers help the leader.
   Mīlitēs ducī subveniunt.

3. Senex juvenem monuit.   The old man advised the youth.
   Senex juvenī persuāsit.   The old man persuaded the youth.

4. Cīvis servum nōn timet.   The citizen is not afraid of the slave.
   Cīvis servō crēdit.   The citizen trusts the slave.

5. Animal gladiātōrem vulnerat.   The animal wounds the gladiator.
   Animal gladiātōrī nocet.   The animal harms the gladiator.

6. Lībertātem amat; lībertātī studet.   He loves liberty; he is eager for liberty.

7. Līber sum; nūllī virō serviō.   I am a free man; I serve no man.

8. Plēbs senātum nōn amāvit, plēbs   The common people did not like the senate; the
   senātuī invīdit.   plebian class hated (envied) the senate.

9. Fīlius patrī cārus est.   The son is dear to his father.

10. Imitātiō nōn est similis vēritātī.   Pretense is not like truth.

11. Dux bellum hostibus īnfert.   The leader brings war upon the enemy.

B.   Practice sentences

1. Pater fīliō cōnsilium dedit.

2. Fīliō cōnsilium placuit; tibi nōn
   placuit.

3. Frātrī dē cōnsiliō persuāsī.

4. Puer pedem hodiē vulnerāvit.

5. Puer pedī saepe nocuit.

6. Praemium cupīvistis semper.

7. Praemiō studuistis nōn numquam.

8. Poētae antīquī litterās amāvērunt.

9. Poētae litterīs studuērunt.

10. Rēx amīcīs beneficia intulit.

11. Rēgī superbō invīdimus.

12. Magistrātus cīvibus subvēnit;
    magistrātus cīvēs adjūvit.

13. Augustus amīcīs crēdidit.

14. Nōnne mihi crēdis?

15. Perīculum adest; perīculum exercituī
    īnstat.

16. Cārus amīcus ducī est.

17. Deus hominibus sacer est.

18. Castra oppidīs sunt similia.

19. Silentium dēscendit simile mortī.

20. Poēta amīcus vōbīs est.

21. Imperātor nōbīs nōn est cārus.

22. Futūra sunt omnibus incerta.

23. Pecūnia ūtilis est viātōribus.

24. Servī sumus sī corporī servīmus.

25. Nihil hominibus certum est.

26. Omnia deīs certum est.

C.   Questions on structure

1. What verbs do you find used with the dative case in this lesson?
2. With what adjectives is the dative used?
3. Many times dative and ablative case forms are identical. If the word is used without a preposition, there may be a problem in deciding which case it is. If the word means a person or persons it is more likely to be dative; if it mentions a thing it is more likely to be ablative. What ideas are expressed by ablatives without prepositions? Check the sample sentences in the previous lesson and this one; are datives more commonly words for persons or for things?

See Appendix B, pages 193-94.

III   EXERCISES

A.   Answer the question by the dative case of the noun used in the sentence.

Example: Cui reī *perīculum* simile est? *Perīculō.*

1. Cui reī carmen simile est? _____
2. Cui reī caput simile est? _____
3. Cui reī barba similis est? _____
4. Cui reī gladius similis est? _____
5. Quibus rēbus flūmina similia sunt? _____

6. Quibus rēbus verba similia sunt? _____
7. Cui reī nox similis est? _____
8. Cui reī diēs similis est? _____
9. Quibus rēbus exercitūs similēs sunt? _____
10. Quibus rēbus oculī similēs sunt? _____

B.   Supply the correct form of *each* of the words in parentheses to fill the blank (three times).

1. Stultus _____ nōn crēdit. (philosophus; sapiēns; poēta nōtus)
2. Dīves _____ studet. (pecūnia; rēs (pl.); glōria facilis)
3. Servus _____ servīre dēbet. (māter bona; virī; imperātor)
4. Pater _____ amat. (fīlia; fīlius; soror dulcis)
5. Pecūnia _____ placet. (mīles; fēmina; juvenēs pigrī)

C.   Change the sentence substituting the intransitive verb (patterning with the dative) that is nearest in meaning to the verb of the sentence. Keep the same person, number, and tense.

1. Vīnea agricolam dēlectāvit.
2. Sapiēns stultum monet.
3. Philosophus vēritātem cupit.
4. Lupus agnōs vulnerāvit.
5. Multās rēs cupīvimus.
6. Nēmō mē adjūvit.

7. Serpēns tē vulnerāvit.
8. Rēgem superbum nōn amātis.
9. Mē nōn timēs.
10. Fortūnam omnem nōn timeō.
11. Frūstrā līberīs monuimus.
12. Omnēs dēlectāre studēs.

D.   Metaphrase

1. Ducibus praemia . . . . . . nt.
2. Ā ducibus praemia . . . . . . ntur.
3. Multīs rēbus vir. . . . . . . tur.
4. Multīs virīs rēx . . . . t.
5. Patribus lēx . . . . . . t.

6. Nōminibus puerī . . . . . . ntur.
7. Puellīs puer . . . . t.
8. Vōbīs. . . . . . . mus.
9. Pedibus certīs. . . . . . . tis.
10. Gladiīs juvenis . . . . . . .tur.

E. Give the Latin equivalent.

1. The man gives his son the remaining money.
2. The boys thank (give thanks to) their father.
3. The rich farmer spoke in such a way to his lazy sons.
4. The king wants to give proper laws to the country.
5. The next day we sent letters to the young man.
6. I cannot show you an easy road through our town.

7. The tired soldiers were transported into the camp again.
8. The commander gave the army a reward sometimes.
9. You gave me the book; you did not send it to my sister.
10. However, few kind words are said to slaves.

IV PATTERN PRACTICE SEVENTEEN

1. The youth reveals his plan.	Cōnsilium ostendit juvenis.
2. The youth reveals his plan to his brother.	Frātrī cōnsilium ostendit juvenis.
3. His brother likes the plan.	Frāter cōnsilium amat.
4. The plan pleases his brother.	Frātrī cōnsilium placet.
5. His brother is eager for the plan.	Frāter cōnsiliō studet.
6. His sisters do not accept the plan.	Sorōrēs cōnsilium nōn accipiunt.
7. His sisters do not trust the plan.	Sorōrēs cōnsiliō nōn crēdunt.
8. The youth does not persuade his sisters.	Sorōribus juvenis nōn persuādet.
9. Yet the youth has warned his sisters.	Sorōrēs tamen juvenis monuit.
10. The youth helped the unhappy girls.	Juvenis puellās miserās adjūvit.
11. The youth aided the unhappy girls.	Juvenis puellīs miserīs subvēnit.
12. The slave served the unhappy girls.	Servus puellīs miserīs servīvit.
13. The slave did not hurt the dog.	Servus canī nōn nocuit.
14. The slave did not wound the dog.	Servus canem nōn vulnerāvit.
15. The dog did not delight the slave.	Servum canis nōn dēlectāvit.
16. The dog did not please the slave.	Servō canis nōn placuit.
17. The slave hated the treacherous dog.	Servus canī perfidō invīdit.
18. The slave did not hate the general.	Servus ducī nōn invīdit.
19. The slave served his general well.	Servus ducī bene servīvit.
20. The leader is dear to his slave.	Est servō cārus dux.
21. The commander is dear to the god.	Est cārus deō dux.
22. The god is sacred to the army.	Est deus sacer exercituī.
23. The gods are sacred to mortals.	Sunt deī mortālibus sacrī.
24. God brings death to mortals.	Deus mortem mortālibus īnfert.
25. Death threatens all mortals.	Mors mortālibus omnibus īnstat.

V   PRĪMA SĒDITIŌ[1]

Temporibus antīquīs plērīque mīlitēs Rōmānī erant[2] plēbēī[3] quī,[4] dum pāx est, agricolae in agrīs labōrābant.[2] Dum exercitus Rōmānus pūgnat et mīlitēs in castrīs absunt, saepe aedificia et agrōs accendērunt hostēs.   Quandō mīlitēs domum rediērunt, habuērunt nūllum cibum, nūllam casam, nūllam pecūniam.   Ēsse et vīvere nōn potuērunt nisī aes aliēnum[5] fēcērunt.   Paene nēmō plēbēius aere aliēnō erat[2] līber.   Prō patriā et prō lībertāte saepe et ḅene pūgnāvērunt, at domī lībertātem vērē nōn habuērunt - multī etiam factī sunt servī: servīvērunt cīvibus suīs[6] quod aes aliēnum solvere nōn potuērunt.   Tandem, igitur, prō patriā pūgnāre nōn jam cupīvērunt.

Auxilium ā cōnsulibus petīvit plēbs.   Neque id dare cōnsulibus placuit, neque senātus Rōmānus plēbī subvenīre cupīvit.   Itaque plēbs senātuī invidēre coepit.   Tum omnis plēbs Rōmam relīquit - nōn profectī sunt contrā hostēs sed ad Sacrum Montem[7] trāns Aniēnem[8] flūmen prōgressī sunt.   Ibi sińe duce castra posuērunt et multōs diēs mānsērunt.

Timor urbem tenuit; nūllum exercitum habēre potuērunt nisī mīlitēs plēbēī rediērunt.   Maximē patrēs Rōmānī, id est, senātus, veritī sunt quod multī hostēs in Italiā erant[2] proximī quī bellum Rōmānīs statim īnferre potuērunt.   Mīsērunt igitur ad plēbem ōrātōrem Menēnium Agrippam,[9] virum plēbī cārum quod apud eōs nātus erat.[10]   Sīc locūtus est ōrātor:

"Ōlim multa membra īrāta erant[2] quod omnia ventrī[11] dedērunt, sed venter omnia accēpit ēgitque nihil.   Cōnsilium igitur cēpērunt: nec manūs ad ōs cibum tulērunt, nec ōs accēpit, nec dentēs cōnfēcērunt.   Sed, dum reliqua membra ventrem famē vincere cōnantur, corpus paene mortuum est tōtum.   Tum reliqua membra ventrī iterum subvēnērunt quod maximē erat ūtilis tōtī corporī.   Sēditiō[1] corporis[12] contrā ventrem similis est īrae plēbis[12] in patrēs et similī modō ad fīnem venīre dēbet."

Hōc[13] modō Agrippa plēbī persuāsit et cum patribus facta est pāx.   Duo magistrātūs novī— tribūnī[14] appellātī sunt—sunt deinde factī quī[4] plebi auxilium contrā patrēs semper dedērunt et lībertātem omnibus cīvibus Rōmānīs sustinuērunt.

Notā bene

1. *sēditiō*: "rebellion," "insurrection," "uprising," "strike"
2. *erat, erant*: "was," "were" -*ba*-: sign of continued past "were"

3. *plēbēius -a -um*: adjective based on *plēbs*; also used as noun for a member of plebeian class

4. *quī*: "who"
5. *aes aliēnum*: money belonging to someone else is a "debt"
6. *cīvibus suīs*: "fellow citizens"
7. *Mōns Sacer*: "Sacred Mount"
8. *Aniēnem*: Anio (River)
9. *Menēnius Agrippa*: use nominative form in English
10. *nātus erat*: past perfect tense: "had been born"
11. *venter, ventre* m.: "stomach"
12. *corporis* and *plēbis*: genitive case forms (see next lesson) "of the body," "of the people"
13. *hōc*: abl., "this"
14. *tribūnus*: Roman official, "tribune"

Respondē Latīnē

1. Quī erant mīlitēs Rōmānī?
2. Cūr post bella nihil habuērunt multī?
3. Cūr aes aliēnum fēcit plēbs?
4. Quid prō plēbe agit senātus?
5. Cūr multī Rōmānī prō patriā pūgnāre nōn cupīvērunt?
6. Quō prōcessit plēbs?
7. Quis erat Menēnius Agrippa?
8. Cui Menēnius persuādēre voluit?
9. In fābulā quid agit venter? ōs? dentēs?
10. Quō modō membra ventrem vincere cōnāta sunt?
11. Quid tandem ēgērunt membra?
12. Quid dēbuit plēbs agere?
13. Quī pācem fēcērunt?
14. Quī fuērunt līberī?
15. Cui reī similis est sēditiō corporis?
16. Quibus est fortūna data?

VI   OPTIONAL READING

Frūstrā aut pecūniae aut imperiīs aut opibus aut glōriae student. — Cicero

Nēmō potest duōbus dominīs servīre. — N. T. (Matthew)

Solitūdō placet Mūsīs; urbs est inimīca poētīs. — Petrarch (?)

Ingrātus ūnus omnibus miserīs nocet. — Publilius Syrus

(Populus) stultus honōrēs
saepe dat indīgnīs et fāmae servit ineptus. — Horace

VII   WORD STUDY

1. Give the Latin source and explain the relationship in meaning to the sources of these derivatives: plebeian, sedition, civic, civil, instant, student, credible, sacrifice, invidious.

2. Give English derivatives from: famēs, membrum, lībertās, similis, aliēnus, ūtilis, persuādeō, senātus, sacer, crēdō, famēs.

3. To what Latin words already studied are these related: lībertās, reliquus, ūtilis, subveniō, īnstō, serviō, īnferō, senātus, studeō, invideō?

4. The preposition *contrā* is used in both Latin and English as a prefix. In English it has also the form "counter." Give three examples of words using it in either form.

5. *Cōnsul* is an example of a word which, while it has come into English without change in spelling, has changed in meaning. The Roman consul was one of the two chief executives of the Roman state. What does a "consul" today do?

6. What is the difference in meaning between "mood" and "mode," both of which are derived from *modus*?

VIII   VOCABULARY

Nouns	*Adjectives*	*Verbs*

Nouns

modus, modō m.

membrum, membrō n.

cīvis, cīve m.
cōnsul, cōnsule m.
famēs, famē f.
(irreg. abl. III
    declension)
lībertās, lībertāte f.
plēbs, plēbe f.

senātus, senātū m.

Adjectives

aliēnus, aliēna, aliēnum
cārus, cāra, cārum
reliquus, reliqua, reliquum
sacer, sacra, sacrum

similis, simile
ūtilis, ūtile

Function Words

ōlim
vērē
tum

contrā + acc.

Verbs

īnstō, īnstāre, īnstitī, īnstātus (dat.)
cōnor, cōnārī, cōnātus

invideō, invidēre, invīdī, invīsus (dat.)
noceō, nocēre, nocuī, nocitus (dat.)
placeō, placēre, placuī, placitus (dat.)
studeō, studēre, studuī (dat.)
persuādeō, persuādēre, persuāsī,
    persuāsus (dat.)

crēdō, crēdere, crēdidī, crēditus (dat.)

serviō, servīre, servīvī, servītus (dat.)
subveniō -venīre -vēnī -ventus (dat.)

īnferō, īnferre, intulī, illātus

LESSON TWENTY-ONE

Rērum hūmānārum domina Fortūna.
-- Cicero

"Lady Luck, mistress of human affairs."

Vōx populī, vōx Deī. — Common phrase

"The voice of the people, the voice of God."
(Popular will is a divine mandate.)

Purpose: to learn the forms of the genitive case and how to show possession

I PATTERN READING

A. Sample sentences

1. Librōs magistrī in mēnsā pōnō.

   I am placing the teacher's books on the table.

2. Librī puerōrum puellārumque in mēnsā sunt.

   The boys' and girls' books are on the table.

3. Frāter meae sorōris est fīlius patris meī.

   My sister's brother is my father's son.

4. Arma exercitūs hostibus sunt nōva.

   The weapons of the army are strange to the enemy.

5. Animālibus est cibus.

   The animals have food.

6. Virtūtem habent animālia.

   Animals have courage.

7. Virtūtem animālium laudāmus.

   We praise the courage of animals.

8. Fortūna rēs hominum regit.

   Fortune guides the affairs of men.

9. Cīvitātī antīquae sunt multa templa deōrum.

   The ancient state has many temples of the gods.

B. Practice sentences

1. Est pater meus.

2. Sum fīlius patris meī.

3. Sumus fīliī patrum nostrōrum.

4. Est māter mea.

5. Sum fīlia mātris meae.

6. Sumus fīliae mātrum nostrārum.

7. Quaerō puerī puellaeque patrem.

8. Quaerō patrem puerōrum puellārumque.

9. Cujus templum vidēmus? Jovis templum.

10. Quōrum templa vidēmus? Deōrum templa.

11. Multī hominēs bona cōnsilia habent.

12. Multīs hominibus sunt bona cōnsilia.

13. Cōnsilia multōrum hominum nōn perfecta sunt.

14. Fortūna bona hominibus fēlīcibus est.

15. Dominō est magna vīlla.

16. Vīllam dominī mīror.

17. Gladius est mīlitī.

18. Gladius mīlitis āmittitur.

19. Hostium arma capta sunt ā nōbīs.

20. Nōs omnēs hostium exercitūs secūtī sumus.

21. Ab castrīs exercituum abiērunt hostēs.

22. Nōmen mīlitis audīvistis.

23. Nōmina mīlitum audīvistis.

24. Nōmen diēī puer didicit.

25. Nōmina diērum puer didicit.

26. Vōx populī, vōx Deī omnibus sacer est.

C.   Questions on structure

1. What is the usual environment of the genitive case?
2. Find examples of two ways of showing possession.
3. What letters do the genitive plural forms have in common?
4. What similarities to other case endings do genitives have?

See Appendix B, pages 192 and 194.

II   FORM CHART

A. Genitive Case

	I	II	III		IV	V
Sg.	puell*ae*	puer*ī*	mīlit*is*	urb*is*	man*ūs*	di*ēī*
Pl.	puell*ārum*	puer*ōrum*	mīlit*um*	urb*ium*	man*uum*	di*ērum* ·

B. Nouns of the III declension you have studied which have -*ium* as the ending of the genitive plural are:

ars	mōns	auris	orbis	īnfāns	animal
mēns	dēns	cīvis	vulpēs	parens	
mors	fōns	hostis		serpēns	
nox		fīnis			
urbs					

This type of noun will be designated hereafter in vocabulary as "i" type. All vocabulary entries will now be made, as in reference dictionaries, by nominative, genitive, gender of the nouns.[1]

C. Genitive forms of pronouns

Interrogative:	cujus	of *is, ea, id*:	ejus
	quōrum (quārum)		eōrum (eārum)

---

[1] This procedure should also be followed in vocabulary notebooks.

III EXERCISES

A. The first sentence states that someone owns something. Answer the questions based on it by using the genitive of the possessor. (Example: *Virō nōmen est. Cujus nōmen audīmus? Virī nōmen audīmus.*)

    1. Opus est auctōrī. Cujus opus laudātur? _____ opus laudātur.

    2. Gladiātōrī est cōnsilium. Cujus consilium capitur?

    3. Puerō manūs sunt. Cujus manūs nōn lavantur?

    4. Deō est vōx. Cujus vōx audītur?

    5. Populō nostrō sunt multī agrī. Cujus agrī mīrāmur?

    6. Puellīs sunt mātrēs. Quārum mātrēs amantur?

    7. Exercitibus sunt dūcēs. Quōrum ducēs sequimur?

    8. Sunt animālibus pedēs. Quōrum pedēs vidētis?

    9. Frātribus vestrīs est pīetās. Quōrum pīetās probātur?

    10. Lībertās est rānīs. Quārum lībertās āmittitur?

B. Change the genitives from singular to plural.

    1. Labor hominis omnia vīcit.

    2. Vōcēs puerī et puellae audīvimus.

    3. Ex juvenis casā profectī sumus.

    4. Nōmina poētae antīquī magister docuit.

    5. Hostēs ab exercitūs nostrī duce victī sunt.

    6. Agricolae pauperis pecūnia nōn inventa est.

    7. Lībertātem virī Rōmānī ōrātor petīvit.

C. Change the genitives from plural to singular.

    1. Rērum hūmānārum domina Fortūna est.

    2. Verbīs magistrōrum movēminī.

    3. Fortūna fēminārum bonārum ā deīs oritur.

    4. Mentēs mīlitum ad bellum vertuntur.

    5. Clāmōrēs fēlīcium puerōrum audīmus.

    6. Magnus est fēminārum trīstium timor.

    7. Beneficia cīvium bonōrum laetē accipiuntur.

    8. Opera auctōrum antiquōrum laudantur.

D. Decline in five cases, singular and plural: via, magister, servus, oppidum, rēs, manus, homō, opus, urbs, soror.

E. Answer the question with the correct genitive form of the noun.

    1. animal

    2. equus

    3. Sī { canis } venit, cujus pedēs audiuntur? _____ pedēs audiuntur.

    4. asinus

    5. aper

    6. servus

    7. poēta

    8. Sī { fīlia } vīvit, cujus vīta agitur? _____ vīta agitur.

    9. cīvis

    10. magister

11-20 Repeat sentences 1-10 using the same nouns in the plural.

Sī animālia veniunt, quōrum pedēs audiuntur? _____ pedēs audiuntur.

F.   Give the Latin equivalent.

1. We are not always eager for our studies.
2. A king is compelled to give benefits to the citizens.
3. We bring war upon our enemies also.
4. Wise words are truly dear to a philosopher.
5. Mortals ought to trust the gods.
6. I did many favors (kindnesses) for them.
7. The poor men served the rich.
8. You tried to please everybody (all).
9. You-all hated your enemies so.
10. War harmed our country very much.

IV   PATTERN PRACTICE EIGHTEEN

1. The boy is my friend.   Puer est amīcus meus.

2. The boy is my son's friend.   Puer est amīcus fīliī meī.

3. The boy is my daughter's friend.   Puer est amīcus fīliae meae.

4. The boy is a friend of my son and my daughter.   Puer est amīcus fīliī meī et fīliae.

5. The boy is my brother's friend.   Puer est amīcus frātris meī.

6. The boy is my sister's friend.   Puer est amīcus sorōris meae.

7. The boy is a friend of all boys.   Puer est amīcus puerōrum omnium.

8. The boy is a friend of all girls.   Puer est amīcus puellārum omnium.

9. We see the Roman soldier.   Mīlitem Rōmānum vidēmus.

10. We see the Roman soldier's leader.   Mīlitis Rōmānī ducem vidēmus.

11. Whose leader do we see? The soldier's.   Cujus ducem vidēmus? Mīlitis.

12. We see the leader of the Roman soldiers.   Mīlitum Rōmānōrum ducem vidēmus.

13. Whose leader do we see? The soldiers'.   Quōrum ducem vidēmus? Mīlitum.

14. The leader forms a plan.   Dux capit cōnsilium.

15. The soldiers do not know the leader's plan.   Mīlitēs ducis cōnsilium nesciunt.

16. Whose plan don't they know? The leader's.   Cujus cōnsilium nesciunt? Ducis.

17. The leaders form plans.   Ducēs cōnsilia capiunt.

18. The soldiers do not know the leaders' plans.   Ducum cōnsilia mīlitēs nesciunt.

19. Whose plans don't they know? The leaders'.   Quōrum cōnsilia nesciunt? Ducum.

20. They do not know the affairs of men.   Rēs hominum nesciunt.

21. Luck rules the affairs of men.   Rēs hominum regit Fortūna.

22. Luck is the mistress of human affairs.   Rērum hūmānārum domina Fortūna.

V   LĒCTIO

1. Vīta hominis brevis est. — Pseudo-Seneca

2. Vīta . . . . mortuōrum in memoriā vīvōrum est posita. — Cicero

3. Mors lupī, agnīs vīta. — Anon.

4. Ars est enim philosophia vītae.[1]

5. Dux vītae ratiō. — Motto (Latin equivalent of $\phi\beta\kappa$)

6. Māter artium necessitās. — Anon.

7. Fundāmentum[2] est omnium virtūtum pīetās in[3] parentēs. — Ecclesiastes

8. Crīmina quī[4] cernunt aliōrum nōn sua cernunt. — Anon.

9. Silentium est sīgnum sapientiae et loquācitās[5] est sīgnum stultitiae. — Petrus Alphonsus

10. Patria . . . . commūnis est omnium . . . parēns. — Cicero

11. Templa deōrum immortālium, tēcta[6] urbis, vītam omnium cīvium, Italiam tōtam ad exitium . . . . vocās.[7] — Cicero

12. Laudās fortūnam et mōrēs antīquae plēbis. — Horace

13. Quālis dominus, tālis et servus. — Petronius

14. Imāgō animī sermō[8] est: quālis vīta, tālis ōrātiō. — Pseudo-Seneca

15. Jūstitia omnium est domina et rēgīna virtūtum. — Cicero (adapted)

16. Mēns et animus et cōnsilium et sententia cīvitātis posita est in lēgibus. — Cicero

17. Rōma caput mundī. — Lucien

18. Sēditiō cīvium hostium est occāsiō. — Publilius Syrus

Notā bene

1. *ars vītae* pattern together here.
2. *fundāmentum -ī* n.: "foundation"
3. *in*: "toward"
4. *quī*: "who"
5. *loquācitās*: *quī multum loquitur, loquax (loquācis) est; loquācitātem habet.*
6. *tēcta*: *tēctum-ī* n., that which is covered, protected; a "house"
7. *vocās*: the "you" is the leader of a plot to overthrow the Roman government.
8. *sermō, sermōnis*: "talk," "conversation"

VI   WORD STUDY

1. As your Latin vocabulary grows larger, you are learning more words which are related to one another. By becoming aware of these relationships, you will make the learning of vocabulary easier. For instance, you now have learned several words of the *reg*-family: *regō, reg*ere, rēx, *rēg*is, *rēg*īna-ae (also *rēctus* from *regō*)

   Similarly: dūcō, dūcere; dux, ducis

   morior, mors, mortālis, immortālis

   Also the m. and f. pairs: fīlius, fīlia   dominus, domina

2. Often an abstract noun, denoting a quality, is constructed on another noun, an adjective, or a verb. Many of these can be easily recognized: for example, in this lesson,

philosophia based on *philosophus*

stultitia   based on *stultus*

You have seen the *-tās* group of nouns already (pages 84 and 85). What abstract nouns with this suffix are based on: cīvis, vērus, celer, līber, necesse?

3. Give the Latin source and meaning of: mundane, ratio, rational, criminal, incriminate.

4. Give derivatives from: dominus, parēns, templum, imāgō, necessitās, commūnis, brevis, sīgnum, hūmānus, occāsiō.

VII   VOCABULARY

Nouns

domina, dominae f.
memoria, memoriae f.
rēgīna, rēgīnae f.
sapientia, sapientiae f.

dominus, dominī m.
mundus, mundī m.

exitium, exitiī n.
sīgnum, sīgnī n.
templum, templī n.

cīvitās, cīvitātis f.
imāgō, imāginis f.
necessitās, necessitātis f.
occāsiō, occāsiōnis f.
parēns, parentis m. (f.) (i)
ratiō, ratiōnis f.

crīmen, crīminis n.

Adjectives

hūmānus, hūmāna, hūmānum
vīvus, vīva, vīvum

brevis, breve
commūnis, commūne
immortālis, immortāle

Verbs

regō, regere, rēxī, rēctus

LESSON TWENTY-TWO

Timor Dominī, fōns vītae. — Motto

"Fear of the Lord (is) the fountain of life."

Homō sum; hūmānī nihil ā mē aliēnum putō. — Terence

"I am a human being; I think nothing concerning humanity is foreign to me."

Purpose: to learn more uses of the genitive case

I VĪLLA COMBUSTA

1. Quō modō aedificium combustum est?

    Ignem ē stabulīs cēpit. (Servus enim, quandō exiit, ignem in stabulō relīquit.)

2. Quandō combustum est?

    Nocte combustum est.

3. Quid ex ignī servātum est?

    Vītae hominum animāliumque servātae sunt.

4. Cūr dominus abest?

    Dominus negōtium apud alium agricolam habuit.

5. Cūr puer cibum ā terrā capit?

    Tōtum aedificium ignī combustum est; nūllus cibus igitur relictus est.

6. Cūr fēmina puellam tenet?

    Quod puella nunc ē vīllā servāta est.

7. Vidēsne saxa ad mūrum?

    Videō. Sub terrā servus asinum mortuum posuit.

8. Quō modō mortuus est asinus?

    Ē stabulīs fugere nōn potuit; vinculīs retentus est.

9. Cūr aqua in ignem nōn jacitur?

    Nōn satis aquae est.

10. Cui pictūra placet?

    Nēminī placet quod nimis trīstis est.

171

II   PATTERN READING

A.   Sample sentences

1. Membra sunt partēs corporis.	The members are parts of the body.
2. Pars exercitūs profecta est.	Part of the army set out.
3. Satis cūrae dominus habet.	The master has enough (of) worry.
4. Aliquid cūrae habet fīlia.	His daughter has some (thing of) worry.
5. Nihil cūrae habet uxor.	His wife has no (nothing of) worry.
6. Vir magnae virtūtis est.	He is a man of great courage.
7. Mūrum decem pedum mūnīvērunt.	They built a ten foot wall.
8. Bona est causa itineris.	There is a good reason for the journey.
9. Dulcis est amor patriae.	Love of one's country is sweet.
10. Agricolae labōre magnus numerus hominum dīves factus est.	A great number of people became rich by the work of the farmer.

B.   Practice sentences

1. Omnis exercitus ad urbem vēnit.

2. Pars exercitūs ibi mānsit.

3. Omnēs exercitūs ad castra profectī sunt.

4. Partēs exercituum in urbibus mānsērunt.

5. Tōtum diem in urbe ambulāvimus.

6. Partem diēī in urbe ambulāvistis.

7. Satis temporis habent puerī.

8. Nimis temporis habent senēs.

9. Aliquid temporis habent juvenēs.

10. Nihil temporis habent virī.

11. Philosophus est vir magnae sapientiae.

12. Asinus est animal magnae stultitiae.

13. Lupus animal magnae celeritātis est.

14. Dux vir magnae virtūtis est.

15. Rōmānus est vir magnae vēritātis.

16. Mīlitēs timōrem hostium dēposuērunt.

17. Populus timōrem rēgis dēposuit.

18. Puellae timōrem serpentium dēposuērunt.

19. Sapientēs timōrem fortūnae dēposuērunt.

20. Mīlitēs mūrum decem pedum mūnīvērunt.

21. Castra centum pedum hostēs mūnīvērunt.

22. Poētae laudāvērunt amōrem patriae, labōrem cīvium, senātūs virtūtem.

23. Tōtus orbis terrārum tālem imperātōrem laudāvit.

24. Amor laudis omnēs trahit.

25. Dē laude amīcitiae in librīs Rōmānīs legimus.

26. Homō sum; nihil hominis ā mē aliēnum putō.

27. Cīvis es; nihil cīvitātis ā tē aliēnum putās.

28. Māter est; īnfantium nihil ā sē aliēnum putat.

29. Philosophī sumus; nihil sapientiae ā nōbīs aliēnum putāmus.

30. Agricolae estis; nihil rūris ā vōbīs aliēnum putātis.

C.   Questions on structure

1. Which genitives are used with nouns indicating part or quantity?
2. Which genitives are used with nouns describing an action?
3. Which genitives indicate qualities of another noun?
4. With what part of speech are genitives most often associated?

See Appendix B, pages 194-95.

III   FORM CHART

A. Adjectives

Adjectives in general have the same genitive case forms as nouns of the corresponding declension. For adjectives of the third declension, the genitive plural is always -*ium*.

	Singular			Plural	
	M. and F.	N.		M. and F.	N.
Nom.	omnis	omne		omnēs	omnia
Acc.	omnem	omne		omnēs	omnia
Abl.	omnī	omnī		omnibus	omnibus
Dat.	omnī	omnī		omnibus	omnibus
Gen.	omnis	omnis		omnium	omnium

For adjectives of the I-II declension the endings are the same as those of the nouns, except for a small group of irregular adjectives which have a dative singular -$\bar{\imath}$, and a genitive singular -$\bar{\imath}us$. So far you have used in this group:

ūnus, nūllus, neuter, sōlus, tōtus. All follow the pattern of *ūnus*:

	M.	F.	N.
Nom.	ūnus	ūna	ūnum
Acc.	ūnum	ūnam	ūnum
Abl.	ūnō	ūnā	ūnō
Dat.	ūnī	ūnī	ūnī
Gen.	ūnīus	ūnīus	ūnīus

B. Pronouns

Personal pronouns have genitive forms which are never used for possession (the adjectives *meus, noster, tuus, vester* are used) but are used for some of the other ways genitives relate to nouns. The forms are:

meī	tuī
nostrum	vestrum

IV   EXERCISES

A.   Answer the question by a genitive patterning with *imāgō*. Whatever is mentioned in the statement is a representation, rather than the thing itself.

1. Nōn est corpus hūmānum. Quid est? Est imāgō corporis hūmānī.
2. Nōn est caput pulchrum.   Quid est? Est imāgō _____ _____
3. Nōn est pēs magnus.   Quid est? ___ _____ _____ _____
4. Nōn est lingua longa.   Quid est?
5. Nōn est ōs ingēns.   Quid est?

6. Nōn est barba inūtilis.   Quid est?
7. Nōn est oculus clārus.   Quid est?
8. Nōn est dēns ūtilis.   Quid est?
9. Nōn est manus dextra.   Quid est?
10. Nōn est auris parva.   Quid est?

Repeat with plurals.

(Example: Non sunt corpora hūmāna. Quae sunt? Sunt imāginēs corporum hūmānōrum.)

B.   Give in five cases singular and plural:

vīta brevis   lēx antīqua   animal fidēle   omne templum
sonus clārus   cīvis Rōmānus   omnis diēs   senātus bonus
vir fortis   nōmen aliēnum

C.   Metaphrase the following:

1. Pecūnia servum . . . .   11. Gladius amīcum . . . .
   Pecūnia servōrum . . . .   12. Gladius mīlitum . . . .

2. Pars mīlitum . . . .   13. Pars pedum . . . .
   Pars mīlitem . . . .   14. Vestis virum . . . .

3. Pictūra manum . . . .   15. Exercitus ducum . . . .
   Pictūra manuum . . . .   16. Servus manum . . . .

4. Deum omnem . . . .   17. Auxilium fortium . . . .

5. Beneficium dominōrum . . . .   18. Lībertās servum . . . .

6. Pater puerum . . . .   19. Virtūs hominum . . . .

7. Māter frātrum . . . .   20. Mors dīvitum . . . .

8. Opus auctōrum . . . .   21. Nihil hūmānōrum . . . .

9. Fābulam poētārum . . . . . .   22. Nihil deum . . . .

10. Tempus diērum . . . .

D.   Answer the question by a genitive patterning with *pars*.

1. Sī littera nōn est tōtum opus, quid est? Pars operis est.
2. Sī hōra nōn est tōtus diēs, quid est? Pars _____ .
3. Sī oculus nōn est tōtum caput, quid est? _____ .
4. Sī verbum nōn est tōta sententia, quid est?
5. Sī urbs nōn est tōta patria, quid est?
6. Sī saxum nōn est tōtus mōns, quid est?
7. Sī mīles nōn est tōtus exercitus, quid est?
8. Sī soror nōn est tōta fāmilia, quid est?
9. Sī via nōn est tōta urbs, quid est?
10. Sī terra nōn est tōtus mundus, quid est?

E.   Supply three words, singular or plural, which fit into each frame.

1. Nihil _____ dīcō.   4. Nimis _____ est.
2. Satis _____ habēs.   5. Partem _____ spectātis.
3. Aliquid _____ vidēmus.

Give the Latin equivalent.

1. I own the book; my book was found on the table.
2. You own a horse; your horse ran through the middle of the street.
3. Marcus owns a dog; his dog hates the slave.
4. The farmer's business was then completed in a fair manner.
5. The boys' teacher also gave them various sweets on account of their hard work.

V   PATTERN PRACTICE NINETEEN

1. Father has many sons.   Pater multōs fīliōs habet.

2. Father has a large number of sons.   Pater magnum numerum fīliōrum habet.

3. Father has a large number of daughters.   Pater magnum numerum fīliārum habet.

4. Father has a large number of brothers.   Pater magnum numerum frātrum habet.

5. The man has a large number of sisters.   Vir magnum numerum sorōrum habet.

6. The man has a great number of posses-   Vir magnum numerum rērum habet.
   ions.

7. The man has enough time.   Vir satis temporis habet.

8. The man is paying enough money.   Vir satis pecūniae solvit.

9. His son is paying no money.   Fīlius nihil pecūniae solvit.

10. His daughter is paying some money.   Fīlia aliquid pecūniae solvit.

11. The rich man pays too much money.   Dīves nimis pecūniae solvit.

12. The master pays part of the money.   Dominus partem pecūniae solvit.

13. The master is a man of great courage.   Dominus est vir magnae virtūtis.

14. The master is a man of great   Dominus est vir magnī studiī.
    enthusiasm.

15. The philosopher is a man of good   Philosophus est vir bonae ratiōnis.
    reasoning.

16. The farmer is a man of great industry.   Agricola est vir magnī labōris.

17. The citizen is a man of great justness.   Cīvis est vir magnae jūstitiae.

18. The mother is a woman of great hope.   Māter est fēmina magnae speī.

19. The women forget their fear of fortune.   Fēminae timōrem fortūnae dēpōnunt.

20. The women forget their fear of snakes.   Fēminae timōrem serpentium dēpōnunt.

21. The women forget their fear of animals.   Fēminae timōrem animālium dēpōnunt.

22. The women forget their fear of soldiers.   Fēminae timōrem mīlitum dēpōnunt.

23. They do not forget their fear of the   Timōrem Dominī nōn dēpōnunt.
    Lord.

24. The fear of the Lord is the source of   Timor Dominī, fōns vītae.
    life.

VI   NIHIL NOVĪ

Ōlim servus, Parmēnō[1] nōmine, malōs rūmōrēs semper nārrāvit.   Dominus ejus, igitur, quandō exīre ob negōtium dēbuit, graviter incēpit: "Ad urbem proficīscor, Parmēnō, servā[2] domum.   Et memoriā tenē![2]   Nēmō rūmōrēs amat malōs.   Rēs est magna tacēre."

Servus: "Sī dī[3] mē amant," inquit, "domine,[4] rūmōrēs malōs numquam iterum nārrāre cupiō."

Dominus prōcessit cōnfēcitque negōtium; tandem, multōs post diēs rediit.   Eī servus occurrit et clāmat, "Gaudeō quod tē tūtum videō."

Dominus, "Et ego quoque, Parmēnō!   At quid novī est?"

Respondit servus, "Malōs rūmōrēs nōn jam nārrō.   Tua verba in memoriā semper habeō.   Sed hīc nihil novī."

"Nihilne?   Quid est?   Certē aliquid āctum est!"

Parmēnō—contrā: "Nihil, domine.[4]   Et ecce, nōn jam rūmōrēs malōs nārrō."

"Id mihi certē placet.   Sed vērē nihil novī est?"

"Oh, canis tua Bispella mortua est.   Sed nihil novī."

"Miseram Bispellam!   Quō modō periit?"

"Carnem equōrum mortuōrum ēdit et hōc[5] modō aegra facta est.   Sed nihil aliud novī."

"Carnem equōrum?   Ubi eam Bispella invēnit misella?"[6]

"Corpora equōrum, ut putō, in stabulīs combustīs fuērunt."

"In stabulīs combustīs?   Stabulane combusta sunt?"

"Combusta.   Sed nihil aliud novī est."

"Unde stabula accēnsa sunt?"

"Ut putō, domine, ignem ē vīllā cēpērunt.   Sed satis . . . ."

"Ignem ē vīllā!   Prō dī immortālēs![7]   Combustane est et vīlla?"

"Nōn falsam rem dīxistī."

"Periī!   Quō modō accēnsa est?"

"Nēmō prō certō scit, domine.   At, ut putō, ignem cēpit ē facibus[8] quae[9] in pompā[10] portātae sunt."

"Quā in pompā?   Estne fīlia mea, Jūlia, nupta?"[11]

"Immō vērō, domine.   Nōn nupta; mortua est Jūlia.   Sed . . . "

"Mortua!   Periī!   Quō modō īnfēlix mortua est?"

"Nesciō quō modō.   Sed, ut putō, ob dēdecus sē[12] occīdit."

"Ī in malam rem![13]   Quod[14] dēdecus?"

"Nōnne aud'īstī?[15]   Vīlicus[16] tōtam pecūniam tuam abstulit."

"Tōtam? Ei mihi! Vīlicus vērō mihi semper fidēlis fuit. Tamquam frātrem eum amāvī. Cūr pecūniam meam abstulit?"

"Ut putō, domine, quod uxor tua eī persuāsit."

"Dīxistīne meam uxōrem? Cūr uxor mea?"

"Ut putō, domine, quod cum vīlicō ipsa[17] fūgit. Sed, ut dīxī, nihil novī est!"

Notā bene

1. *Parmēnō -menis*, m.: "Parmeno," name of slave
2. *servā, tenē, vidē*: see page 120
3. *dī = deī*: the phrase is a mild oath, "So help me"
4. *domine*: see page 120
5. *hoc*: "this"
6. *misella*: diminutive of *miser*: "poor little"
7. *Prō dī immortālēs*: *prō* is adverbial; "by heaven," "by the gods"
8. *fax, facis* f.: "torch"
9. *quae*: "which"
10. *pompa -ae*, f.: "parade," "procession"
11. *nupta est*: *nūbō*: "marry"
12. *sē*: "herself"
13. *ī in malam rem*: "go to," "the deuce with you"
14. *quod*: "what" - adjective
15. *audī'stī*: contracted form of *audīvistī*
16. *vīlicus*: "keeper of villa," "overseer"
17. *ipsa*: "she herself"

Respondē Latīnē

1. Quālēs rēs nārrat Parmēnō?
2. Quid dominus jussit?
3. Quid cupīvit servus?
4. Quandō rediit dominus?
5. Cūr servus gāvīsus est?
6. Quid dīxit iterum iterumque servus?
7. Quantae calamitātēs dominō fuērunt?
8. Quid prīmō āctum est?
9. Quid ēgit vīlicus?
10. Quis vīlicō persuāsit?
11. Quid dēdecus fuit?
12. Quis mortua est? Cūr?
13. Unde stabula accēnsa sunt?
14. Cūr vīlla combusta est?
15. Quō modō equī occīsī sunt?
16. Quō modō canis periit?

VII   OPTIONAL READING

Stulte, quid est somnus gelidae nisī mortis imāgō? — Ovid
Dulcis amor patriae, dulce vidēre suōs. — Catullus
Discordia ōrdinum venēnum est urbis. — A. Capitolinus (?)
Ūnum est inexpūgnābile mūnīmentum, amor cīvium. — Seneca

Nēmō mortālium omnibus hōrīs sapit. — Pliny, the Elder
Jūcunda memoria est praeteritōrum malōrum. — Cicero
Gravis īra rēgum est semper. — Seneca

VIII   WORD STUDY

1. Note the increasing number of verbs which are compounds of already familiar ones: ex + eō;   per + eō;   ob + currō;   etc. Show how the meaning of these words develops from the parts. (*Per + eō* is a polite way of describing an unhappy event.)
2. The preposition *ob* is used in many words as a prefix. It appears in several forms, among them: *oc-, of-, op-.* Give five English words using this prefix. It may mean "against" or "toward" as well as its meanings as a preposition.
3. Give derivatives from: ignis, negōtium, domus, occurrō, stabulum, pompa, falsus, exeō.
4. Explain the Latin source and relation to it in meaning of: conservation, preserve, perish, combustion, nuptials, and decoration.
5. Note how the opposite of words is indicated: decus, dēdecus; fēlīx, īnfēlīx.

IX   VOCABULARY

Nouns

Jūlia, Jūliae f.

domus, domī (or) domūs[1] f.
numerus, numerī m.

negōtium, negōtiī n.
stabulum, stabulī n.
vinculum, vinculī n.

ignis, ignis m. (i)
pars, partis f. (i)
rūmor, rūmōris m.
uxor, uxōris f.

decus, decoris n.
dēdecus, dēdecoris n.

Adjectives

aeger, aegra, aegrum
falsus, falsa, falsum
īnfēlīx (īnfēlīcis)

Verbs

servō, servāre, servāvī, servātus

gaudeō, gaudēre, gāvīsus[2]

combūrō, combūrere, combussī, combustus
occurrō -currere -currī -cursus (dat.)

exeō, exīre, exiī, exitus
perō, perīre, periī, peritus

Function Words

ut

immō
hīc

quam ob rem

ob + acc.

---

[1] Usually fourth declension, *domus* has some forms in second also.
[2] This verb is regular in present, deponent in perfect. It is called "semi-deponent."

FIFTH REVIEW

Repetītiō est māter studiōrum. — School motto

"Repetition is the mother of learning."

I. VOCABULARY AND MODEL SENTENCE REVIEW

Replace one or more of the italicized words in these ten model sentences with suitable words to vary the meaning. Give 20 new sentences, using each model sentence at least once, some twice or more times.

1. *Poēta* nāscitur, ōrātor fit.
2. Nīl *hominī* certum est.
3. *Mors omnibus* īnstat.
4. *Rērum hūmānārum* domina Fortūna.
5. Vōx *populī*, vōx *Deī*.
6. *Repetītiō* est māter *studiōrum*.
7. *Homō* sum; *hūmānī* nihil ā mē aliēnum putō.
8. *Deō, Rēgī, Patriae.*
9. Frūstrā labōrat quī *omnibus placēre studet*.
10. In *omnī* rē vincit *imitātiōnem vēritās*.

II. STRUCTURE REVIEW

1. List all case endings that are identical for more than one form and tell the possible cases indicated.
2. Mention four ways that the dative case may be used.
3. Mention four ways that the genitive case may be used.
4. How do adjectives of the third declension differ from nouns?
5. What adjectives of I–II declension differ from nouns in the genitive and dative case endings?

III. FORM REVIEW

A. Answer the questions, using the case of the noun or pronoun and adjective in parentheses that each question calls for.

1. (dominus)
   Quis servōs habet?
   Cui servī sunt?
   Cujus servī labōrant?
   Quem servī audiunt?

2. (rānae)
   Quibus Juppiter rēgem dedit?
   Quālem rēx male rēxit?
   Quae rāmum ascendērunt?
   Ad quās deus rēgem mīsit?

3. (vincula)
   Quae rēs equōs tenent?
   Quibus rēbus hominēs malī tenentur?
   Quārum rērum sonus audītur?
   Quās rēs hominēs timent?

4. (māter)
   Cujus fīliī sunt fidēlēs?
   Cui fīliī placent?
   Quis semper fīliōs amat?
   Ā quā fīliī laudantur?

5. (crīmen)
   Quid dominum miserum facit?
   Cujus reī fāma in omnī ōre est?
   Cui reī gladius ūtilis est?
   Quid hominēs honestī nōn timent?

6. (exercitus)
   Quid dux accipit?
   Quō īnstrūmentō dux vincit?
   Cui dux persuādet?
   Cujus perīculum vidētur?

7. (diēs)
   Quārum rērum nōmina scrībimus?
   Quam diū prōcēdimus?
   Quibus rēbus nōmina dantur?
   Quandō fodimus?

8. (magnum gaudium)
   Quō modō afficior?
   Quid quaerō?
   Cujus reī sīgna videō?
   Cui reī saepe studeō?

9. (regīna dīves)
   Quem populus amāvit?
   Cui fortūna data est?
   Cujus beneficia nota sunt?
   Ā quā beneficia data sunt?

10. (agnī īnfēlīcēs)
    Ad quōs lupus mentem vertit?
    Quibus lupus nocet?
    Quōrum timōrem lupus videt?
    Quī ā lupō quaeruntur?

11. (mōrēs vestrī)
    Quārum rērum pars nōn probātur?
    Dē quibus rēbus scrībimus?
    Quās rēs nōn laudātis?
    Quae rēs vōbīs nōn placent?

12. (carmina laeta)
    Quārum rērum sonum audītis?
    Quibus rēbus sonus similis est?
    Quās rēs canimus?
    Quibus rēbus dēlectāmur?

13. (hostēs perfidī)
    Quibus arma dantur?
    Quibuscum Rōmānī pūgnant?
    Quōrum numerus magnus est?
    Quōs Rōmānī vulnerant?

14. (magistrātūs nostrī)
    Quōs laudāmus?
    Quibus crēdimus?
    Ā quibus negōtia pūblica facta sunt?
    Quōrum nōmina nōta sunt?

15. (spēs bona)
    Cujus reī satis nōn habēmus?
    Quid amāmus?
    Cui reī studēmus?
    Dē quā rē ōrātor dīcit?

B.   See how many answers you can supply to these questions, in a time limit of three minutes. (This can be done as a class competition.)

Cujus nōmen audīs? _____ nōmen audiō. (Example: <u>Mīlitis</u> nōmen audiō.)
Quōrum nōmina audīs? _____ nōmina audiō. (Example: <u>Mīlitum</u> nōmen audiō.)

C.   Answer the questions with either genitive or dative.

1. Sī mīles pecūniam solvit, cujus pecūnia solvitur?
2. Sī imperātor exercitum jubet, cujus exercitus jubētur?
3. Sī poēta carmen scrībit, cujus carmen scrībitur?
4. Sī magistrātus lēgem tulit, cujus lēx lāta est?
5. Sī parēns fīliōs amat, cujus fīliī amantur?

6. Sī auctor opus laudat, cui opus est?
7. Sī dux virtūtem ostendit, cui virtūs est?
8. Sī cīvitās membra habet, cui membra sunt?
9. Sī servus dominō servit, cui servus est?
10. Sī ōrātor verba facit, cui verba sunt?
11 - 20. Do 1 - 10 in the plural.

D. Answer the question with the dative (sg. or pl.) showing possession.

1. Caput aprī videō. Cui caput est?
2. Pennās corvōrum mīror. Quibus pennae sunt?
3. Arma mīlitum cernō. Quibus arma sunt?
4. Praemiō frātris invideō. Cui praemium est?
5. Opus auctōrum nōtōrum laudō. Quibus opus est?
6. Templum deī ostendō. Cui templum est?
7. Domum fēminae mūniō. Cui domus est?
8. Aurēs lupī teneō. Cui aurēs sunt?
9. Decus patriae quaerō. Cui decus est?
10. Mūnera amīcōrum petō. Quibus mūnera sunt?

E. Decline in all cases, singular and plural.

rumor malus	Graecia immortālis (sg.)	modus communis	aetās nostra
tempus antīquum	Athēnae immortālēs (pl.)	magister nūllus	animal omne
castra Rōmāna (pl.)	negōtium difficile	frāter sōlus	uxor cāra
spēs mea (sg.)	senātus gravis	manus inūtilis	magna pars

F. Give the Latin equivalent. (optional)

1. The rich man had enough money; he soon lost it.
2. The poor man had a little money; he kept it carefully (with care).
3. The master's small daughter never saw her mother's picture.
4. The rest of the men showed their wives the villas.
5. He completed the decoration (ornaments) of the temple and went away to his own land.
6. A great number of Romans thanked the goddess Fortune for (*ob*) so many favors.
7. The fear of death threatens all mortals at some time.
8. The leader of our armies captured the enemies' camp.
9. Many slaves were eager then for the death of (their) masters.
10. No danger (nothing of danger) frightened men of great courage.
11. Juppiter is at the same time king of gods and men.
12. The end of winter is pleasing to all.

G. The optional oral practice on noun and adjective declensions may be used in this review.

IV. WORD STUDY REVIEW

A. There are many "word families" in addition to those already discussed in word studies. Go over your vocabulary lists and find at least *five* additional "word families." List at least two words in each "family" or group.

B. List all compound verbs you have had to date.

C. List all suffixes studied so far, with one example in English and one in Latin for each.

V OPTIONAL ORAL REVIEW PRACTICE ON DECLENSIONS

After the noun is announced give the singular forms. Wait for the check, then give the plural. After that is checked the next noun will be announced.

PUELLA

puella	puellae
puellam	puellās
puellā	puellīs
puellae	puellīs
puellae	puellārum

DIĒS

diēs	diēs
diem	diēs
diē	diēbus
diēī	diēbus
diēī	diērum

ANIMAL

animal	animālia
animal	animālia
animālī	animālibus
animālī	animālibus
animālis	animālium

EQUUS

equus	equī
equum	equōs
equō	equīs
equō	equīs
equī	equōrum

LIBER

liber	librī
librum	librōs
librō	librīs
librō	librīs
librī	librōrum

HOMŌ

homō	hominēs
hominem	hominēs
homine	hominibus
hominī	hominibus
hominis	hominum

VERBUM

verbum	verba
verbum	verba
verbō	verbīs
verbō	verbīs
verbī	verbōrum

GLADIUS GRAVIS

gladius	gravis	gladiī	gravēs
gladium	gravem	gladiōs	gravēs
gladiō	gravī	gladiīs	gravibus
gladiō	gravī	gladiīs	gravibus
gladiī	gravis	gladiōrum	gravium

PATER

pater	patrēs
patrem	patrēs
patre	patribus
patrī	patribus
patris	patrum

STUDIUM FACILE

studium	facile	studia	facilia
studium	facile	studia	facilia
studiō	facilī	studiīs	facilibus
studiō	facilī	studiīs	facilibus
studiī	facilis	studiōrum	facilium

NOX

nox	noctēs
noctem	noctēs
nocte	noctibus
noctī	noctibus
noctis	noctium

DUX NOSTER

dux	noster	ducēs	nostrī
ducem	nostrum	ducēs	nostrōs
duce	nostrō	ducibus	nostrīs
ducī	nostrō	ducibus	nostrīs
ducis	nostrī	ducum	nostrōrum

CORPUS

corpus	corpora
corpus	corpora
corpore	corporibus
corporī	corporibus
corporis	corporum

MAGNUM OPUS

magnum	opus	magna	opera
magnum	opus	magna	opera
magnō	opere	magnīs	operibus
magnō	operī	magnīs	operibus
magnī	operis	magnōrum	operum

MANUS

manus	manūs
manum	manūs
manū	manibus
manuī	manibus
manūs	manuum

OMNIS TERRA

omnis	terra	omnēs	terrae
omnem	terram	omnēs	terrās
omnī	terrā	omnibus	terrīs
omnī	terrae	omnibus	terrīs
omnis	terrae	omnium	terrārum

VI. OPTIONAL READING

Ex ōre parvulōrum vērītās. —Anon.

Ēnse petit placidam sub lībertāte quiētem. —Motto (Massachusetts)

Nōn ōvum tam simile ōvō. —Quintilian

Animus ejus erat īgnārus artium malārum. —Sallust

Stultōrum plēna sunt omnia. —Cicero

Silent lēgēs inter arma. —Cicero

nōn compos mentis —Medical term

pāx vōbīscum —Ecclesiastical phrase

Common phrases: per sē
                     ad nauseam
                     prō et con
                     ex parte

APPENDIX A

SUPPLEMENTARY READING

JŪSTĀ DĒ CAUSĀ
(after Lesson Fifteen)

Apud Rōmānōs vir uxōrem semper dēpōnere poterat[1] jūstā dē causā. Sed quālis erat[1] jūsta causa?

Ōlim ad praetōrem, jūdicem[2] in eīs causīs,[3] accessit vir, quī[4] incēpit:

"Uxor mea nōn dulcis sed īnsāna est; eam dēpōnere volō."

"Īnsāna?" rogāvit praetor. "Cūr id dīcis?"

Vir magnā vōce respondit: "Quod caprum[5] tenet in cubiculō[6] ubi dormīmus. Nōnne satis dēmēns[7] est?"

"Num caprum amās?" rogāvit jūdex.

"Perferre possum caprum," inquit vir, "sed aeger sum quod caper olet[8] et eum odōrem perferre nōn possum."

Tum praetor: "Sī olet, cūr fenestram nōn aperīs[9]?"

"Id agere nōn possum," respondit vir. "Quandō ego fenestram aperiō, omnēs avēs[10] meae per fenestram ēvolant!"[11]

Notā bene

1. *poterat*: "could"; *erat*: "was"
2. *praetor -e* m: "official"
   jūdex, jūdice m: "judge"
3. *causa -ā* f.: "cause," "reason,"
   also "case"
4. *quī*: "who"
5. *caper, caprō* m.: "goat"
6. *cubiculum -ō* n.: "bedroom"
7. *dēmens = sine mente = īnsānus*
8. *olet = odōrem habet*
9. *aperiō -īre*: "open"
10. *avis, ave* f.: "bird"
11. *ēvolō -āre*: *ē + volāre* ("fly")

NĀVIS

(after Lesson Sixteen)

In urbe Graecā fābula saepe nārrātur dē aedificiō quae[1] ab omnibus "nāvis"[2] appellāta est.

Fuit juvenis quī[1] cēnās[3] nimis amāvit. Ūnō diē amīcōs suōs ad cēnam invītāvit. Omnia praeparāta sunt; vīnum cibusque nōn neglēcta sunt.

Multō diē amīcī ad cēnam convēnērunt. Ad mēnsās trēs accubuērunt.[4] Prīmum allāta[5] sunt ostreae, lactuca, pānis, ōva,[6] dulcī cum vīnō; deinde carō, avēs, piscēs holeraque.[7] Iterum iterumque ā servīs vīnum apportātum est. In vīnō nūlla aqua fuit. Juvenēs vīnum pūrum bībērunt. Multī magnā vōce clāmāvērunt et jocōs nārrāvērunt.

Tandem posita sunt dulcia, nucēs, pōma.[8] Tum juvenis ēbrius ascendit in mēnsam et salīre incēpit. Sed quod tam ēbrius fuit, diū salīre nōn potuit. Dē mēnsā magnō cum clāmōre cecidit.[9] Rīsērunt cēterī et clāmāvērunt:

"Ēbrius es, stulte! Nimis bībistī."

"Ēbrius nōn sum," īrātus exclāmāvit. "Nōn quod ēbrius fuī cecidī, sed quod ea mēnsa mōta est."

"Quō modō," inquiunt, "stulte, movētur mēnsa? In nāvibus mēnsae saepe moventur, sed in amīcī aedificiō nōn in nāve sumus."

Sīc ēbrius, "Sī tantum in nāvibus mēnsae moventur, nōs in nāve sumus."

Tunc servum rapuit. "Ubi sumus?" quaesīvit, "Nōnne in nāve sumus?"

"Ita," respondit servus territus, "ita, domine, ut dīcis, in nāve."

"Aha," exclāmāvit homō, "ēbrius nōn sum. Mēnsa igitur mōta est." Tum mēnsam innocentem pede magnā vī[10] pulsāvit. Statim ea propulsa est.

Juvenis "Ecce " inquit, "ut[11] dīxit, mēnsa movētur. Vērē in nāve sumus. Vēnit magna tempestās![12] Omnēs ferte auxilium! Omnia in aquam jacite! Tantum hōc[13] modō tūtī esse possumus!"

Magnīs clāmōribus juvenēs ēbriī jacere incēpērunt per fenestrās omnia — mēnsās, lucernās, vestēs. Servī territī nihil facere potuērunt. Tum homō parvam aquam cōnspexit quae ab mēnsā flūxit.

"Ei! Nāvis submergitur," is clāmāvit. "Quid nunc in aquam jacere possumus?"

Tantō clāmōre multī ante aedificium convēnērunt. Tandem custōdēs vocātī sunt juvenēsque raptī sunt. Proximō diē eī in jūs appellātī sunt.[14] Omnēs ob vīnum aegrī erant.[15] Multī sōlī stare nōn potuērunt, sed ab amīcīs sustentī sunt. Jūdex, gravis sapiēnsque senex, quaesīvit:

"Cūr tantum tumultum incitāvistis?[16]　Bonōs cīvēs ē somnō excitāvistis?[16]　Cūr id fēcistis?"

"Vēnit magna tempestās," inquit ūnus juvenis.　"Quod ab eā tempestāte tūtī esse voluimus, omnia in aquam jēcimus."

Jūdex īrātus:　"Nūlla tempestās fuit; ēbrius es!"

"O!" respondit juvenis.　"Vērē maxima tempestās fuit.　Ecce!　Ob tempestātem etiam nunc omnēs aegrī sumus!"

Notā bene

1. *quae, quī*: "which", "who"
2. *nāvis -e* f: "ship"
3. *cēna: ad cēnam hominēs cibum cēpērunt et vīnum bībērunt*
4. *accubuērunt: (accumbō -ere)* "recline"
5. *allātus*: from *ad + ferō*
6. *ostreae, lactuca, pānis, ōva*: "oysters, lettuce, bread, eggs"
7. *piscēs holeraque*: "fish and vegetables"
8. *nucēs, pōma*: "nuts, fruit"
9. *cecidit: (cadō -ere)* "fall"
10. *magnā vī: vīs, vim, vī*: "force," "strength"
11. *ut*: "as"
12. *tempestās*: cf. derivative
13. *hōc*: "this"
14. *in jūs appellātī sunt*: "summoned into court"
15. *erant*: "were"
16. *incitō -āre; excitō -āre*: cf. derivatives; "stir up", "rouse"

APPENDIX B

EXPLANATION OF STRUCTURE

In Latin one of the chief indications of the structure of a sentence is the *form* of words. While English relies heavily on word order and function words to establish relationships and therefore meaning (see Introduction, pages 3-5), Latin uses changes in the form, especially endings, to show the relationship of a word to the rest of a sentence.

It is through these same *forms* of words that parts of speech can be most easily recognized in Latin—in fact, this is the most reliable way to distinguish nouns, adjectives, pronouns, adverbs, and verbs, the only way possible without first knowing the meaning of the word. Each of these five parts of speech will be taken up in this Appendix with the forms and uses summarized.

Before beginning with these, just a brief word about the other "parts of speech." They are few, unchanging in form, but important because they are used constantly.

Prepositions relate nouns and pronouns to the rest of the sentence. For details see under noun uses.

Conjunctions tie parts of sentences together. Both of these may be considered "function words" in Latin.

Adverbs which are formed from adjectives are easily recognized by their form (see Part II), but other adverbial modifiers which do not have regular type endings must be learned as vocabulary items.

Exclamations of surprise, dismay, joy, grief comprise a few, occasional words usually labeled *interjections*; they are not related to the structure of the sentence and are learned as vocabulary items.

NOUNS

I. Nouns in Latin belong to a group of words that have CASE forms. The case is shown by the *ending* of the noun; when a noun has a certain ending it is said to be in a particular case. (The same endings also indicate number and gender.)

II. The endings denote

A. *Case*

The case identifies the *use* of the noun in the sentence, that is, its relationship to the other words in the sentence (e.g., as subject or object).

PUER PUELLAM VIDET.	The boy sees the girl.
PUERUM PUELLA VIDET.	The girl sees the boy.

B. *Number*

The singular or plural form of the case is indicated by differences in endings. (Only singular nouns are used until Lesson Seven of this book.)

singular:	puell*a*	homō	puer*um*	nomen
plural:	puell*ae*	homin*ēs*	puer*ōs*	nomin*a*

C. *Gender*

The gender of a noun is primarily related to the form classification to which it belongs, rather than to its meaning. Nouns which belong to a form class showing no change between subject and object (nominative and accusative cases) are classed as neuter. All other nouns are classed as masculine or feminine. Aside from male and female organisms, which for the most part are masculine or feminine, respectively, all other words are either "masculine" or "feminine": that is, they belong to certain form classes having certain sets of endings and requiring certain adjective endings to pattern with them.
(See below on adjectives.)

oppidum	*neuter*	urbs	*feminine*	vīcus	*masculine*
oppidum	(town)	urbem	(city)	vīcum	(village)

III. CLASSIFICATION OF NOUNS

A. Nouns may be classified as *personal* or *non-personal*. This classification is based on meaning, but it has an effect also on the patterns in which the noun may be found. For example, only personal nouns have a vocative form. Also contrast the personal and non-personal:

> MĪLES *CUM HOSTE* PŪGNAT.   The soldier is fighting with his enemy.
> MĪLES *GLADIŌ* PŪGNAT.   The soldier fights with a sword.

B. *Declensions*. Nouns may be classified by sets of endings according to the form classification in which they occur. Within a given declension, a fixed set of endings indicates the case and number of the noun. There are five main groups or declensions, each with a characteristic vowel which predominates in it. (See complete charts, Appendix C.)

Declension	I	II	III	IV	V
Vowel	ā	ō	e (i)	ū	ē

In each declension are five main cases, each having forms for singular and plural, ten endings in all.

C. The three most frequently used cases are NOMINATIVE, ACCUSATIVE, and ABLATIVE.

Nominative endings: the singulars have widely varied forms.
the plurals are vowel and -*ī* or
vowel and -*s (oi =ī, aī =ae)*
neuters are -*a*

Accusative endings: the singulars are short vowel and –*m*
the plurals are long vowel and -*s*
neuters are -*a*

In III, IV, and V declensions nominative and accusative plural are alike.

Ablative endings: the singular is the vowel of the declension.
the plurals are -*īs* or -*bus*.

IV. Uses of nominative, accusative, and ablative cases occurring in Lessons One to Six.

A. NOMINATIVE   (Something is presented.)

USE 1a

Environment (i.e., surrounding words): a verb in active form other than
EST (SUNT)

EQUUS PUERUM VIDENT.   The horse sees the boy.
PUERUM VIDENT *FĒMINAE*.   The women see the boy.

Function: this is the doer of the action
Name: subject
Question words: QUIS, QUID, who? what? (pl. QUĪ, QUAE)

USE 1b

Environment: a verb having passive forms

MĪLES SPECTĀTUR.   The soldier is being watched.
MĪLITĒS SPECTANTUR.   The soldiers are being watched.

Function: this is the receiver of the action
Name: subject
Question words: QUIS, QUID, who? what? (QUĪ, QUAE)

USE 1c

Environment: EST (SUNT) or similar verb

EQUUS EST.   It's a horse.
EQUĪ SUNT.   There are horses.

Function: something is presented or identified
Name: subject
Question words: QUIS, QUID (QUĪ, QUAE)

USE 2

Environment: EST (SUNT) or a similar verb and another noun in the nominative case

VIR *AGRICOLA* EST.   The man is a farmer.
                             The farmer is a man.

FĒMINAE NŌN SUNT *AGRICOLAE*.   Women are not farmers.

Function: one noun is identified by the other. (The word order of Latin gives
no clue as to which noun is subject or predicate nominative. Sometimes the context makes it clear; at other times it is ambiguous.)
Name: predicate nominative or A = B construction
Question words: QUIS, QUID (QUĪ, QUAE)

B. ACCUSATIVE   (The goal of action)

USE 1

Environment: a verb other than EST (SUNT) in active form (transitive)

PUERUM VIDET.   He sees a boy.
PUERŌS VIDET.   He sees the boys.

Function: this receives the action of the verb
Name: direct object
Question words: QUEM, QUID, whom? what? (QUŌS, QUĀS, QUAE)

USE 2
    Environment: with an intransitive verb;
                with a transitive verb and object

      ŪNAM HŌRAM SEDET.   She sits still for one hour.
      SAXUM *MULTŌS PEDĒS* JACIT.   She throws a stone many feet.

Function: modifies the verb adverbially, in time or space
Name: adverbial accusative (shows extent in time or space)
Question words: QUAM DIŪ, how long? QUAM LONGĒ, how far?

USE 3
    Environment: a verb and one of the prepositions: AD, ANTE, IN (in the
                sense of "into," "against"), INTER, PER, POST, SUB,
                SUPER, TRĀNS (also OB, PROPTER, PRAETER,
                CIRCUM, APUD)

      AD *FLŪMEN* CURRIT.   He runs to the river.

Function: modifies the verb adverbially
Name: adverbial accusative, accusative with prepositions
Question words: UBI, where?   QUŌ, to what place?

C. ABLATIVE (The chief uses are adverbial. Nouns in the ablative pattern with
            verbs in a sense similar to that of adverbs.)

USE 1
    Environment: a verb; no preposition (The noun in the ablative is a word
                designating a time.)

      MĪLES *AESTĀTE* PŪGNAT.   A soldier fights in summer.

Function: the ablative modifies the verb in time
Name: ablative of time
Question word: QUANDŌ, when?

USE 2
    Environment: a verb, active or passive; no preposition   (The noun in the
                ablative is non-personal.)

      VIR *MANŪ* LABŌRAT.   The man works by hand (with his hands).

Function: modifies the verb in the sense of "by means of," "with," "by"
Name: ablative of means
Question word: QUŌ ĪNSTRŪMENTŌ, with what (tool, instrument)? by
                what means?

USE 3[1]
    Environment: a verb and the preposition CUM (The noun in the ablative
                is usually personal.)

      JUVENIS *CUM AGRICOLĀ* LABŌRAT. The youth is working with a
                                        farmer.

[1] *SINE*, the opposite of *CUM* in meaning may be used in the same way as *CUM* both with personal and nonpersonal words.

MĪLES *CUM HOSTIBUS* PŪGNAT.   The soldier fights with his enemies.

Function: modifies the verb in the sense of "together with"
Name: ablative of accompaniment
Question words: QUŌCUM   (QUIBUSCUM), with whom?

USE 4

Environment: a verb and the preposition CUM   (The noun in the ablative
may express a feeling or quality. If an adjective modifier is
present, CUM may be omitted.)

GLADIĀTOR *CUM STUDIŌ* PŪGNAT.   The gladiator fights with
enthusiasm (eagerly).

GLADIĀTOR *MAGNŌ (CUM) STUDIŌ*   The gladiator fights very
PŪGNAT.   eagerly.

Function: modifies the verb in the sense of "with what feeling," "in what
way"
Name: ablative of manner
Question word: QUŌ MODŌ, how?

USE 5

Environment: a verb and one of the prepositions: Ā, AB; Ē, EX; DĒ; IN;
SUB; PRŌ; PRAE   (The noun in the ablative is often, but not
always, a place.)

IN *FLŪMINE* NATAT PUER.   The boy is swimming in the river.

Function: modifies the verb in the sense of the preposition, in location
(the meaning may be extended)
Name: ablative of place, or with prepositions
Question words: UNDE, from where? UBI, where?

USE 6

Environment: a verb in passive form and the preposition Ā, AB. (The noun
in the ablative is always personal.)

PUER *Ā FĒMINĀ* SPECTĀTUR.   The boy is watched by the woman.

Function: this shows by whom the action of the passive verb is done
Name: ablative of (personal) agent
Question words: Ā QUŌ (Ā QUIBUS), by whom?

V.   Uses of the two remaining major cases, DATIVE and GENITIVE

A. Forms

1) Dative

The dative singular ending is chiefly -*ī*, with the stem vowel (except II declension which is the same as the ablative) (aī = ae).   The plural is identical
to ablative plural.

2) Genitive

The singular genitive ending is -*ī* combined with stem vowel or stem vowel
plus -*s*. The plural is -*rum* or -*um* and the stem vowel.

B. Uses of *Dative* (This is a third party, interested in and affected by the action of verb, but less directly than accusative. It is most often a personal noun.)

USE 1
Environment: a verb meaning give, tell, show, etc.; often an accusative direct object

PATER *FĪLIĪS* PECŪNIAM DAT.	The father gives his sons money.
PATER *FĪLIŌ* DĪCIT.	Father speaks to his son.

Function: shows person to whom something is given, said, etc.
Name: indirect object
Question words: CUI, QUIBUS, to whom?

USE 2
Environment: certain intransitive verbs, as listed in vocabulary

SERVUS *PUERŌ* NŌN NOCET.	The slave does not harm the boy.
CŌNSILIUM *GLADIĀTŌRIBUS* PLACET.	The plan is pleasing to the gladiators.

Function: dative is used with intransitive verbs while accusative is used with transitive verbs
Name: dative with intransitives
Question words: CUI, QUIBUS, to whom? to what? whom? what?

USE 3
Environment: EST or SUNT (or other tenses)

AGRĪ BONĪ *PATRĪ* SUNT.	Father has good fields.

Function: shows ownership - the person for whom something exists
Name: dative of possession
Question words: CUI, QUIBUS

USE 4
Environment: some compound verbs

DUX BELLUM *HOSTIBUS* ĪNFERT.	The general makes war on the enemy.

Function: it is associated with the idea contained in the prefix
Name: dative with compound verbs
Question words: CUI, QUIBUS

USE 5
Environment: certain adjectives

TŪ *MIHI* CĀRUS ES.	You are dear to me.
QUID ŪTILE *REĪ PŪBLICAE* EST?	What is useful for the state?

Function: it names person or group with reference to which the adjective applies
Name: dative with adjectives
Question words: CUI, QUIBUS, to whom? for whom? for what?

USE 6

Environment: any verb, transitive or intransitive

PATER *FĪLIŌ* TIMET.   The father fears for his son.

Function: it names the person with reference to whom the action occurs or
             who is interested in or indirectly affected by the action
Name: dative of reference
Question words: CUI, QUIBUS, for whom?

C.   Uses of *Genitive*   (It relates one noun to another; it is the adjectival case.)

USE 1

Environment: another noun

PUERŌRUM LIBRŌS INVĒNĪ.   I found the boys' books.

Function: genitive names the owner of what is mentioned by the other noun
Name: possessive genitive
Question words: CUJUS (QUŌRUM, QUĀRUM), whose?

USE 2

Environment: another noun

MŪRUM DECEM *PEDUM* MŪNĪVĒRUNT.   They built a ten-foot wall.

Function: describes the other noun
Name: genitive of description
Question words: QUANTUS,   how big? how much?

USE 3

Environment: another noun; words like SATIS, NIMIS, ALIQUID, used
             substantively

PARS *EXERCITŪS* AD URBEM VĒNIT.   Part of the army came to the
                                    city.

PUERŌ SATIS *PECŪNIAE* DEDĪ.   I gave the boy enough money.

Function: names the whole of which the other noun is the part
Name: genitive of the whole; partitive genitive
Question words: CUJUS, QUŌRUM, QUĀRUM, of what?

USE 4

Environment: another noun, often one naming an action or feeling (verbal
             idea)

TIMOR *MORTIS* EUM CĒPIT.   Fear of death seized him.

Function: it is in the relationship of object, receiver of action named in the
             other noun
Name: objective genitive
Question words: CUJUS, QUŌRUM, QUĀRUM, of what? of whom?

USE 5
Environment: another noun, usually one naming a verbal idea

POĒTAE AMŌREM *MĀTRIS* LAUDANT.   Poets praise a mother's love.

Function: it is in the relationship of subject, the doer of the action named
in the other noun
Name: subjective genitive
Question words: CUJUS, etc.

(There are other less frequent uses of the genitive with a few special verbs
and adjectives that will occur occasionally in the reading.)

ADJECTIVES

I. Adjectives belong to a group of words that have case forms similar to those of nouns.
They are distinguished from nouns, which have one set of endings, in having more
than one set of endings to show not only case and number but also differences of
gender. They may also have forms showing degrees of comparison.

II. Forms

There are two types of adjectives: (For complete charts see Appendix C, page
193, in Part II.)

A. Adjectives of the I-II declension, so-called because their endings are the same
as those of nouns of these declensions

B. Adjectives of the third declension, with endings like i-type nouns

III. The chief function of adjectives is to modify nouns, giving information describing,
limiting, or qualifying the nouns.

A. This modification is shown by "agreement" with the gender, number, and case
of the noun: i.e., the adjective form varies according to the gender, number,
and case of the noun with which it patterns.

PATER ME*US*   MĀTER ME*A*   NŌMEN ME*UM*

VIRUM FORT*EM*   FĒMINAM FORT*EM*   ANIMĀLĪ INGENT*Ī*

B. Since the gender of the noun determines the set of endings used for the adjective,
the importance of the gender of nouns becomes apparent. Knowledge of gender
is an essential. In many instances it must simply be memorized, but a few
general statements may be of help.

1. Nouns of the I declension are usually feminine (excepting men's occupations).
2. Nouns of the II declension are usually masculine; a group in *-um* are neuter.
3. Nouns of the III declension are highly variable; all genders are found. Only a
few follow a set pattern; they are:

   a. *-tās (-tāte)*, *-tūs (-tūte)*, *-tūdō (-tūdine)*, *-iō (-iōne)* endings are feminine
   b. most *-or (-ōre)* (abstract) endings are masculine (not *soror, arbor,
   uxor*)
   c. most *-us, -n, -e, -l, -r* (nominative) endings are neuter

4. Nouns of the IV declension are usually masculine (but *manus*, f.).
5. Nouns of the V declension are mostly feminine (*diēs* usually m.).

C. Position of adjective

Order is a secondary sign of which nouns an adjective modifies; many times the two are fairly close together.

1. Most adjectives of description follow the noun: a few like *Rōmānus* must follow.

> PUER *BONUS* MĒ AUDIT.   The good boy listens to me.

2. Adjectives of size and number usually precede.

> *MULTĪ* PUERĪ IN VIĀ CURRUNT.   Many boys are running in the road.

3. In prepositional phrases a common variation is:

> *MULTĪS* CUM PUERĪS   *MAGNĀ* CUM CELERITĀTE

Since endings are the chief signal of what noun the adjective patterns with, a high degree of flexibility is permissible for emphasis and for poetic and rhetorical effects.

D. Substantive use of adjective

An adjective may stand alone without an expressed noun, or be used in place of a noun. A masculine or feminine form indicates persons, neuters a quality or thing.

> *OMNĒS* VENĪMUS.   We are all coming.
> LABOR *OMNIA* VINCIT.   Hard work overcomes all things.
> *BONUM* FUGITUR.   The good is avoided.
> *NOSTRĪ* VINCUNT.   Our men are winning.

E. Question words for adjectives

> QUĀLIS, QUĀLE, what kind of? (descriptive adjectives)
> QUANTUS, QUANTA, QUANTUM, how large? (adjectives of size)
> QUOT, how many?   (for numbers)

IV. Special forms

1. Irregular

A group of adjectives have dative singular endings in *-ī* and genitive singular endings in *-ius*. They include:

> SŌLUS, TŌTUS, NŪLLUS, ŪLLUS, ŪNUS, UTER, UTERQUE, NEUTER, ALIUS, ALTER

2. For demonstratives, see pronouns

3. Numerals

Some numerals are declined (ŪNUS, DUO, TRĒS, plural of MILLE, compounds of CENTUM, see Appendix C); most are not declined.

4. Indeclinable adjectives, showing no ending changes: among them,

> TOT, QUOT, SATIS, NIMIS

VERBS

I. Verbs belong to the group of words that have certain sets of endings that indicate person, number, and voice. (Other segments combined with these indicate tense, aspect, and mood.)

II. Endings denote:

A. *Number*

The ending indicates whether the verb, and the subject with which it is in agreement, is singular or plural.

The ending -*t* (used in Lessons One - Six) indicates singular number.
The ending -*nt* (Lesson Seven) indicates plural number.

VIR LABŌRA*T*.	The man is working.
VIRĪ LABŌRA*NT*.	The men are working.

B. *Person*

The same endings also indicate that the subject is the person called "third." That is:

FĒMINA ANIMAL VIDE*T*.	The woman sees an animal.
PUELLAM NŌN VIDE*T*.	She does not see the girl.
VIRĪ FLŪMEN VIDE*NT*.	The men see the river.

See below for other persons.

C. *Voice*

1. The endings -*t* and -*nt* also indicate that the subject is doing the action or is in the state the verb describes. This is called ACTIVE VOICE of the verb.

PUER BONUS ES*T*.	The boy is good.
PUELLA CANEM PĒLLI*T*.	A girl is chasing the dog away.
VIRĪ MŪRŌS MŪNIU*NT*.	The men are building walls.

2. The ending -*tur* (Lesson Six) indicates that the singular subject is the receiver of the action of the verb.

The ending -*ntur* (Lesson Seven) indicates that the plural subject is the receiver of the action the verb describes.

Ā PUELLĀ CANIS PELLI*TUR*.	The dog is chased away by the girl.
Ā VIRĪS MŪRĪ MŪNIU*NTUR*.	Walls are being built by the men.

This is called PASSIVE VOICE of the verb. See below for other persons.

For the most part, the same idea may be stated in either an active or passive construction.

PUER EQUUM PELLIT.	The boy chases the horse away.
Ā PUERŌ EQUUS PELLITUR.	The horse is being chased away by the boy.

3. The changes from active to passive are:

    a) object (receiver of action) becomes subject;
    b) verb ending changes from *-t* to *-tur*;
    c) the doer of the action becomes ablative;
       (if a person,with *ā*, *ab*; if a thing, with no preposition. For this use of ablative see under nouns uses 2 and 6.)

III. Other form changes denote:

A. *Tense*

The tense of a verb is indicated by internal segments plus certain stem changes. (See below for individual tenses.) Tense shows both

1. the *time* the action occurred (past, present, future)
2. and the *aspect* of completeness or incompleteness of action.

Example: the present tense is incomplete at the present time;
        the perfect is complete at the present time.

VĪNCIT   he is winning
VĪCIT   he won

B. *Mood*

The same signs that indicate tense also indicate in what mood the tense occurs.

    The *indicative* mood is used to make an assertion or inquire into a fact.

VENIT.   He is coming.   VENITNE?   Is he coming?

    The *imperative* mood is used to give a command.

VENĪ!   Come!   VENĪTE, OMNĒS!   Come, all of you!

    The *subjunctive* mood is used to contrast with assertion.

VENIAT.   May he come.

(Tenses of the indicative mood are taken up in various lessons from Eleven to Thirty-four; the imperative in Twenty-seven; the subjunctive tenses in Thirty-six to Forty.) See summaries below.

IV. CLASSIFICATION OF VERBS

A. Verbs may be classified as *transitive* or *intransitive,* according to patterns in which they occur.

1. Transitive verbs pattern with direct objects; they may be thought of as "two-party" verbs (subject-object). Transitive verbs have regular passive voice forms.

    PUERĪ PUELLĀS *VOCANT.*   The boys call the girls.
    Ā PUERĪS PUELLAE *VOCANTUR.*   The girls are called by the boys.

2. Intransitive verbs do not pattern with direct objects and do not regularly have passive forms.

    MŪRUS LONGUS *EST.*   It's a long wall.
    PUELLAE AD VĪLLAM *CURRUNT.*   The girls are running toward the farm house.

B. *Conjugations*

Verbs may be classified according to the form class or conjugations to which they belong. There are four conjugations, each with its characteristic vowel. This vowel appears before the *-re* ending of the infinitive. (In the *-t* form of the present tense it is always shortened.)

I ā	II ē	III e (i)	III-(i) e (i)	IV ī
ambul*āre*	mov*ēre*	ag*ere*	cap*ere*	aud*īre*
ambulat	movet	agit	capit	audit

V. INDICATIVE TENSES

A. The six indicative tenses occur in statements of fact and direct questions. Questions are distinguished from assertions by:

1. Interrogative word, pronoun or adjective or adverb: QUIS, QUID, QUEM, QUŌ MODŌ, QUANDŌ, etc.

2. -NE attached to the first word, usually a verb, of the question.

3. Special adverbs:
NŌNNE expecting an affirmative answer
NUM expecting a negative answer

NŌNNE VENĪS? You're coming, aren't you?
NUM VENĪS? You're not coming, are you?

B. Changes of ending of the verb indicate changes of person, number, and voice. These sets of *personal endings* are used in all but one tense of the indicative.

(1) *Active*

Person	Singular		Plural	
1	(I)	*-ō, -m*	(we)	*-mus*
2	(you)	*-s*	(you)	*-tis*
3	(he, she, it)	*-t*	(they)	*-nt*

(2) The use of pronouns is not required in Latin to indicate person, but they may be used for emphasis.

(3) *Passive*

Person	Singular	Plural
1	*-(o)r*	*-mur*
2	*-ris*	*-minī*
3	*-tur*	*-ntur*

General rule for *vowel length*, preceding these endings:

(4) Long vowels are shortened before:
another vowel, *-nt*, final *-m*, *-r*, and *-t*;
or length of vowel is retained in:
second person singular, first and second person plural, active and passive, and third person singular passive.

C. *Present tense* (active and passive)

1. Formation

   a) General pattern

   Present stem of verb, ending in vowel of conjugation (no tense-mood sign) plus

   personal endings, active or passive

   b) Modifications

   (1) Conjugation vowel omitted before -ō and -or in I and III
   (2) The vowel in III is -i- (not -e-); only in passive, second singular is it -e- *(mitteris)*
   (3) In III, third plural, the vowel is -u -nt *(ur)*
   (4) In III(i) and IV, third plural is -iu -nt *(ur)*.

   For complete paradigm of each conjugation see text, page 100 and 105, and Appendix C, in Part II.

   c) Irregular verbs use the same sets of endings but have variations in stem and vowel patterns. See Appendix C, in Part II.

2. Meaning

   The present tense expresses an action in present time, considered in a continuing or incomplete aspect. It may indicate

   a) an action (or state of being) going on now and not completed

   PUERĪ AD URBEM PRŌCĒDUNT.   The boys are going toward the city.

   b) a general truth

   VESTIS VIRUM FACIT.   Clothes make the man.

   c) vivid narration of action in past time

D. *Principal parts*

In dictionaries, verbs are listed with "principal parts" which provide key forms, showing the conjugation and the stems necessary in forming all the tenses of the verb.

These parts are:

	I	II	III	III (i)	IV
Present active indicative (1 sg.)	portō	habeō	agō	capiō	audiō
Present active infinitive	portāre	habēre	agere	capere	audīre
Perfect active indicative (1 sg.)	portāvī	habuī	ēgī	cēpī	audīvī
Perfect passive participle	portātus	habitus	āctus	captus	audītus

The conjugation is indicated by the first two parts together. The present stem with characteristic vowel appears in the second, the perfect active stem in the third, perfect passive in the fourth.

Since knowledge of these stems is essential, the principal parts of all verbs studied up to Lesson Sixteen are given, by conjugation, on pages 134-35; thereafter they are included in the vocabulary listing.

E. *Perfect tense*

1. Formation of *active*

   perfect active stem of verb (see third principal part) plus special set of personal endings for this tense only:

	Singular	*Plural*
1	-ī	-imus
2	-istī	-istis
3	-it	-ērunt

2. Formation of *passive*

   (This is not a true passive, because it does not have passive endings.)

   It is a compound form consisting of the perfect passive participle (fourth principal part) and the present tense of *sum*.

   Since the participle part of the compound is an adjectival form, its endings will show agreement with the subject of the verb (nominative case, sg. or pl., m., f., or n., in *-us*, *-a*, *-um* type of adjective).

   MĪLES VULNERĀT*US* EST. *MĪLITĒS* VULNERĀT*Ī* SUNT.
   FĒMINA VULNERĀT*A* EST. *FĒMINAE* VULNERĀT*AE* SUNT.
   ANIMAL VULNERĀT*UM* EST. *ANIMĀLIA* VULNERĀT*A* SUNT.

   All verbs (including irregulars) form the perfect tense in the same way.

3. Meaning

   The perfect tense has two separate and distinct meanings. (Many languages, including English, use two different tenses to fill these two purposes.)

   a) Simple narration of an action in past time (now past and complete)

   VĒNĪ, VĪDĪ, VĪCĪ.   I came, I saw, I conquered.

   b) Description of an action, often of the immediate past, regarded as complete in present time (present perfect)

   VIĀTŌRĒS, QUOD DIŪ *AMBULĀVĒRUNT*, NUNC FESSĪ SUNT.

   The travelers are tired now because they have walked for a long time.

VOCABULARY

(The first occurrence of each word is indicated by lesson number, L1, for example. If the number is in parentheses, the word is not required for learning in that lesson.)

A

ā, ab, abs: prep. with abl., *from, away from, by* L4

abeō -īre-iī-ītus: *go away from* L19

abhorreō-horrēre-horruī: *be averse to, shrink from* (1st Rev)

absum-esse-fuī-futūrus: *be away, be away from, be absent* L10

accēdo-cēdēre-cessī-cessus: *go toward, approach, accede to* L13

accendō-cendere-cendī-cēnsus: *set on fire, catch fire, inflame* L16

accipiō-cipere-cēpī-ceptus: *receive, take, accept* L6

accūsō (1): *blame, accuse, reproach* L13

acerbus-a-um: *sharp, sour, bitter, harsh* (L18) L27

āctum, āctī, n: *something done, action, transaction* (L18)

ad: prep. with acc., *to, toward, at, near* L5

adjuvō-juvāre-jūvī-jūtus: *help, assist* L9

adnatō (1): *swim to, swim towards* L15

adscrībō-scrībere-scrīpsī-scrīptus: *add to, assign, ascribe* L27

adsum-esse-fuī-futūrus: *be present, be at hand, be at* L10

aedificium, aedificiī n: *building* L2

aeger, aegra, aegrum: *sick* L22

aes, aeris n: *bronze, money*
   aes aliēnum: *debt* (L20)

aestās, aestātis f: *summer* L3

aetās, aetātis f: *age, time, period of life* L18

afficiō-ficere-fēcī-fectus: *act on, do to, affect* L8

ager, agrī m: *field, open country* L2

agnus, agnī m: *lamb* L5

agō, agere, ēgī, āctus: *do, act, accomplish, drive, impel, spend time, give attention to*
   age: *come now;* quid agitur: *what is going on* L1

agricola, agricolae m: *farmer, country man* L2

aiō, (ait, aiunt): defective verb, few other forms, *say* L13

ālea, āleae f: *die, dice, game of chance* (L16)

aliēnus-a-um: *belonging to another, another's, strange* L20

aliquandō: adv., *sometimes* 4th Rev

aliquis, aliquid: *somebody, anyone, something, anything* L18

alius, alia, aliud: *other, another*
   aliī. . .aliī: *some. . .others* L15

almus-a-um: *loving, nurturing, nourishing, kind* (2nd Rev)

altus-a-um: *high, deep* L14

amanuēnsis, amanuēnsis m: *secretary* (L18)

ambō, ambae, ambō: irreg. forms, cf. duo, *both of two* (L13)

ambulō (1): *walk, walk around* L4

amīcitia, amīcitiae f: *friendship* L12

amīcus, amīcī m: *friend*
   amīcus-a-um: *friendly* L4

āmittō-mittere-mīsī-missus: *let go, lose, send away* L17

amō (1): *love, like, take delight in* L8

amor, amōris m: *love, longing* L12

amphora, amphorae f: *amphora* jar for wine or oil, usually with two handles (L12)

an: conj., *whether, or,* often paired with <u>utrum</u> L16

Anio, Aniēnis m: *Anio* River, near Rome (L20)

animal, animālis n: *animal* L2

animus, animī m: *mind, courage, attitude, spirit, intellect* (2nd Rev)

annus, annī m: *year* L7

ante: prep. with acc., *before, in front of* L5

antīquus-a-um: *ancient, of old times, former, old* L18

aper, aprī m: *boar, wild pig* L9

appellō (1): *call by name, address, speak to, name* L6

apud: prep. with acc., *among, at home of, in presence of, in, with, at time of* L15

aqua, aquae f: *water* L5

arbor, arboris f: *tree* L4

arma, armōrum n pl: *arms, weapons* L19

ars, artis f (i): *art, skill, work of art* L21

ascendō-cendere-cendī-cēnsus: *go up, climb, ascend, mount* L13

asinus, asinī m: *donkey* L12

at: conj., *but, on the other hand* L14

Athēnae, Athēnārum f pl: *Athens* L18

atque (ac): conj., *and, and also* L19

auctor, auctōris m: *author, originator, founder, writer, artist* L2

audiō, audīre, audīvī, audītus: *hear, listen to* L1

auferō, auferre, abstulī, ablātus: *carry off, remove, take away* (L15), L35

Augustus, Augustī m: *Augustus,* honorary title of Octavius Caesar after he became the first Roman Emperor, also name of month once known as <u>Sextilis</u> L18
   Augustus-a-um: *of Augustus*

aureus-a-um: *golden, of gold* (L18) L39

auris, auris f (i): *ear* L12

aurum, aurī n: *gold* (3rd Rev) L39

aut: conj., *or*
   aut. . .aut: *either. . .or* L12

autem: conj., *moreover, besides, however* L13

auxilium, auxiliī n: *help, aid, support,* pl. *auxiliary troops* L15

avidus-a-um: *eager, greedy, ravenous* L14

B

balbūtiō, babūtīre: *stammer, stutter, speak indistinctly* (L11)

barba, barbae f: *beard* L2

beātus-a-um: *blessed, happy* (L15) L23

bellum, bellī n: *war* L7

bene: adv. of bonus *well, ably, rightly* L3

beneficium, beneficiī n: *kindness, favor* L19

bibō, bibere, bĭbī: *drink* L11

bis: adv., *twice* L19

Bispella, Bispellae f: *Bispella*, name of pet (L22)

bonus-a-um: *good, fine, pleasant*

　　　bona, bonōrum n pl: *goods* L16

brevis-e: *short, brief* L18

C

C. = Gaius (L18)

cadō, cadere, cecidī, cāsus: *fall, happen, fall down, set* as sun, *subside* (3rd Rev) L28

caecus-a-um: *blind, hidden* (3rd Rev)

caedēs, caedis f: *cutting down, slaughter, killing* (1st Rev) L35

Caesar (C. Jūlius), Caesaris m: *Caesar* (L18)

canis, canis m and f: *dog* L1

canō, canere, cecinī, cantus: *sing, compose (a poem), play* L14

capiō, capere, cēpī, captus: *take, take up, seize, capture, take on, form, gain, take into the mind* L4

caput, capitis n: *head, person, chief thing* L5

carmen, carminis n: *song, poem* L14

carō, carnis f: *flesh, meat* L14

cārus-a-um: *dear, precious, costly* L20

casa, casae f: *cottage, hut, small dwelling* L10

castra, castrōrum n pl: *camp, encampment* L19

cathedra, cathedrae f: *professor's chair, chair of one in authority* (L4)

Catullus (C. Valerius), Catullī m: *Catullus*, a Roman poet (L18)

causa, causae f: *cause, reason, good reason, law case* L10

cēdō, cēdere, cessī, cessus: *move, yield, withdraw, retreat* (4th Rev) L38

celer, celeris, celere: *fast, swift, fleet, quick* L9

celeritās, celeritātis f: *speed, swiftness, haste* L14

centum: indecl., *a hundred* Int.

cernō, cernere, crēvī, crētus: *perceive, discern, distinguish, decide, prove* L12

certāmen, certāminis n: *contest, struggle, fight* (L17)

certō(1): *fight, strive, struggle* (4th Rev)

certus-a-um: *sure, certain, reliable* L11

Christiānus-a-um: *Christian, having to do with Christianity* (L18)

cibus, cibī m: *food* L14

Cicero (M. Tullius), Cicerōnis m: *Cicero*, a famous Roman (L18)

cīvilis-e: *civil, public* (L18)

cīvis, cīvis m(i): *citizen* L20

cīvitās, cīvitātis f: *state, body of citizens, citizenship* L21

clāmō (1): *shout, cry out, declare* L10

clāmor, clāmōris m: *outcry, shout, noise* L15

clārus-a-um: *clear, bright, famous* L18

coepī, coeptus: (defective) *began* L18

cōgō, cōgere, coēgī, coāctus: *compel, force, drive together, collect* L13

color, colōris m: *color, coloring* (L18) L35

combūrō-būrēre-bussī-bustus: *burn, burn up, consume* L22

committō -mittere-mīsī-missus: *entrust, commit, engage in, commence* (1st Rev) L33

commūnis-e: *common, pertaining to community, general* L21

compos, compotis: *possessing, sharing* (5th Rev)

cōn = contrā: (5th Rev)

concēdō-cēdere-cessī-cessus: *yield, grant, concede, allow* L19

concordia, concordiae f: *harmony, agreement, concord* (L3)

cōnficiō-ficere-fēcī-fectus: *do, complete, weaken, consume* L14

cōnor, cōnārī, cōnātus: *try, attempt* L20

cōnsilium, cōnsiliī n: *plan, advice* L4

cōnspiciō-spicere-spexī-spectus: *look at, catch sight of, notice* L7

cōnsul, cōnsulis m: *consul*, one of the Roman heads of state L20

cōnsumō (1): *complete, use up* (4th Rev)

contrā: prep. with acc. and adv., *against, opposite to, in reply (to), on the contrary, in turn* L20

cor, cordis n: *heart* (2nd Rev) L35

Corinthus, Corinthī f: *Corinth*, great city of Greece (4th Rev)

Cornēlius, Cornēliī m: *Cornelius* L16

corpus, corporis n: *body, corpse, person* L2

corvus, corvī m: *crow, raven* L14

crās: adv., *tomorrow* L19

crēdō, crēdere, crēdidī, crēditus: *believe, trust, entrust* L20

crēdulus-a-um: *easy of belief, credulous* (L18)

crēscō, crēscere, crēvī, crētus: *grow, increase, arise* (L3) L25

crīmen, crīminis n: *accusation, crime, fault* L21

crustulum, crustulī n: *cookie* (L19)

cum: prep. with abl., *with, together with* L3

cupiō, cupere, cupīvī, cupītus: *want, be eager for, wish* L10

cūr: interrog. adv., *why* L10

cūra, cūrae f: *care, concern, worry, attention* L17

currō, currere, cucurrī, cursus: *run, hurry, go rapidly* L5

cursus, cursūs m: *course, race course, race* (4th Rev) L33

D

D. = Decimus (L18)

dē: prep. with abl., *from, down from, about, according to* L5

dēbeō, dēbēre, dēbuī, dēbitus: *owe, ought* L13

decem: indecl., *ten* Int.

decimus-a-um: *tenth* Int.

　　　Decimus -ī m: *Decimus*, proper name L13

decōrus-a-um: *suitable, proper, beautiful* (L17)

decus, decoris n: *ornament, grace, honor* L22

dēdecus, dēdecoris n: *disgrace, dishonor, shameful action* L22

dēfodiō-fodere-fōdī-fossus: *dig up, bury* (L16)

deinde: adv., *then, next* L10

dēlectō (1): *please, delight* L2

dēns, dentis m(i): *tooth* L14

dēpōnō-pōnere-posuī-positus: *put down, lay aside, get rid of* L13

dēscendō-scendere-scendī-scēnsus: *go down, climb down* L13

dēscrībō-scrībere-scrīpsī-scrīptus: *write down, copy* (L18)

deus, deī m: *god, deity* L14

dexter, dextra, dextrum: *right, on the right hand* L16

dīcō, dīcere, dīxī, dictus: *say, tell, assert* L7

diēs, diēī m (sometimes f): *day, time* L3

difficilis-e: *hard, difficult* L9

dīligō, dīligere, dīlēxī, dīlēctus: *have high regard for, respect,\have affection for, love* (L18) L32

discēdō-cēdere-cessī-cessus: *depart, go away from, leave* L16

discō, discere, didicī: *learn* L12

discordia, discordiae f: *discord, lack of harmony, disagreement* (L22)

diū (diūtius, diūtissimē): adv., *for a long time* L15
     quam diū: *how long* L5

dīves, dīvitis: *rich, wealthy* L16

dō, dare, dedī, datus: *give, bestow, grant* L19

doceō, docēre, docuī, doctus: *teach, inform* L12

dolor, dolōris m: *pain, grief, sorrow, regret* L4

domina, dominae f: *mistress of the household, lady of the house, lady* L21

dominus, dominī m: *lord, master* L21

Domitiānus, Domitiānī m: *Domitian*, Roman emperor (81-96A.D.) (L18)

domus, domī or domūs f: *house, home* L22

dormiō, dormīre, dormīvī, dormītus: *sleep, be inactive* 4th Rev

dūcō, dūcere, dūxī, ductus: *lead, guide, take, consider* L12

dulcis-e: *sweet, agreeable, charming* L14

dum: conj. with indicative, *while* L11

duo, duae, duo: irreg. decl. (see App. C), *two* Int.

dux, ducis m: *leader, guide, commander* L19

E

ē: see ex

ēbrius-a-um: *intoxicated* (L11)

ecce: excl., *look, see,* L10

edō, ēsse, ēdī, ēsus: *eat, eat up* L19

effugiō-fugere-fūgī-fugitus: *flee from, escape* (L13)

ēgelidus-a-um: *lukewarm, somewhat warm* (L18)

ego: pron. (irreg.), I (*me*) L11

ei: excl., *oh!* (L14)

elephantus, elephantī m: *elephant* (L11)

enim: conj., *for, indeed* L15

ēnsis, ēnsis m: *sword* (5th Rev)

eō, īre, iī, (īvī) ītus: *go* L18

equus, equī m: *horse* L1

ēripiō-ripere-ripuī-reptus: *take away, snatch away* (L16) L40

errō (1): *wander, err, make a mistake* (3rd Rev)

error, errōris m: *wandering, error, mistake* (L8)

et: conj., *and, and also* L2
    et. . .et: *both. . .and* L8

etiam: conj., *and also, too, besides* L3

ex, ē: prep. with abl., *from, out of, on account of, of* L4

exemplum, exemplī n: *example, model* L12

exeō-īre-iī-ītus: *go out, leave* L22

exercitus, exercitūs m: *army, trained group* L19

exitium, exitiī n: *destruction* L21

expellō-pellere-pulī-pulsus: *drive out, force away* L18

experientia, experientiae f: *trial, experience* (L1)

exstruō-struere-strūxī-strūctus: *build up, construct* (4th Rev)

extinguō-tinguere-tinxī-tinctus: *put out, extinguish* (L16)

extrā: prep. with acc., *outside, on the outside* (4th Rev)

F

fābula, fābulae f: *story* L7

facilis-e: *easy* L9

faciō, facere, fēcī, factus: *make, do, act* L1

factum, factī n: *act, deed* L7

fallō, fallere, fefellī, falsus: *deceive, elude, escape the notice of, disappoint* (L18) L35

falsus-a-um: *deceptive, false* L22

fāma, fāmae f: *rumor, reputation, report, fame* L17

famēs, famis f: *hunger* L20

fāmilia, fāmiliae f: *slaves of household, household, family* L6

fax, facis f: *torch* (L22)

fēlēs, fēlis f: *cat* (3rd Rev) L30

fēlīcitās, fēlīcitātis f: *happiness* (L9)

fēlīx, fēlīcis: *fortunate, happy, lucky* L9

fēmina, fēminae f: *woman* L1

fenestra, fenestrae f: *window, opening* L14

ferō, ferre, tulī, lātus: *carry, bear, endure, bring, produce, get* L14
    fertur: *it is handed down, it is said*

fessus-a-um: *tired, feeble* L13

fidēlis-e: *faithful, trusty* L9

fidēs, fideī f: *faith, faithfulness, trustworthiness, trust* (1st Rev) L23

fīlia, fīliae f: *daughter* L6

fīlius, fīliī m: *son* L6

fingō, fingere, fīnxī, fictus: *mould, fashion, make up* (3rd Rev) L30

fīniō, fīnīre, fīnīvī, fīnītus: *finish, end, cease* (4th Rev) L36

fīnis, fīnis m (i): *limit, end*, pl. *boundaries, territories* (within the boundaries) L16

fīō, fīerī, factus (see faciō): *be made, become* L18

firmus-a-um: *firm, steady, solid* (3rd Rev)

flūmen, flūminis n: *river* L2

fluō, fluere, flūxī, flūxus: *flow* L5

fodiō, fodere, fōdī, fossus: *dig, dig up* L2

folium, foliī n: *leaf* L15

fōns, fontis m (i): *spring, fountain, water source*
L5

fortis-e: *brave, manly, strong* L9

fortūna, fortūnae f: *luck, fortune* (good or bad) L9

frāter, frātris m: *brother* L6

frūstrā: adv., *in vain, vainly* L15

fugiō, fugere, fūgī, fugitus: *flee, run away, fly* L8

fundāmentum, fundāmentī n: *foundation* (L21)

futūrus-a-um: future participle of <u>sum</u>, *future* (3rd
Rev)

G

gaudeō, gaudēre, gāvīsus: *rejoice, be glad* L22

gaudium, gaudiī n: *joy, gladness* L6

gelidus-a-um: *cold, icy* (L22)

gerō, gerere, gessī, gestus: *carry, wear, have,
carry on, wage* L2

gladiātor, gladiātōris m: *gladiator* L4

gladius, gladiī m: *sword* L3

glōria, glōriae f: *glory, fame, boasting* L17

Graecia, Graeciae f: *Greece* L18

Graecus-a-um: *Greek* L18

grammatica, grammaticae f: *grammar* (L11)

grātia, grātiae f: *favor, gratitude, thanks, grace* L11

gravis-e: *heavy, serious, hard* L9

H

habeō, habēre, habuī, habitus: *have, hold, possess,
have in mind* L3

habitō (1): *live in, dwell* L15

harēna, harēnae f: *sand, sandy place, arena* L4

hic, haec, hoc: irreg. pro. and adj., *this*, pl. *these;*
may be used for third person pronoun, *he* etc.;
the latter (opp. to *ille*) (L20) L23,27

hīc: adv., *here, in this place* L22

hiems, hiemis f: *winter, storm* L3

Hispānia, Hispāniae f: *Spain* L18

historia, historiae f: *history* (L18)

historicus-a-um: *of history, historical* (L18)

hodiē: adv., *today* L18

homō, hominis m (and f): *human being, man* L8

honestus-a-um: *honorable, of honor, respectable* L9

honor, honōris m: *honor* (L18) L24

hōra, hōrae f: *hour, time* L5

Horātius, Horātiī m: *Horatius*, member of a well-
known Roman family (L26)

     Q. Horātius Flaccus: *Horace*, a Roman poet (L18)

horribilis-e: *horrible, terrible* L15

hostis, hostis m (and f) (i): *enemy* L3

hūmānus-a-um: *human, of a human being, of man*
L21

humilis-e: *humble, lowly, low* (3rd Rev)

I

ibi: adv., *there, in that place* L16

īdem, eadem, idem: pro. and adj., *the same* (L18)
L27

igitur: conj., *therefore, then* L10

īgnārus-a-um: *ignorant of, not knowing* (5th Rev)

ignis, ignis m(i): *fire* L22

imāgō, imāginis f: *representation, image, reflection,
statue, ghost* L21

imitātiō, imitātiōnis f: *imitation, pretense, counter-
feit* L6

imitor, imitārī, imitātus: *copy, act like, imitate* L18

immō: adv., *on the contrary* L22

immortālis-e: *immortal, not subject to death* L21

impediō-pedīre-pedīvī-pedītus: *hinder, impede, get
in way of* (L3)

imperātor, imperātōris m: *general, chief commander,*
(in later Roman period) *emperor* L18

imperium, imperiī n: *command, power to command,
chief command, empire* (L20)

in: prep. with abl., *in, on;* prep. with acc., *into, onto,
upon, against, toward, in regard to* L4, 5

inceptiō, inceptiōnis f: *beginning, start* L9

incertus-a-um: *not sure, uncertain, unreliable,
disturbed, doubtful* L11

incipiō-cipere-cēpī-ceptus: *begin, start* L14

indignātiō, indignātiōnis f: *indignation, displeasure*
(L18)

indīgnus-a-um: *unworthy* (L20)

industria, industriae f: *hard work, diligence* (1st Rev)

ineptus-a-um: *unsuitable, inept, foolish* (L18)

īnfāns, īnfantis m (and f) (i): *baby, small child* L10

īnfēlīx, īnfēlīcis: *unhappy, unlucky, unfortunate* L22

īnferō-ferre-tulī-illātus: *bring in, bring upon, bring*
L20

īnfīnītus-a-um: *unending, boundless* (L5)

ingēns, ingentis: *huge, great* L10

ingrātus-a-um: *disagreeable, ungrateful* (L20) L35

inimīcus-a-um: *unfriendly, hostile* (L18)

injūria, injūriae f: *injury, harm, wrong* L6

innocēns, innocentis: *innocent* (L17)

inops, inopis: *weak, needy, lacking* (L19) L29

inquam (inquis, inquit, inquiunt): defective, *say* (with
direct quotation) L11

īnstō-stāre-stitī-stātus: *stand over, press upon,
impend, threaten* L20

īnstrūmentum, īnstrūmentī n: *tool, implement*
     quō īnstrūmentō: *with what? how?* L3

integritās, integritātis f: *soundness, fine character*
(1st Rev)

inter: prep. with acc., *between, among* L5
     inter sē: *with one another*

intereā: adv., *meanwhile* (L8)

intrā: prep. with acc., *within, inside* (L18) L37

intrō (1): *enter, go into, occupy* (3rd Rev)

inūtilis-e: *useless* L15

inveniō-venīre-vēnī-ventus: *come upon, find, discover*
L16

invideō-vidēre-vīdī-vīsus: *envy, hate, begrudge, scorn*
L20

invidus-a-um: *envious* (L18)

ipse, ipsa, ipsum: pro. and adj., *himself, herself, itself,
themselves, the very* (L22) L27

īra, īrae f: *anger, wrath* (L20) L27

īrāscor, īrāscī, īrātus: *grow angry, be angry* (4th Rev)

īrātus-a-um: *angry, enraged* L15

irreparābilis-e: *irretrievable, unable to be gotten back*
(L8)

irrīdeō-rīdēre-rīsī-rīsus: *laugh at, make fun of* (L18)

is, ea, id: pro. and adj., *this, that,* used for *he, she, it, they* (L3) L11

Italia, Italiae f: *Italy* L18

iterum: adv., *again* L11

J

jaciō, jacere, jēcī, jactus: *throw, hurl, bring forth* L11

jam: adv., *yet, now, already* L15
    nōn jam: *no longer*

jocus, jocī m: *joke* (3rd Rev)

jubeō, jubēre, jussī, jussus: *order, command* L13

jucundus-a-um: *delightful, agreeable, cheerful* (L18) L25

jūdicium, jūdiciī n: *judgement, trial, court of law* L18

Jūlia, Jūliae f: *Julia* (L22)

Jūlius, Jūliī m: *Julius;* also the month of July, named for Gaius Julius Caesar L4

Juppiter, Jovis m: *Jupiter* L15

jūstitia, jūstitiae f: *justice* L19

Juvenālis (D. Jūnius), Juvenālis m: *Juvenal,* a Roman satirist (L18)

juvenis, juvene: *young*
    juvenis, juvenis m: *young man, young person* L2

L

labor, labōris m: *hard work, effort, toil, hardship* 1st Rev

labōrō (1): *work, work hard, suffer* L2

laetus-a-um: *happy, joyful* L3

lateō, latēre, latuī: *lie hidden, be concealed* L16

Latīnus-a-um: *Latin* L18

latrō (1): *bark* (L10)

lātus-a-um: *wide, broad* L6

laudō (1): *praise, commend, approve of, admire* L2

laus, laudis f: *praise, good report* L12

lavō, lavāre, lāvī, lautus (lōtus): *bathe, wash* L1

legō, legere, lēgī, lēctus: *read* L7

lepidus-a-um: *charming, witty* (L18)

lepus, leporis m: *hare* (L17)

Lesbia, Lesbiae f: *Lesbia,* a woman's name in poetry (L18)

levis-e: *light, frivolous, trivial, rapid* 2nd Rev

lēx, lēgis f: *law* L17

liber, librī m: *book* L7

līber, lībera, līberum: *free* L15

lībertās, lībertātis f: *freedom, liberty* L20

lingua, linguae f: *tongue, language* L11

littera, litterae f: *letter of alphabet,* pl. *letter, epistle, literature* L18

(T.) Līvius, Līviī m: *Livy,* Roman historian (L18)

locus, locī m (pl. may be n): *place, location, room* L17

longus-a-um: *long, far off* L6

loquācitās, loquācitātis f: *talkativeness* (L21)

loquor, loquī, locūtus: *speak, talk about, tell* L17

lūceō, lūcēre, lūxī: *shine, be light* (L19)

lucerna, lucernae f: *lantern, lamp* L16

Lūcia, Lūciae f: *Lucia, Lucy* L6

Lūcius, Lūciī m: *Lucius, Luke* L6

lūdō, lūdere, lūsī, lūsus: *play, make sport of, mock* L19

lūdus, lūdī m: *game, play, school* (L18)
    lūdī scaenicī: *stage play* (L18)

lūmen, lūminis n: *light, source of light* (used of eyes, moon, sun) (L2) L28

lupus, lupī m: *wolf* L5

lūsus, lūsūs m: *playing, fun* (L3)

lūx, lūcis f: *light* (L2) L23

M

M. = Mārcus (L18)

māchina, māchinae f: *machine, device* (L4)

magister, magistrī m: *master, leader, teacher* L19

magistrātus, magistrātūs m: *magistracy, office of magistrate, magistrate, official* L18

magnus-a-um: *large, big, great,* L2

male: adv., *badly* L3

maledīcō-dīcere-dīxī-dictus: *speak ill of, slander, curse* (L15)

malus-a-um: *bad, evil, unfortunate* L9

maneō, manēre, mānsī, mānsus: *remain, stay* L7

manus, manūs f: *hand, forcefulness, band of men, power* L1

Mārcus, Mārcī m: *Marcus, Mark* L4

Martiālis (M. Valerius), Martiālis m: *Martial,* a Roman poet (L18)

māter, mātris f: *mother* L6

maximē: adv., *very greatly, especially* L11

maximus-a-um: *greatest, most* (L16) L29

mediocritās, mediocritātis f: *moderation, mean* (L18)

medius-a-um: *middle, middle of* L12

membrum, membrī n: *limb, part of the body, portion, member* L20

memoria, memoriae f: *memory, remembrance* L21

mēns, mēntis f (i): *mind, attention, intelligence, intention* L5

mēnsa, mēnsae f: *table, food* L11

merīdiēs, merīdiēī m: *midday, noon.* (L5)

meus, mea, meum: *my, mine* L9

mīles, mīlitis m: *soldier* L3

mīlle, (pl) mīlia: *a thousand* Int.

mīmus, mīmī m: *farce* (L18)

minimē: adv., *least, not at all* L14

ministrō (1): *attend, serve, minister to* (3rd Rev)

mīror, mīrārī, mīrātus: *wonder at, admire, be amazed at* L17

misellus-a-um: *poor little, unhappy little* (L22)

miser, misera, miserum: *unhappy, wretched, miserable* L14

miseria, miseriae f: *wretchedness, misery* (3rd Rev)

mittō, mittere, mīsī, missus: *send, let go, let loose, throw* L6

modus, modī m: *way, manner, sort* L20

moneō, monēre, monuī, monitus: *remind, warn, advise, give advice to* L8

mōns, montis m(i): *mountain* L5

mōnstrō (1): *point out, show* (L1)

mordeō, mordēre, momordī, morsus: *bite, devour* (1st Rev)

morior, morī, mortuus (fut. morītūrus): *die* L17

mors, mortis f (i): *death* L16

mortālis-e: *mortal, subject to death* L19

mortuus-a-um: *dead* (L10)

mōs, mōris m: *custom, manner*, pl. *manners, behavior* L13

moveō, movēre, mōvī, mōtus: *move, remove* L6

mox: adv., *soon, then* L13

mulier, mulieris f: *woman* (L18)

multus-a-um: *much*, pl. *many, a great deal of* 1st Rev

mundus, mundī m: *world* L21

mūnīmentum, mūnīmentī n: *rampart, fortification, defense* (L22)

mūniō, mūnīre, mūnīvī, mūnītus: *build, strengthen, fortify* L6

mūnus, mūneris n: *duty, service, gift* L12

murmurō (1): *murmur, mutter* (L13)

mūrus, mūrī m: *wall* L6

Mūsa, Mūsae f: *Muse*, one of the nine goddesses of the arts (L20)

musca, muscae f: *fly* (L11)

mūtō (1): *change, move from its place, exchange* L12

mūtus-a-um: *silent, speechless* (L14)

N

nārrō (1): *tell, relate, speak* L7

nāscor, nāscī, nātus: *be born, originate from* L17

natō (1): *swim, float* L5

nātūra, nātūrae f: *nature* (1st Rev) L23

nausea, nauseae f: *seasickness, disgust* (5th Rev)

-ne: indicates sentence is a question L1

nec: see neque

necessitās, necessitātis f: *necessity, need* L21

negō (1): *say no, say. . .not, deny* (L18) L29

negōtium, negōtiī n: *business, matter, affair* L22

nēmō, nēminis (gen. usually nūllīus, abl. nūllō) m (and f): *nobody, no one* L9

neque (nec): *and not*

    neque (nec) . . .neque (nec): conj., *neither. . . nor* L14

nesciō, nescīre, nescīvī, nescītus: *not know, be ignorant of* L12

neuter, neutra, neutrum: irreg. gen. and dat., *neither of two, neither one* L17

nihil (nihilō) n: other forms rare, *nothing* L12

    nihil posse: *have no power*

    nihilōminus: *nevertheless* (L16)

nīl = nihil (L19)

nimis: indecl., *too, too much* L19

nisī: conj., *unless, if not* L12

nōbilitās, nōbilitātis f: *nobility, excellence* (L18)

nōbilitō (1): *ennoble, render excellent* (L8)

nocēns, nocentis: participle of noceō, *injurious, wicked, guilty* (L17)

noceō, nocēre, nocuī, nocitus: *harm, injure, do harm to* L20

nōlō, nōlle, nōluī: *be unwilling, not wish, not want,* (*don't* as neg. imperative) (L15) L28

nōmen, nōminis n: *name* L2

nōn: adv., *not* L1

nōnne?: expects answer *yes; that's so isn't it?* L14

nōnus-a-um: *ninth* Int.

nōs: irreg. pro., *we, us* L11

noster, nostra, nostrum: *our, ours* L9

nota, notae f: *note, mark* (L18)

nōtus-a-um: *well-known, noted* L13

novem: indecl., *nine* Int.

novus-a-um: *new, recent, strange* L17

    novissimus-a-um: *last, most recent*

nox, noctis f(i): *night, darkness* L16

nūbō, nūbere, nūpsī, nūptus: *marry* (used of the woman) (L22)

nūllus-a-um: irreg. gen. and dat., *no, not any* L9

    nōn nūllī: *some* (L24)

num?: expects answer *no; that isn't so, is it?* L14

nūmen, nūminis n: *divine power, deity* (L2)

numerō (1): *count, consider* L12

numquam: adv., *never* L6

nunc: adv., *now* L11

O

ob: prep with acc., *on account of, for, because of*

    quam ob rem: *for this reason, why* L22

obumbrō (1): *obscure, darken, hide* (L12)

occāsiō, occāsiōnis f: *opportunity, occasion* L21

occīdō-cīdere-cīdī-cīsus: *cut down, kill* L10

occurrō-currere-currī-cursus: *run up to, meet, attack* L22

octāvus-a-um: *eighth* Int.

octō: indecl., *eight* Int.

oculus, oculī m: *eye* L11

ōlim: adv., *once, at one time*, past or future L20

omnis-e: *each, every, all* L9

oppidum, oppidī n: *town* L2

opus, operis n: *work, a work* (book, work of art, etc.) L2

    opus est: *there is need*

ōrātiō, ōrātiōnis f: *speech, oration* (L18) L26

ōrātor, ōrātōris m: *speaker, orator* L18

orbis, orbis m(i): *circle, globe, ring, world* L15

ordō, ordinis m: *rank, line, order, arrangement* (L9) L40

orior, orīrī, ortus: *rise, arise, get up, originate, descend from* L17

ōrnō (1): *decorate, grace, honor* (L2) L25

ōrō (1): *pray, beg* (L13) L43

ōs, ōris n: *mouth, face* L10

ostendō, ostendere, ostendī, ostentus: *show, display* L14

ōtium, ōtiī n: *leisure, relaxation, ease* (L15)

Ovidius (P. Ovidius Nāso), Ovidiī m: *Ovid, a Roman poet* (L18)

ōvum, ōvī n: *egg* (5th Rev.)

P

P. = Publius (L18)

paene: adv., *almost* L16

pāla, pālae f: *spade* L3

parēns, parentis m and f (i): *parent* L21

Parmēnō, Parmēnis m: *Parmeno, a name given to slaves in Roman Comedy* (L22)

pars, partis f(i): *part, share, side, place* L22
  ā dextrā (sinistrā) parte: *on the right (left) side* L16

parvulus-a-um: *very small, insignificant, a little bit of a* (5th Rev.)

parvus-a-um: *small, little* L2

pater, patris m: *father* L6

patior, patī, passus: *suffer, endure, allow, forgive* L17

patria, patriae f: *native country, fatherland* L17

paucī-ae-a: *few* L17

paulō: adv., *a little* L16

pauper, pauperis: *needy, poor, meagre* L16

pāx, pācis f: *peace* L18

pecūnia, pecūniae f: *money* L11

pecūniōsus-a-um: *wealthy, filled with wealth* L16

pellō, pellere, pepulī, pulsus: *drive away, chase away* L1

penna, pennae f: *feather* L14

per: prep. with acc., *through, throughout* L5

perdō, perdere, perdidī, perditus: *lose, destroy* (L15) L35

pereō-īre-iī-ītus: *pass away, perish, be lost* L22

perferō-ferre-tulī-lātus: *endure, carry through* (L15)

perficiō-ficere-fēcī-fectus: *finish, complete, do thoroughly* L16

perfidus-a-um: *treacherous, tricky, dishonest* L14

perīculum, perīculī n: *danger, peril* L6

persuādeō-suādēre-suāsī-suāsus: *persuade, convince* L20

pēs, pedis m: *foot* L4

petō, petere, petīvī, petītus: *seek, look for, ask for, go after* L11

philosophia, philosophiae f: *philosophy* (L18)

philosophus, philosophī m: *philosopher* L2

pictūra, pictūrae f: *picture, representation* L4

pīetās, pīetātis f: *respect, reverence, duty, affection* L13

piger, pigra, pigrum: *lazy, reluctant* L16

piscis, piscis m(i): *fish* (3rd Rev) L23

placeō, placēre, placuī, placitus: *please, be pleasing* L20
  placet: *it is one's opinion*

placidus-a-um: *peaceful, calm* (5th Rev)

plēbēius-a-um: *of the plebs, of the common people* (L20)

plēbs, plēbis f: *common people, lower class citizens, plebeians* L20

plēnus-a-um: *full* (L17) L37

plērīque, plēraeque, plēraque: *the majority, for the most part, very many* L17

poena, poenae f: *penalty, punishment* (L5) L34

poēta, poētae m: *poet* L18

pompa, pompae f: *procession, parade* (L22)

pōnō, pōnere, posuī, positus: *put, place, put aside, propose* L8

populus, populī m: *people, a people* L19

porta, portae f: *gate, entrance* L7

portō (1): *carry, convey, bring* L6

possum, posse, potuī: *be able, can* L13

post: prep. with acc., *after, behind* L5

postquam: conj., *after* L16

praemium, praemiī n: *prize, reward, booty, profit* L19

praesēns, praesentis: *present* (3rd Rev)

praeteritus-a-um: *past, done in past* L13

premō, premere, pressī, pressus: *press, push on, oppress* (1st Rev)

prīmus-a-um: *first* Int.

prīvātus-a-um: *private* (L18)

prō: prep. with abl., *for, on behalf of, in front of, before, in place of* L11
  used adverbially: Prō dī immortālēs : *By the gods!* (L22)

probō (1): *approve, test, try* L13

prōcēdō-cēdere-cessī-cessus: *proceed, advance, go along, go* L4

procul: adv., *far, at a distance* L4

proelium, proeliī n: *battle* (L7) L26

prōferō-ferre-tulī-lātus: *produce, bring forth, bring out* (L14)

proficīscor, proficīscī, profectus: *set out, start* L17

prōgredior, prōgredī, prōgressus: *advance, move toward, go forward* L17

proximus-a-um: *nearest, next* L16

prūdēns, prūdentis: *careful, prudent, cautious* (2nd Rev) L32

pūblicus-a-um: *public, having to do with the people* L18

Pūblīlius, Pūblīliī m: *Publilius* (L18)

Pūblius, Pūbliī m: *Publius* L6

puella, puellae f: *girl, sweetheart* L1

puer, puerī m: *boy, child* L1

pūgnō (1): *fight, strive* L3

pulcher, pulchra, pulchrum: *beautiful, lovely, handsome* L9

pulsō (1): *hit, beat, strike* L11

pūrus-a-um: *pure, clean* L9

putō (1): *think, consider, suppose* L10

Q

Q. = Quintus (L18)

quaerō, quaerere, quaesīvī, quaesītus: *ask, inquire, try to get* 2nd Rev

quālis-e: *of what sort, of what kind, what kind of* correlative with tālis: *as* L9

quam: adv., *how, as. . .as possible* with superl., *than* with compar. L13
  quam diū: *how long* L5
  quam ob rem: *for this reason, why* L22

quandō: *when* L3

quantus-a-um: *how much, how great;* correl. with tantus: *as much as* (L18) L27

quā rē: *on what account, why* (L18)

quārtus-a-um: *fourth* Int.

quattuor: indecl., *four* Int.

-que: conj., *and* L2

quī, quae, quod: rel pro., *who, which, that* (*whom, whose* in inflected forms);
  interrog. adj: *which? what?* (L4) L24

quia: conj., *because* (L18)

quiēs, quiētis f: *peace, quiet, rest* (5th Rev) L32

quīnque: indecl., *five* Int.
quīntus-a-um: *fifth* Int.
quis, quid: interrog. pro., *who? (whom?) which? what?* L1
quisque, quidque: indef. pro., *each one, each, every, everything* (L17) L26
quisquis, quidquid (quicquis, quicquid): indef. pro., *whoever, whatever* (L18) L27
quō: adv., *where (to), to what place* L5
quōcum, (pl. quibuscum): *with whom* L3
quod: conj., *because, since* L3
quō īnstrūmentō: *with what?* tool, implement, thing helping L3
quō modō: *in what way, in what manner, how* L4
quoque: *also, too* L12
quot: indecl., *how many;* correlative with <u>tot</u>: *as* L8

R

rāmus, rāmī m: *branch of a tree* L14
rāna, rānae f: *frog* L15
rapiō, rapere, rapuī, raptus: *seize, snatch, catch* L14
ratiō, ratiōnis f: *reckoning, account, reason, reasonableness, rationality, method* L21
rēctus-a-um: *straight, correct* L10
    ōrātiō rēcta: *direct statement* (L33)
recūsō (1): *refuse* (3rd Rev)
redeō-īre-iī-ītus: *go back, return* L18
referō, referre, rettulī, relātus: *bring back, return, relate* (L18)
rēgīna, rēgīnae f: *queen* L21
regō, regere, rēxī, rēctus: *guide, rule, direct, govern* L21
relinquō, relinquere, relīquī, relictus: *leave, leave behind, abandon* L7
reliquus-a-um: *the rest of, the remaining* L20
repetītiō, repetītiōnis f: *repetition* (5th Rev)
rēs, reī f: *thing, affair, situation, matter, circumstance, possessions* L3
    rēs pūblica: *state, republic* (L18)
respondeō-spondēre-spondī-spōnsus: *answer, reply, correspond with* L16
retineō-tinēre-tinuī-tentus: *hold back, restrain, retain, keep* L15
rēx, rēgis m: *king, ruler* L10
rīdeō, rīdēre, rīsī, rīsus: *laugh, smile, laugh at, make fun of* L11
rogō (1): *ask, inquire, question* L8
Rōma, Rōmae f: *Rome,* the city L4
Rōmānus-a-um: *Roman*
    Rōmānus, Rōmānī m: *a Roman* L3
Rūfus, Rūfī m: *Rufus* L10
rūmor, rūmōris m: *talk, rumor, slander* L22
rūs, rūris n: *country* (vs. city) L18
rūsticus-a-um: *rural, of the country, country* (L16)

S

Sabis, Sabidis m: *Sabis* (L18)
sacer, sacra, sacrum: *sacred, holy* L20
saepe: adv., *often* L9

saliō, salīre, saluī, saltus: *leap, jump* L15
salūs, salūtis f: *safety, health, welfare, refuge, greeting* (L9) L25
sanguīs, sanguinis m: *blood* L10
sānus-a-um: *sane, sound, healthy, wholesome* (L18)
sapiēns, sapientis: *wise, sensible* L9
sapientia, sapientiae f: *wisdom, good sense* L21
sapiō, sapere, sapīvī: *have taste, have wisdom* (L22)
sat = satis (L19)
satis: indecl., *enough, sufficient* L19
saxum, saxī n: *rock, stone* L3
scaenicus-a-um: *of the stage, of the theatre* (L18)
sciō, scīre, scīvī, scītus: *know* L12
scrībō, scrībere, scrīpsī, scrīptus: *write* L7
sē: reflex. pro., sg. and pl., *him (her) (its) self, themselves* (L19) L27
secundus-a-um: *second, following, favorable* Int.
sed: conj., *but* L2
sedeō, sedēre, sēdī, sessus: *sit, be seated* L4
sēditiō, sēditiōnis f: *revolt, withdrawal, strike* (L20)
semper: adv., *always* L10
senātus, senātūs m: *senate* L20
senex, senis: *old;* as noun, *old man* L2
sententia, sententiae f: *opinion, decision, sentence* L8
sepeliō, sepelīre, sepelīvī, sepultus: *bury* (L16) L24
septem: indecl., *seven* Int.
septimus-a-um: *seventh* Int.
sequor, sequī, secūtus: *follow, pursue* L17
serēnus-a-um: *calm, serene, bright* L12
sermō, sermōnis m: *talk, discussion, conversation* (L21) L38
serpēns, serpentis f: *snake, serpent* L10
serviō, servīre, servīvī, servītus: *serve, be a slave to, be subject to* L20
servō (1): *save, preserve, keep* L22
servus, servī m: *slave, servant, serf* L4
sex: indecl., *six* Int.
sextus-a-um: *sixth* Int.
sī: conj., *if* L10
sīc: adv., *so, in this way* L14
sīgnum, sīgnī n: *sign, signal, indication, military standard* L21
silentium, silentiī n: *silence, quiet* L15
sileō, silēre, siluī: *be silent* (5th Rev)
silva, silvae f: *forest, woods* L5
similis-e: *like, similar, similar to* L20
simul: adv., *at the same time* L16
sine: prep. with abl., *without* L6
singulī-ae-a: *one at a time* L15
sinister, sinistra, sinistrum: *left, on the left* (L16)
sōl, sōlis m: *sun* L19
sōlitūdō, sōlitūdinis f: *solitude, loneliness* (L20)
sōlus-a-um: irreg. dat. and gen., *only, alone* L9
solvō, solvere, solvī, solūtus: *let go, let loose, solve, dissolve, pay* L11
somnus, somnī m: *sleep* L16
sonus, sonī m: *sound, noise* L15
soror, sorōris f: *sister* L6
spectātor, spectātōris m: *spectator, observer* L4
spectō (1): *watch, look at* L1
spērō (1): *hope, trust* L12

spēs, speī f: *hope* (2nd Rev)

stabulum, stabulī n: *stable* L22

statim: adv., *at once, immediately* L10

sternō, sternere, strāvī, strātus: *lay low, overthrow* (L3)

stō, stāre, stetī, status: *stand, stand still, stand up* L2

studeō, studēre, studuī: *be eager for, be enthusiastic about, study* L20

studium, studiī n: *enthusiasm, eagerness, study* L4

stultitia, stultitiae f: *stupidity* (L21)

stultus-a-um: *stupid, foolish* L9

stupeō, stupēre, stupuī: *be stunned, be astonished* (L17)

sub: prep. with abl., *under, below,* (indicating position); prep. with acc., *under* (indicating direction) L5

subveniō-venīre-vēnī-ventus: *help, come to the assistance of* L20

sum, esse, fuī, futūrus: *be* L1

super: prep. with acc., *over, above* L5

superbus-a-um: *proud, haughty, arrogant* L18

suprā: prep. with acc., *over, above, beyond, on top of* (L11) L28

surgō, surgere, surrēxī, surrēctus: *rise, get up, raise* L11

sustineō-tinēre-tinuī-tentus: *uphold, support, endure* L13

suus, sua, suum: *his (her) (its) (their) own* L9

Syrus-a-um: *Syrian* (L18)

T

T. = Tītus (L18)

taberna, tabernae f: *shop, wineshop* L11

taceō, tacēre, tacuī, tacitus: *be silent, be quiet* L14

tālis-e: *such, of such a sort* L14

tam: adv., *so, so much* L13

tamquam: *as if* L17

tandem: *finally, at last* L10

tangō, tangere, tetigī, tāctus: *touch, reach, attain* (4th Rev) L25

tantum: adv., *merely, only, just* L14

tantus-a-um: *so great, so much, so big* L13

tardus-a-um: *slow* L17

tēlum, tēlī n: *weapon, javelin* (1st Rev)

templum, templī n: *temple* L21

tempus, temporis n: *time, season, situation* L8

teneō, tenēre, tenuī, tentus: *hold, have, keep* L3

tepor, tepōris m: *warmth* (L18)

terra, terrae f: *earth, land, soil* L7

terreō, terrēre, terruī, territus: *scare, frighten* L6

tertius-a-um: *third* Int.

thēsaurus, thēsaurī m: *treasure, treasury* (2nd Rev)

timeō, timēre, timuī: *fear, be afraid, be afraid of* (3rd Rev)

timor, timōris m: *fear, dread* L15

Tītus, Tītī m: *Titus* L13

tot: indecl., *so many, as many* L8

tōtus-a-um: irreg. dat. gen.; *whole, entire, all* L16

tractō (1): *treat, handle* (L12)

trahō, trahere, trāxī, tractus: *draw, drag, pull, attract* L12

trāns: prep. with acc., *across, beyond* L5

trānsmūtō (1): *change over* (L18)

trēs, tria: *three* Int.

tribūnus, tribūnī m: *tribune,* official of the Roman people (L20)

trīstis-e: *sad, unhappy, mournful, harsh* L3

tū: irreg. pro., *you* (sg.) L11

tum: adv., *then, next in order* L20

tumultus, tumultūs m: *uproar, disturbance* L4

tunc: adv., *then, at that time* L15

tūtus-a-um: *safe, reliable, unharmed* L10

tuus-a-um: *your, yours,* referring to one person L9

tyrannus, tyrannī m: *tyrant, cruel ruler* (L19)

U

ubi: conj., where (?); introd. subord. clause, *where, when* L4

umbra, umbrae f: *shade, shadow, ghost* L16

unde: *from where* L4

ūnicus-a-um: *sole, only, one of a kind* (L18)

ūnus-a-um: irreg. dat. and gen., *one* Int.

urbs, urbis f (i): *city* L4

ut: conj. with indic., *as* L22; conj. with subjunct., *that, in order that, to* L37

ūtilis-e: *useful, suitable* L20

ūva, ūvae f: *grape, bunch of grapes* (L16)

uxor, uxōris f: *wife* L22

V

vacuus-a-um: *empty* (1st Rev) L32

valeō, valēre, valuī, valitus: *be strong, be well, be of value, be worthy, be worth, be powerful* L12 valē: *goodbye*

vehō, vehere, vēxī, vectus: *transport, carry* L12

vel: conj., *or;* vel. . .vel: conj., *either. . .or* L17

vēnātor, vēnātōris m: *hunter* (L10)

venēnum, venēnī n: *poison* (L22)

veniō, venīre, vēnī, ventus: *come* L5

venter, ventris m: *stomach* (L20)

vēr, vēris n: *spring, spring-time* L17

verbum, verbī n: *word* L7

vereor, verērī, veritus: *fear* L17

Vergilius (P. Vergilius Maro) Vergiliī m: *Vergil,* a Roman poet (L18)

vēritās, vēritātis f: *truth* L6

vērō: *certainly, to be sure, but* L14

versus, versūs m: *verse, line of poetry* (L18)

vertō, vertere, vertī, versus: *turn, change* L5

vērus-a-um: *true* L18

vester, vestra, vestrum: *your, yours,* ref. to more than one person L9

vestis, vestis f: *clothing, clothes* L1

vetus, veteris: *old, of old times, aged* L17

via, viae f: *road, street, way* L4

viātor, viātōris m: *traveler* L4

victōria, victōriae f: *victory* (L3) L26

videō, vidēre, vīdī, vīsus: *see, perceive* L1

vīlicus, vīlicī m: *overseer* (L22)

vīlis-e: *cheap, worthless* L12

vīlla, vīllae f: *farm house, country house* L16

vincō, vincere, vīcī, victus: *win, beat, conquer, surpass* L3

vinculum, vinculī n: *chain, bond* L22

vīnea, vīneae f: *vineyard* L16

vīnum, vīnī n: *wine* L11

vir, virī m: *man, hero, husband* L1

virtūs, virtūtis f: *courage, valor, manliness, virtue* 1st Rev

vīs, vim, vī, (pl) vīrēs, vīribus, vīrium f: *force, strength;* pl. *military force, power* (L15) L26

vīta, vītae f: *life* L16

vīvō, vīvere, vīxī, vīctus: *live* L9

vīvus-a-um: *alive, living* L21

vix: adv., *scarcely, hardly, with difficulty* L19

vocō (1): *call, summon* L6

volō, velle, voluī: *be willing, wish, want* L13

voluntās, voluntātis f: *will, wish, good will* (L17) L34

volvō, volvere, volvī, volūtus: *turn, turn around, roll* L11

Vorēnus, Vorēnī m: *Vorenus*, a centurion in Caesar's Gallic army (L3)

vōs: irreg. pro., *you* (pl.) L11

vōx, vōcis f: *voice, tone* L11

vulnerō (1): *wound, injure* L3

vulpēs, vulpis f: *fox* L12